THE SECRET TO LIFE IS STOP B*TCHING

PATRICK FRANCIS

STOPBITCHINGBOOK.COM

TABLE OF CONTENTS

INTRODUCTION: THE LAST SELF-HELP BOOK YOU'LL EVER NEED

"MOST SELF-HELP BOOKS SELL YOU THE DREAM. THIS ONE WAKES YOU UP FROM IT."

How many hours have you wasted complaining about the same problems you had last year? And the year before that? How many self-help books are collecting dust on your shelf while the issues they promised to fix are still ruining your life? What if the real reason you're stuck isn't because you don't know what to do, but because you'd rather talk about your problems than actually solve them?

So Now, You've Got This Book In Your Hands

If you bought this book yourself: Your Amazon history is probably a timeline of abandoned self-improvement attempts. You've got enough unfinished books and journals to decorate your entire house with good intentions. This time will be different though, right? (Spoiler alert: only if you actually do the work instead of just highlighting stuff.)

If a family member or friend gave you this book: They know you're someone who actually wants to improve. Unlike the people who just talk about changing, they've seen you genuinely try. This is their way of saying, "I believe in your journey enough to invest in it." Maybe they read it themselves and thought, "This is exactly what [your name] has been looking for!" It's not an insult—it's recognition that you're the rare person who might actually do something with good advice.

If your romantic partner gave you this book: They probably thought it was hilarious, but comedy usually hits because it has some truth to it. If your relationship was a TV show, it'd probably be called "When Bitching Becomes A Lifestyle" with you as the breakout star. Consider yourself lucky—they chose this book over a conversation that starts with "we need to talk." Get them a copy too and make it interesting: "Whoever complains less this month gets to choose our next vacation spot." This can be couples therapy but with more laughs and fewer awkward silences. Suddenly you're both winning instead of whining.

Why This Book Exists (And Why You Need It)

Hello, my name is Patrick Francis, and I wrote this book because I was sick of my own bullshit. I've failed more times than most people have even tried. I've loved people who later turned me into the villain of their life story. I've spent countless nights wondering if existence was worth the effort. These experiences taught me something valuable: sometimes the most powerful insights come from our lowest moments.

One night at my lowest point, I asked the universe the big question: "What's the secret to life?" The answer wasn't some profound wisdom. It was just two words: **"Stop Bitching."**

I wanted wise words I could post on my Instagram story and immediately forget. Instead, I got something that sounded like it came from someone who was completely fed up with my excuses. At first I was offended, but then I realized—this was exactly the wake-up call I needed.

I've watched this same transformation happen countless times. My friend who spent years complaining about being single found their perfect match a month after they stopped talking about how "there's nobody good out there" and started becoming someone worth dating. The always-broke friend who stopped blaming "the economy" and started a side hustle that now makes more than their day job. The forever-miserable relative who finally found happiness when they stopped waiting for the world to make them happy. I wish I'd had this book in my twenties when my default response to everything was "this sucks" instead of "how do I fix this?" I could have saved myself years of repeating the same patterns and wondering why nothing changed.

Most Self-Help Books Are Useless

Let's be real about most self-help books. They're not designed to actually change your life; they're designed to make you feel like you might change your life someday. They give you just enough hope to keep buying more books without requiring you to do anything difficult.

Most self-help books fall into one of three categories:

"The Universe Is Your Personal Genie" Collection: These magical thinking manuals promise success through positive thoughts alone. Just visualize wealth and—poof!—it appears! Still fai ing? You're just not believing hard enough. The only thing manifesting is your growing sense of inadequacy.

"It's Not You, It's Literally Everyone Else" Library: These validation guides assure you that you're perfect as-is. Your problems? Blame toxic people, society, mercury retrograde, or your childhood. They're like that friend who takes your side even when you're clearly wrcng. "You're right—the entire world IS conspiring against you!"

"5 AM Club of Productivity Superhumans" Manuals: These books insist you can have it all with the perfect morning routine. They make you feel like a failure for hitting snooze while the author is apparently running marathons, writing novels, and achieving enlightenment before your first cup of coffee.

Why This Book Is Different (And Why It Actually Works)

This book won't pat you on the head and tell you everything's fine. It's not going to tell you that your problems are unique or that the world needs to change before your life can improve. It's not going to give you permission to keep complaining while waiting for circumstances to magically shift in your favor.

"The Secret To Life Is Stop Bitching" is like having a friend who cares enough to tell you you're still talking about your ex two months after the breakup and it's time to move on. It might make you uncomfortable. You might get defensive. But deep down, you know they're right.

Here's what makes this book different:

1. **It's based on reality, not fantasy.** This book acknowledges that life is sometimes unfair, people can be jerks, and circumstances can genuinely suck. The difference is in how you respond to those realities. Complaining about problems is like complaining about the weather—it might make you feel better for a minute, but you're still going to get wet in the rain.

2. **It focuses on what you can control.** Most self-help books try to teach you how to influence things beyond your control: other people's opinions, random opportunities, or the perfect timing. This book focuses on the one thing that actually determines your life quality: how you choose to respond to whatever happens.

3. **It's written by someone who's actually been in the trenches.** I'm not some guru who's been successful since birth. I'm someone who's failed repeatedly, complained bitterly, and finally figured out why that approach guaranteed more of the same. This book isn't theory—it's what actually works when life gets real.

4. **It demands action, not just awareness.** Understanding why you're stuck is only 10% of the solution. This book doesn't just help you understand—it gives you specific, practical tools to do something about it. Knowledge without action is just trivia.

5. **It works whether you believe in it or not.** This isn't about faith or positive thinking. The principles in this book work because they're based on how life really is, not on how we wish it would be. You don't have to believe in electricity for the lights to turn on when you flip the switch.

"The 'good old days' are happening right now."

Warning: This Book Requires Actually Doing Stuff

Let's be clear about something: this isn't a passive reading experience. If you're looking for something to skim while half-watching Netflix, put this down and grab a celebrity memoir instead.

This book will ask you to do uncomfortable things. It will challenge you to change behaviors you've had for years. It will require actual effort—not just nodding along and highlighting passages that sound good. Each chapter includes specific actions that work only if you actually do them. Revolutionary concept, I know.

PAUSE HERE AND ANSWER THIS: When was the last time you actually implemented something from a self-help book? Not just thought about it, not just highlighted it, but actually did it consistently for at least 30 days? If you can't remember, that's the problem this book solves.

What You'll Find in These Pages

Each chapter in this book tackles a different area where most of us get stuck in cycles of complaint and excuse-making, providing both the wake-up call and practical tools to do something different.

The Blueprint: How Each Chapter Works

Every chapter is designed to actually help you, not just make you feel good. Each one includes:
1. A straight-to-the-point quote that sets the tone
2. The unfiltered truth about what's keeping you stuck
3. Real-life situations you'll instantly recognize from your own life
4. Practical strategies you can implement immediately
5. Clear action steps that produce results when you actually do them

What You'll Learn: Chapter by Chapter

This book builds a complete system for transforming your life, one chapter at a time:

- **Chapter 1: Stop Bitching** - Quit complaining and start fixing shit (your life will thank you)
- **Chapter 2: The Art of Getting Your Head Out of Your Ass** - Calling out your own bullshit before it ruins your next big break
- **Chapter 3: Building an Emotional Backbone** - Building resilience without losing your humanity in the process
- **Chapter 4: Life Isn't Fair** - Handling life's BS without becoming bitter and impossible to be around
- **Chapter 5: Playing the Long Game** - Why your need for instant results is screwing your future self
- **Chapter 6: How to Handle Haters** - Managing critics without becoming the very asshole you can't stand
- **Chapter 7: Making Any Place Suck Less** - Turning crappy situations into opportunities while others are still whining
- **Chapter 8: Stop Being the Person Everyone Avoids at Parties** - Making people feel energized instead of drained when you're around
- **Chapter 9: Teaching Without Being a Know-It-All** - Sharing your wisdom in ways people actually want to hear
- **Chapter 10: Relationship Detox** - Creating relationships that lift you up instead of wear you down
- **Chapter 11: Dancing with Disaster** - Using life's bullshit as your comeback fuel
- **Chapter 12: When Everything Goes to Hell** - Your survival manual for when life decides to test your limits
- **Chapter 13: Leveling Up Your Life** - Upgrading your existence without the eye-roll-inducing inspirational quotes
- **Chapter 14: Never Ending Story** - Why this journey never ends (and why that's not as depressing as it sounds)

How to Use This Book (Without Overthinking It)

Read this book however you want. Start to finish? Great. Skipping straight to the chapter that feels like it's personally calling your name? Even better. I reference other chapters occasiona lly, but each one stands on its own. I wrote it this way because I know how people actually read books—in random chunks between scrolling Instagram and pretending to work. Come back to it whenever you need a reality check. It's like having a brutally honest friend in your pocket who makes you laugh while telling you exactly what you need to hear, not what you want to hear.

The Only Promise This Book Makes

Most self-help books promise you'll become a millionaire with perfect abs who never feels sad. This book makes just ore promise: if you stop wasting energy on complaints and excuses, you'll have more energy for actually fixing your problems. It's not magic—it's math. Less time spent whining equals more time spent winning. Less energy on blame means more energy for change.

What If...

What if you woke up tomorrow and didn't immediately start mentally listing all the things you hate about your life? What f you could redirect all that mental energy you waste on complaints into actually building something worth talking about? What if six months from now, people started asking what happened to you because you've changed so dramatically?

This isn't fantasy—it's what happens when you stop bitching and start living. It's the natural result of redirecting wasted er ergy toward actual solutions.

The Choice Is Yours

So what's it gonna be? This isn't just another book to skim and forget. It's a decision point. Either you're ready to stop the endless cycle of complaints and excuses, or you're comfortable staying exactly where you are. There's no middle ground here. No "I'll try this approach when things calm down" or "I'll start after the holidays." Either you're done with your own bullshit, or you're not.

The shelf of unfinished self-help books is waiting for this one to join it. The question is: Are you finally ready for something different? Are you tired enough of your own excuses to actually do something about them?

Turn the page and let's find out.

The Cost of Waiting

Every day you spend complaining steals from your future. While you're perfecting your victim story, someone with bigger obstacles and fewer advantages is out there getting what you want. Not because they're special—because they refuse to waste time on useless complaints. How many more years of the same frustrations are you willing to accept? Because change doesn't happen when you've read enough—it happens when you've finally had enough.

UP NEXT: Chapter 1 is about to hit you with the fundamental truth that will change everything: Stop Bitching, Start Living. You'll discover why complaints are the most expensive habit you've never calculated, how your brain becomes addicted to bitching, and the exact tools to break free from the complaint cycle that's keeping you stuck.

CHAPTER 1: STOP BITCHING, START LIVING (THE ONLY ADVICE ANYONE WILL EVER NEED)

"IN LIFE, THERE ARE 2 OPTIONS: BOSS UP OR BITCH UP. BE THE DIRECTOR OF YOUR OWN MOVIE, OR PLAY AN EXTRA IN SOMEONE ELSE'S."

PART 1: THE COMPLAINT CYCLE: WHAT IT COSTS YOU

Warning: This isn't another self-help book about manifesting dreams through positive thinking. This is the conversation your real friends are too afraid to have with you. I'm the friend who catches you checking your ex's Instagram at 3AM and snatches your phone. While other gurus get rich selling $49.99 journals to "process your healing journey," I'm offering something that actually works: reality. This book will explain why you keep ending up in the same situations because of your mentality. Every minute spent documenting problems is a minute not spent solving them. Want to keep refreshing other people's lives while yours stays the same? Put this book down. Ready to stop bullshitting yourself and actually change? Keep reading.

Quick note: I won't be using real names in this book for relevant stories. Not because I'm trying to protect the innocent, but because I don't want my friends texting me "Did you seriously put my personal shit in your book?" Also, why immortalize someone's temporary problems in a timeless book? That's just evil.

THE PRICE TAG OF COMPLAINING:

Let me tell you a story: I had 2 friends that ended their relationships around the same time... Right before Valentine's Day... go figure. Six months later, their lives couldn't be more different. Friend 1 is dating someone new, in better shape than before, and genuinely moving forward. Friend 2? Still saying they're battling insomnia when in reality they're scrolling TikToks before switching to Instagram for the 5th time that night to check who followed their ex.

What made the difference? It wasn't luck or circumstances - it was where they invested their energy. Friend 1 channeled their post-breakup emotions into hitting the gym, developing actual hobbies (not Instagram-friendly fake ones), and meeting real people face-to-face. Meanwhile, Friend 2 became obsessed with complaining and reliving bad memories. Their "healing process" consisted of weekend partying, strategically posting club photos at 1AM with captions like "living my best life" – all while secretly hoping their ex would see it, spiral into jealousy, and send that magical "I miss you" text.

Spoiler alert: it never came.

Plot Twist: I was Friend 2.

This is the real cost of complaint addiction. Every hour spent in negativity is an hour stolen from your future success. That time wasted thinking about past failures and crafting elaborate revenge scenarios? It could have been invested in literally anything that would make you more knowledgeable, fulfilled, and valuable to yourself and others.

Complaining isn't just annoying—it's fucking expensive in terms of time, energy, and opportunity. While you're crafting the perfect rant about how unfair your situation is, someone else with the exact same problem is already halfway to solving it.

Your excuses and dreams can't coexist. One must go.

The Problem: Trapped in the Complaint Cycle

7:03 AM: Wake up. First thought: "God, I'm tired."
7:05 AM: Check phone. "Everything's going to shit."

7:10 AM: Roll over. "My back hurts."

7:12 AM: Can't find the right clothes. "I have nothing to wear."

7:15 AM: Update status: "Universe really testing me today..." with eye-roll emoji.

Recognize yourself? This complaint ritual plays out in millions of homes every morning. Before even finishing their first cup of coffee, most people have already built a list of problems to bitch about all day.

By lunch, they've sent multiple texts about how their job is "soul-crushing," complained about traffic (as if it's some shocking new development), and wasted thirty minutes telling anyone who'll listen how exhausted they are — conveniently leaving out the fact that they were scrolling through mindless videos all night.

THE COMPLAINT BLINDSPOT: The biggest joke? Most chronic complainers have absolutely no idea they're doing it. They spew negativity in every conversation without offering a single solution. Not one. While they think they're just "venting" or "keeping it real," everyone else sees them as negative vibes.

Everyone hates traffic, yet nobody sees the irony of their complaint. If you're on the highway at 5:30 PM, you're not the victim of traffic—you're a willing participant. You're literally what you're complaining about.

Watched this happen just last week. Six friends at a table. Food hadn't even arrived. Within 10 minutes, they were neck-deep in discussing everything wrong in their lives with no solutions mentioned. Then when someone tries to offer a solution, they feel offended.

Want to know the most telling part? There's always that one person who doesn't join in. They just sit there, maybe nodding, maybe sharing one small thing before moving on. Pay attention to that person - they're usually the one actually doing something with their life. They're not wasting energy on the misery competition because they're too busy actually fixing the things everyone else at the table is just complaining about.

The Complaint Approach vs. Action Approach

Motivation is unreliable. Discipline shows up regardless.

Situation: Bad boss Complaint Approach: "My boss is such a micromanaging asshole. He never trusts me to do anything right." Spends 45 minutes texting friends about it.

Action Approach: "My boss micromanages everything. I'll document my work clearly, have a direct conversation, or update my resume." Spends 45 minutes doing one of those things.

Situation: Dating app frustration Complaint Approach: "These apps are full of garbage people. Nobody decent is on here." Screenshots worst profiles to share in group chat.

Action Approach: "These apps aren't working for me. I'll try a different one, improve my profile, or meet people through activities I enjoy." Joins a photography club.

Situation: Money problems Complaint Approach: "I'm always broke. The economy is rigged against people like me." Scrolls social media looking at things can't afford Action.

Approach: "I need to increase my income or decrease expenses. Let me make a plan." Creates budget, researches side hustles

Situation: Weight gain Complaint Approach: "My metabolism is broken. Nothing works for me." Orders takeout while complaining .

Action Approach: "I need a sustainable approach. Let me track what I eat for a week and find one small change to make." Actually does it

This isn't just about attitude. This is about where your precious time and energy go. Same 24 hours. Same problems. Completely different results.

This is your complaint headquarters—the definitive guide to recognizing and eliminating bitching. Consider this chapter the foundation that everything else in this book builds upon. Eliminating complaints creates the mental bandwidth needed for all the transformation that follows.

The Complaint Hall of Fame: Five Toxic Archetypes You Definitely Know

Let's identify the complaint super-villains currently occupying space in your life. I guarantee you'll recognize at least two of these toxic archetypes:

The Drama Monarchs – These royals of crisis turn the smallest problems into major catastrophes. A red light held too long? "This day is RUINED and the universe SPECIFICALLY HATES ME." They'll text everyone with updates about how this tiny delay proves their life is cursed. Someone doesn't reply for 20 minutes? That's not a busy person—it's 'proof they hate me and our relationship is over and I'll die alone.' Rain on their day off isn't weather—it's a personal attack from the sky ruining their entire week.

The Misery Competitors – These people measure suffering against everyone else's to ensure they win the championship of suffering. "Let me tell you why my situation is worse than yours!" They scan conversations for chances to one-up others with superior suffering. "You think your job is stressful? Well, mine pays better but my commute is longer and my boss texted me on Sunday, so I'm clearly the real victim here."

The Chronic Broadcasters – These people don't just experience problems—they need to alert the entire world. Every inconvenience requires a social media update, six text conversations, and telling the barista making their coffee. Their problems aren't real until they've been thoroughly documented, shared, and received appropriate sympathy reactions. They don't want solutions—they want an audience.

The Selective Memory Masters – These professional complainers have an uncanny ability to forget anything positive while maintaining a detailed catalog of every negative experience since middle school. Tell them about the nine things that went right today, and they'll immediately steer the conversation to the one thing that went wrong. Their brains are like negativity magnets, attracting and storing only the worst parts of every experience.

The Responsibility Dodgers – These complaint specialists have a PhD in blame distribution. Nothing is ever their fault—it's their boss, the economy, the weather, their metabolism, their parents, or the alignment of the planets. Their complaints serve a crucial purpose: protecting them from ever having to admit they might be partially responsible for their own circumstances.

Complaints aren't just annoying everyone—they're serving as personal bodyguards protecting precious delusions. When someone complains to get validation, what they're really saying is "Please confirm that my excuses are totally legitimate and not complete bullshit." It's like asking friends to co-sign a loan for a failing business of lies.

Complaints also function as shields against responsibility— medieval armor protecting against the deadly arrows of accountability. "I would have succeeded if my boss wasn't such a jerk" is just a fancy way of saying "I refuse to examine my own role in this situation because that would require actual work."

PART 2: THE FUNDAMENTAL TRUTH: YOUR BRAIN ON BULLSHIT

Complaining is like frantically searching for your phone while talking on it—wasting energy on a problem that could be solved with a bit of mental clarity.

WARNING: No Participation Trophies Beyond This Point. No more excuses. No more venting. No more "processing" bullshit.

Let's be real - millions of people casually browse self-help books hoping for life-changing wisdom. Here's the only self-help advice that doesn't require downloading an app, attending a $5,000 weekend retreat in the desert, or chanting affirmations while burning sage in the bathroom. This isn't a gentle nudge toward self-improvement—it's a full-body tackle into reality.

Ready for it? Here it comes: **STOP. CONSTANTLY. BITCHING.**

Stop auditioning for the role of victim in your life story.

Here's the secret most self-help gurus hide behind their $997 "platinum mastermind" packages. All that energy spent bitching? That's valuable mental energy down the toilet! It's like running on a treadmill but staying in the same spot. People are sweating, breathing hard, using up all their energy... and haven't moved an inch. All they've done is made themselves tired and pissed off.

The most frustrating part? While some folks are typing up that long-ass Facebook rant about how nobody understands their struggle, somebody with the exact same problem has already fixed it, started a business, and is on vacation. The difference isn't circumstance—it's mindset. One person used frustration as fuel while the other used it as marinade for their misery.

This changes everything. Full stop.

Here's the truth: Even doing the wrong thing beats just complaining! A wrong turn still puts you on a different street with new possibilities. Complaints, however, keep you stuck in a roundabout. You go in circles, thinking you're moving forward just because the scenery spins past your window.

Let's get something straight – nobody needs a PhD in neuroscience to see how this works. A complaint habit isn't just annoying everybody unfortunate enough to be trapped near you at dinner; it's literally rewiring your brain to become a professional victim. And here's the kicker – the more you bitch, the harder it gets to stop, like trying to quit drinking while working as a bartender.

The Bitching Cycle (That Ruins Lives)

FIRST: NORMAL LIFE HAPPENS The coffee shop gets an order wrong. Traffic exists. Internet drops for eight minutes. A completely normal, everyday thing happens - the kind of thing that happens to literally every person on the planet.

For chronic complainers, though? This isn't just an inconvenience. This is an ASSAULT. This is EVIDENCE that the universe has singled them out for special torture. The body physically can't tell the difference between "lukewarm latte" and "being chased by a bear." Same adrenaline. Same cortisol spike. Completely different threat level.

THEN: THE SYMPATHY HUNTING BEGINS Now they need witnesses to their suffering. They text friends. They post about it. They tell coworkers. They're basically collecting signatures for their petition of misery.

And when people respond with "that sucks" or a sad face emoji? That's the good stuff right there. The brain lights up like Times Square on New Year's. That little hit of validation feels so good it's practically narcotic.

Pretty soon they're hunting for things to complain about just to get that sweet hit of sympathy. It's like discovering a slot machine that pays out every time - except instead of money, it pays in people feeling sorry for them.

FINALLY: COMPLAINT-COLORED GLASSES DEVELOP This is where it gets really sad. The brain basically installs a filter that only lets in the negative stuff. At a restaurant - they don't notice the free appetizer, only that the server took too long with the check. A promotion at work - instead of celebrating, they immediately focus on the amount of extra work they'll have.

It's not "being realistic" like they tell themselves. It's being trapped in a reality of their own making where everything is always awful all the time. The most messed up part? There's actually good stuff happening around them constantly, but they literally can't see it anymore. Their brains have become negativity magnets.

Think about going hiking with two friends. Same trail. Same day. One spends the whole time pointing out how beautiful everything is. The other complains nonstop - too hot, too many bugs, trail too steep. Literally the exact same experience, completely different realities.

Rewiring the Complaint Factory: The Brain Makeover

Good news: the human brain isn't permanently screwed—it's more like Play-Doh than concrete. Anyone can reshape it, but they'll need better tools than "just think positive," which works about as well as fighting a house fire with a squirt gun.

Want to kick a complaint addiction? Give the brain the good feelings it's looking for, just from better sources. The brain doesn't care if the feel-good chemicals come from bitching or from finishing a workout, completing a project, or helping someone. It's like switching a kid from candy to fruit—they still get something sweet, but it's actually good for them.

Next comes the attention game. The brain is like a puppy— it chases whatever gets pointed at. Most complainers have trained their brains to chase every problem. The key is to start pointing at different things. This isn't fake positive thinking; it's more like being the director of a brain movie and changing where the camera points.

When that familiar complaint bubbles up like heartburn after too many tacos, stop it in its tracks. Picture a stop sign, pinch yourself, or ask "What would someone who isn't a whiny complainer do right now?" It's like jamming a stick in the gears of the complaint factory.

The real power move? Putting space between what happens and how we react. Count to ten. Take a breath. Do anything except jump straight to bitching. Every time someone fights the urge to complain, they're rewiring their brain to be less dramatic and more helpful.

The Complaint Conveyor Belt: How Small Problems Become Life-Consuming Dramas

Facebook complaints are just Yelp reviews for a life people keep choosing to live in. One star, would not recommend, but still won't leave.

It typically starts with something trivial—like someone taking too long to text back. The complainer's brain immediately catastrophizes: "They're OBVIOUSLY not into me!" Instead of just getting on with the day or sending a direct message to address the concern, they screenshot the conversation and send it to three friends for analysis. These friends respond with appropriate outrage, validating the reaction and amplifying the perception of being wronged. That sweet hit of validation feels better than getting an actual reply.

So naturally, they post a vague story on Instagram ("Some people just show you who they really are 🙄"), bring it up during brunch ("You won't believe what happened to me"), and mention it on their next date with someone new ("My ex had serious communication issues"). They've transformed a momentary disappointment into a personal brand.

Let's break this down in real numbers: They've spent 5 minutes obsessing over the late reply, 10 minutes capturing screenshots and texting friends, 15 minutes discussing the outrage in group chat, 5 minutes crafting the perfect vague Instagram story, and another 10 minutes rehashing it at brunch.

Before long, they've spent 45 minutes talking about a 5-second problem that affected them for all of 2 minutes. They've stretched that negative experience to nearly an hour of their day—not because the problem was significant, but because complaining gave them a small hit of validation each time.

The time wasted on pointless negativity could be spent building something, connecting with someone, or becoming someone worth talking about. That same 45 minutes could have been a workout, half a job application, or progress on a creative project.

Most Problems Aren't Special (And That's Good News)

Most problems aren't special. Not even a little bit. They're like store-brand cereal – same damn thing as the expensive stuff, just in a boring box. That massive issue keeping people up at night? Billions have faced it before, and billions more will after everyone's dust.

THE MEMBERSHIP CLUBS YOU'VE JOINED (WHETHER YOU WANTED TO OR NOT)

The Terrible Boss Club: Got a micromanaging boss who steals credit? Congratulations on joining a club with more members than Christianity, Judaism, and Islam combined.

The Can't Afford It Club: You can't buy what you want? Welcome to the human condition since commerce began. People have been unable to afford things they want since the invention of wanting things.

The Dating Disaster Club: Frustrated with your love life? Congrats, you've joined the most populous club in history. Even royalty throughout time struggled to find someone who wasn't just after their crown.

The Aging Body Club: Outraged that your knees crack and you can't eat like you did at 20? Welcome to the oldest club in human history—literally everyone who's ever lived has membership.

The Family Drama Club: Think your relatives are uniquely dysfunctional? This club is so crowded it makes Times Square on New Year's Eve look spacious.

THE MASSIVE OPPORTUNITY YOU'RE MISSING

The good news? Common problems already have proven solutions. It's like walking into a test and finding all the answers posted online.

Right now, someone with your exact same problem is already halfway to fixing it while you're still crafting the perfect complaint post. The difference isn't luck. It's that they're googling solutions while you're rehearsing your victim story. They're building while you're bitching.

PART 5: THE HIDDEN COSTS OF COMPLAINING

The Social Media Complaint Factory

Nobody's actually living the life they post online. They're crying in their car between perfect beach selfies and 'living my best life' captions.

Social media is the world's most efficient complaint amplification system. It rewards misery and punishes progress through a simple formula:

A rant about bad customer service = 43 comments and endless engagement An actual accomplishment = 6 likes and your Aunt saying "proud of you hun"

The algorithm has cracked the code: outrage gets more engagement than joy. Every notification from your complaint post delivers a tiny rush of validation. Your brain doesn't distinguish between genuine connection and shallow attention, so you naturally keep posting negative content to harvest more of those addictive responses.

Meanwhile, we're all comparing our actual lives (unwashed hair, dirty laundry, real problems) to everyone else's highlight reel.

The Innovation Killer: How Complaining Blocks Creative Genius

Ever notice how history books don't have chapters dedicated to professional complainers? Nobody's building monuments to people whose greatest achievement was pointing out what's wrong.

Ever wonder why some people can find chances to grow everywhere while others just find problems? It's not luck - it's what they focus on. When someone's busy complaining about how something sucks, they can't see how it could be better. Attention is limited - every minute spent crafting the perfect complaint is a minute not spent fixing the problem.

Innovation doesn't come from complaining about what's wrong - it comes from being so tired of what's wrong that people roll up their sleeves and fix it. Every major breakthrough came from someone who was less interested in describing the problem than in solving it.

The moment someone switches from "This sucks" to "How could this be better?" they use completely different parts of their brain. They move from emotional reactions to actually solving problems. This isn't just about attitude; it's about which part of the brain is running the show. When people complain, their emotional brain is in charge. When they solve problems, their thinking brain takes over.

PART 6: HEALING VS. HOLDING ON TO SHIT

Processing vs. Poisoning: The Crucial Difference

Processing emotions is like washing dishes right after dinner—a small effort that keeps a space clean. Complaining is like letting those dishes rot for weeks, then inviting friends over to witness the disgusting sink while asking, 'Can you believe I have to live like this?'

Here's the thing: there's a huge difference between actually dealing with feelings and just being a toxic whiner. Most people's idea of "processing emotions" is just bitching with fancier vocabulary. Processing emotions means noticing when you're pissed off, figuring out why, then doing something about it. Poisoning means wallowing in how awful everything is, practicing the sad story until it's memorized perfectly, and infecting everyone around you.

Processing emotions is like taking out the trash—a necessary chore that keeps the mental house clean. "I'm frustrated about this situation. Why? What can I do about it?" Have ONE focused conversation about it, acknowledge the feeling, then move on like an actual adult. It's the emotional equivalent of a quick shower—get in, get clean, get out.

Poisoning is when someone turns complaints into their personality. 'This ALWAYS happens to me! Everything is TERRIBLE!' They tell the same story to anyone who'll listen, with no plans to actually fix anything. It's like deliberately keeping problems around just to have something to talk about.

The difference? Processing leads to resolution. Poisoning leads to festering. One moves people forward; the other keeps them stuck in a hamster wheel of their own design, running furiously but going absolutely nowhere.

Productive vs. Unproductive Feedback: The Art of Useful Criticism

There's a Grand Canyon-sized gap between offering useful feedback and just bitching. One builds bridges; the other burns them.

Not all negative communication is created equal. A critical distinction exists between productive feedback that creates positive change and unproductive complaining that just pollutes the atmosphere.

Want to know the difference between feedback that actually changes things and just being another whiny voice in the void? It's all in the delivery. Effective feedback is specific, balanced, solution-oriented, and well-timed. Ineffective complaining is vague, one-sided, problem-focused, and poorly timed. One opens doors to improvement; the other slams them shut.

Most people's idea of "feedback" is just complaint karaoke—singing the same tired tune of how wronged they feel with zero consideration for the audience. "You ALWAYS ignore me for your STUPID phone!" Great job, Shakespeare. That'll definitely make someone want to change.

Here's how to actually get shit done: Start with what actually happened, not a dramatic interpretation of it. "I noticed you were on your phone during our entire dinner last night" hits different than "You clearly think TikTok is more important than our relationship." One is a fact; the other is auditioning for a soap opera nobody wants to watch.

Then talk about real impact, not just feelings explosions. "When we don't talk during our limited time together, I feel disconnected" works better than "YOU MAKE ME FEEL WORTHLESS AND INVISIBLE."

Finally, make an actual request instead of a passive-aggressive question. "Could we agree to put phones away during meals?" is an invitation to solve a problem together. "Why don't you try actually caring about me for once?!" is just throwing a verbal grenade and wondering why the relationship keeps exploding.

The Complaint Translation Guide: The Bullshit Decoder Ring

Complaints need subtitles because what comes out of people's mouths isn't remotely close to what's actually happening in their lives.

When people complain, they're rarely saying what they actually mean. Here's your decoder ring for the most common complaint patterns:

COMPLAINT: "This ALWAYS happens to me!" ACTUAL TRANSLATION: "I've done absolutely nothing to prevent this totally predictable situation from happening again, but I expect different results every time." WHAT IT REVEALS: Refusal to spot patterns or accept that random stuff happens to everyone.

SELF-CHECK: "Has this happened before? What specific action did I take to prevent it?" REAL-WORLD EXAMPLE: Someone who constantly complains about traffic making them late, yet refuses to leave earlier, check traffic apps, or take alternate routes.

COMPLAINT: "I don't have time to fix this." ACTUAL TRANSLATION: "I found 3 hours for Instagram, 2 hours for Netflix, and 45 minutes to text everyone about how overwhelmed I am, but sure, I'm totally booked solid when it comes to actually solving my problems." WHAT IT REVEALS: Your real priorities - which apparently include everything except fixing the problems you keep complaining about.

SELF-CHECK: "What did I actually spend time on yesterday? Could even 15 minutes have gone toward this problem?"

COMPLAINT: "Nobody understands what I'm going through." ACTUAL TRANSLATION: "I want to believe my problems are so unique and special that nobody could possibly have solutions that would work for me." WHAT IT REVEALS: Your need to feel special is stronger than your desire to feel better.

SELF-CHECK: "Have other humans experienced similar challenges? What did they do that worked?"

THE QUICK TEST: Next time you're about to complain, ask: 1. Am I stating facts or just adding dramatic interpretation? 2. What do I actually need right now? (Usually it's validation or attention) 3. What would fixing this require? (Usually it's action you're avoiding)

Most complaints are just emotion-management strategies masquerading as communication. They're designed to get you sympathy without requiring you to change anything.

The Physical Price of Bitching: The Body's Complaint Tax

Complaints aren't just annoying everyone nearby—they're literally aging complainers faster than avocados left out in the sun.

HOW YOUR BODY PROCESSES COMPLAINTS

The human body can't tell the difference between actual danger and just bitching about stupid stuff. When someone complains about a coworker's annoying habits, their body reacts exactly like they're in danger.

The Stress Hormone Factory Every time someone starts complaining, their body floods with stress hormones. They pump out cortisol like they're about to fight a tiger, when really they're just mad that a barista wrote the wrong name on their cup. That hormone is meant for life-threatening situations, not coffee cup typos.

The Physical Symptoms Checklist:

Stress Belly: That extra weight around your middle? It's directly linked to chronic stress hormones from constant complaining.

Sleep Problems: Hard to rest when your brain is busy rehearsing tomorrow's grievances. Poor sleep makes everything worse, creating a cycle where physical symptoms trigger more complaints, which worsen physical symptoms.

Mystery Aches: Those random pains aren't mysterious at all. Chronic stress creates inflammation, which shows up as joint pain, muscle tension, headaches, and digestive issues.

Breaking this cycle isn't just about improving your attitude—it's about protecting your health. The good news? These physical changes can reverse surprisingly quickly once you stop the complaint habit.

PART 7: SHUTTING UP & SHOWING UP: THE SOCIAL IMPACT

The Anti-Bitching Arsenal: Three Weapons That Actually Work "Complaining is like eating chips in a library. Might feel good for a minute, but everyone around you is annoyed and nobody wants to sit near you afterward."

Breaking a complaint habit isn't like giving up soda—it's more like quitting an addiction while still being surrounded by it. Forget "just think positive" bullshit advice. Stop treating complaints like precious pets. They're parasites eating your life one bitching session at a time. Here are three techniques that actually work, from easiest to most challenging:

WEAPON 1: THE 24-HOUR QUARANTINE When a complaint bubbles up, write it down instead of saying it out loud. Check it again in 24 hours. Half your grievances will look ridiculous by then, and the rest might actually deserve action.

WEAPON 2: THE "SO WHAT NOW?" MANEUVER Train yourself to immediately follow any complaint with "and here's what I'm going to do about it." This transforms you from a weather reporter ("It's raining problems!") to an actual problem-solver.

Instead of: "The dating scene in this city is pathetic." Try: "The dating scene here is challenging, so I'm joining that book club this weekend."

Have no solution? Then at minimum add "so I'll think about this for 15 minutes tomorrow." Even a tiny action plan beats endless bitching.

WEAPON 3: THE GRATITUDE JUDO FLIP When you feel a complaint bubbling up, immediately flip it by identifying specific things to appreciate in that exact moment. Skip the generic "thankful for my blessings" crap and get ultra-specific: "The sun hitting my face right now feels amazing."

During genuinely awful moments, embrace ridiculously small wins: "At least my phone's charged" or "At least I look good today." People who commit to this practice report their entire outlook transforming—fewer complaints, more gratitude, with business success naturally following the mindset shift.

THE 30-DAY CHALLENGE: Use one technique per week for a month. Week 1: Count complaints (baseline). Week 2: 24-Hour Quarantine. Week 3: Add "So What Now?" Week 4: Master the Gratitude Judo flip. Track your progress. The visual chain of success becomes motivation not to break the streak.

In Chapter 4, you'll see how fairness complaints are premium versions of the bitching you're eliminating now. The tools you're learning here will be your foundation for handling the more sophisticated complairts that show up later.

The Network Effect of Negativity

Negativity spreads faster than those nude celebrity photos everybody claimed they didn't look at. One complaint and suddenly everybody's infected.

THE EMOTIONAL PANDEMIC

Chronic bitching isn't just ruining the complainer's life - it creates a ripple effect that spreads through entire social networks. When people constantly complain, they're not just expressing dissatisfaction - they're literally programming everyone around them to adopt their outlook.

ENVIRONMENTS MOST VULNERABLE TO COMPLAINT CONTAGION

IN FAMILIES: The dinner table becomes ground zero for negativity vibes. Parents who constantly complain about work teach children that careers are burdens rather than opportunities. Those children grow up expecting to hate their jobs because that's the model they've observed.

IN RELATIONSHIPS: Professional complainers pull their partners into their misery pit. Spend enough time with a negative person, and even the most optimistic partner starts seeing the world through shit-colored glasses. Your brain isn't complicated—you eventually start acting like whoever you spend the most time with.

IN WORKPLACES: One negative team member can drag down productivity for everyone. A study of healthcare teams found that groups with even one chronic complainer experienced higher error rates, lower patient satisfaction, and increased staff turnover.

THE GOOD STUFF SPREADS TOO

The flip side? Positivity is just as contagious as bitching, maybe even more so.

Your good mood affects everyone you interact with. You smile at the person in line behind you, who then holds the door for someone else, who compliments a stranger's outfit. Good vibes multiply just like the bad ones.

THE RIPPLE EFFECT OF POSITIVE THINKING

Optimism creates a powerful ripple effect in our environments. When you maintain a solution-focused mindset, you naturally influence those around you to adopt similar approaches. This isn't just feel-good philosophy—it's practical psychology.

In workplaces, positive thinking transforms team dynamics. When one person consistently approaches challenges with "How can we solve this?" instead of "This is impossible." the entire group gradually shifts toward solution-finding rather than problem-dwelling. Teams that focus on possibilities rather than limitations consistently outperform their negative counterparts.

Positive interactions also strengthen relationships in measurable ways. When you respond to someone's good news with genuine enthusiasm rather than complaints about your own situation, you build connection. These positive exchanges create what psychologists call "emotional deposits" that make relationships more resilient during difficult times.

Solution-focused conversations create momentum that complaint-centered ones never can. When you discuss what could work instead of what's broken, you activate creative thinking in yourself and others. This momentum builds as small solutions lead to bigger ones, creating a positive cycle that replaces the negative one.

Perhaps most importantly, positive environments attract more opportunities. People naturally gravitate toward those who energize rather than drain them. When you become known as someone who finds solutions instead of just pointing out problems, doors open. Colleagues bring you interesting projects, friends include you in their ventures, and new connections seek you out.

Look at any group chat that banned negativity for a month. Messages suddenly shift from "this sucks" to "here's what I tried." Problems that lingered for years get solved in days when people stop wasting energy bitching and start using it to fix shit instead.

The Social Consequences: What Happens When You're Known as a Complainer

The harsh truth? Right now, there's a group chat you're not in where your "friends" are making weekend plans. They didn't forget you. They actively decided life is better without your running commentary on how everything sucks.

People don't ghost complainers overnight—they gradually fade them out. First come delayed text responses. Then shorter replies. Finally, the dreaded "We should hang out sometime!"— social code for "not if I can help it."

We've all sat in rooms where someone suggests inviting the chronic complainer and everyone makes that same pained face. Then someone brave says what everyone's thinking: "I don't have the emotional energy for three hours of negativity today."

THE 3-STEP REPUTATION REPAIR PLAN

1. **Make one acknowledgment:** "I realize I've been negative lately. I'm working on that." No grand speeches.
2. **Follow the 3:1 rule:** For each complaint that slips out, offer three constructive comments.
3. **Stay consistent for 90 days:** The human brain needs repeated evidence to update its expectations.

In a world where everyone's emotional bandwidth is as limited as airplane WiFi, complainers get muted first. This isn't cruelty—it's self-preservation. Every relationship is an energy exchange, and complaints are massive withdrawals with minimal deposits.

PART 8: WHAT LIFE LOOKS LIKE WITHOUT THE BULLSHIT

Your Complaint Retirement Plan

The universe responds to actions, not feelings.

Nobody built a statue of a critic. They're too busy building statues of people who were too occupied doing shit to complain about it.

QUIT YOUR DAY JOB

It's time to quit Professional Bitching & Moaning LLC. You've been Employee of the Month in the Complaint Department way too long. The benefits package sucks, the coworkers are miserable, and there's zero room for advancement.

Effective immediately, start your new career at Actually Solving Shit, Inc.

This isn't just cute wordplay. It's moving from being shaped by circumstances to shaping them. From victim to creator. From passenger to driver.

ONE YEAR LATER: YOUR NEW REALITY

Picture this: Same job, city, and challenges. But you haven't complained for 365 days. Here's your new life:

Morning traffic still exists, but doesn't ruin your day. Your group chats contain plans instead of problems When stuff breaks, you fix it instead of photographing it for your misery portfolio. That idea you've had for years? You're six months into building it. Your friendships are fewer but deeper—quality over quantity. You sleep better because your brain isn't rehearsing tomorrow's grievances. **People actually listen when you speak because your words have weight now.**

This isn't fantasy—it's what happens when you redirect complaint energy toward solution energy. Same person, same circumstances, completely different results.

I'll start tomorrow are the most dangerous words you can say.

The world has enough critics. What it needs is builders. So close your mouth, open your eyes, and get to work.

The 60-Second Bottom Line

Life gives you exactly two options: 1. Keep bitching and stay exactly where you are 2. Shut up and fix what you can

Same 24 hours. Same problems. Different results.

THE "STOP WHINING" FORMULA

Convert your complaints into actions:

Instead of: "This traffic is killing me." **Try:** "I'll leave 15 minutes earlier or find a podcast worth listening to."

Instead of: "My boss is an asshole." **Try:** "I need to have a direct conversation or update my resume."

Instead of: "Dating apps are a waste of time." **Try:** "I'll try meeting people through things I actually enjoy doing."

This formula works for literally any complaint. The moment you shift from problem-describing to solution-creating, you activate entirely different neural pathways.

WHAT HAPPENS WHEN YOU QUIT COMPLAINING

When someone stops being the person everyone avoids: People pick up your calls again Opportunities appear "out of nowhere" (they were always there, just invisible through complaint-colored glasses) Your energy doubles (you're not wasting it on emotional drama) Your work gets noticed (because you're producing results, not just noise Your dating life improves (nobody swipes right on professional victims

Taking off those shit-colored glasses reveals a world with plenty of good stuff that was being filtered out while building a wall of complaints. The world doesn't suddenly improve - your ability to see beyond problems does.

Ready to stop talking about your problems and start solving them? Chapter 2 shows you how to cut through your own bullshit stories. Here's the thing: once you stop the constant complaining, you create mental space to see something even more important - the stories you've been telling yourself that keep you stuck. Your complaint habit has been hiding these stories from you, providing convenient distractions from the deeper self-deception.

When you stop bitching about external circumstances, you're forced to confront internal bullshit. That's where the real work begins. The complaint habit and self-deception are partners in crime - one keeps you focused outward while the other works behind the scenes. Breaking the complaint cycle is your first step toward seeing yourself clearly.

UP NEXT: Think you're finally done with the hard part? That's cute. The real work is just beginning.

Now that you've stopped filling the air with complaints, you're about to face the real enemy: your own bullshit stories. In Chapter 2, you'll discover the five lies you tell yourself that keep you stuck—including the big one that's sabotaging your goals right now without you even noticing.

CHAPTER 2: THE ART OF GETTING YOUR HEAD OUT OF YOUR ASS (AND SEEING DAYLIGHT AGAIN)

THE HUMAN ABILITY TO BULLSHIT ONESELF IS TRULY FUCKING IMPRESSIVE. MOST PEOPLE HAVE CONVINCED THEMSELVES THEY'RE 'ALMOST THERE' FOR SO LONG THAT THEIR EXCUSES HAVE BIRTHDAYS NOW.

PART 1: BEYOND COMPLAINTS - THE PRICE OF SELF-DECEPTION

REAL TALK: People can spot everyone's bullshit but their own like they've got fucking superhero vision. That "dream business" they've been "about to start" for three years? That fitness transformation they'll begin "after the holidays" (which holidays? ALL OF THEM apparently? That relationship pattern they keep repeating while wondering why they're still single? Let's call this what it is - heads so far up asses they could probably see tonsils. Pure delusion. Nothing more.

The complaint-free foundation from Chapter 1 was just the beginning. Complaints were never the main problem—they were the smoke screen hiding the real issue: the elaborate web of lies we tell ourselves. The stories about why we can't, shouldn't, or would-if-only. The comfortable delusions that let us feel good while accomplishing nothing.

The ultimate irony: I delayed writing this chapter for days while sitting on a draft about not making excuses. My procrastination masterclass while writing about self-deception proves I'm uniquely qualified—not because I've mastered these skills, but because I'm fighting the same battles as everyone else.

Why This Matters: The Self-Deception Tax

The average person wastes 3-5 YEARS of their life on goals they never actually take meaningful action toward. Think about that. Years. YEARS. Not hours or days. YEARS of one precious life, gone forever, while maintaining the comforting delusion of being "about to start." That's not just sad—it's a catastrophic waste of limited time on this planet.

This is your self-deception headquarters—the definitive guide to spotting your own bullshit. The most dangerous lies aren't the ones you tell others—they're the ones you tell yourself while nodding along like a fucking bobblehead.

These two things - complaints and self-deception - go together like drunk texting and regret. When someone stops numbing themselves with complaints, they're forced to face the uncomfortable truth: they've been lying to themselves more consistently than a politician during election season. They're about as trustworthy, too.

Those complaints people spew aren't just annoying everyone around them—they're serving as personal bodyguards protecting precious delusions. When someone complains to get validation from others, what they're really saying is "Please confirm that my excuses are totally legitimate and not complete bullshit." It's like asking friends to co-sign a loan for a failing business of lies. Complaints also function as shields against responsibility— medieval armor protecting against the deadly arrows of accountability. "I would have succeeded if my boss wasn't such a jerk" is just a fancy way of saying "I refuse to examine my own role in this situation because that would require actual work." Let's not forget how complaints let you position yourself as the victim in a cosmic tragedy rather than the author of your own mediocre story. "The universe is against me" sounds so much more dramatic and exonerating than "I consistently make poor choices and refuse to learn from them."

PART 2: SPOTTING YOUR OWN BULLSHIT AND DELUSIONS

We've all done it. Given perfect advice to a friend that we completely ignore ourselves. "You should really leave that toxic relationship" - said while texting an on-again-off-again ex for the 17th time this month. "You need to start saving more" - spoken while one-clicking another Amazon purchase that's absolutely unnecessary. "You should stand up to your boss" - mumbled right before saying "sounds great!" to a manager's request to work another weekend. Stop the mental masturbation and start doing the actual work.

Most people are fucking EXPERTS at diagnosing everyone's bullshit but their own. They can spot someone else's self-sabotage from outer space yet can't see their own when it's tattooed on their forehead.

Some people's heads are so far up their asses they're practically wearing themselves as hats. Basically human Russian nesting dolls at this point. The good news, though: nobody's alone in this, and extraction is entirely possible. Everyone's got their head up their ass about something. The only difference is some people are actively working on getting unstuck, while others are settling in for the long haul.

HARD TRUTH: The average person spends over 2 hours daily on what could generously be called "productive procrastination." That stuff that FEELS like work but produces exactly zero actual results. Color-coding task lists. Reorganizing notes. Researching the perfect app before writing a single word. That's over a month per year of sophisticated time-wasting disguised as productivity. A MONTH. Enough time to learn a language. Instead, you perfect the art of busy nothingness.

Self-Delusion in Action

Most people's self-awareness has worse reception than a flip phone in an elevator. Time to upgrade that mental hardware.

Everyone has their signature flavor of self-deception. Here are the main characters in this psychological circus, presented as a field guide to the wild beasts of self-deception. Learn to recognize these creatures in their natural habitat—your mind.

The Productivity App Collector This creature hoards organization apps like trophies—17 different to-do list apps downloaded during late-night "getting my life together" moments. More time spent comparing Notion vs. Evernote than completing actual tasks. Their mantra: "I just need the right system" as they download yet another task manager at 11:43 PM on a Tuesday. They've spent 14 hours this month customizing their productivity dashboard that they've used for exactly 7 minutes of actual work. Their phone storage is 80% productivity apps they opened once.

The Tab Hoarder Their browser resembles an anxiety attack—74 open tabs for "research" on projects they'll start "any day now." Computer fans working overtime to keep open pages they haven't viewed in weeks but are "definitely getting back to." They have 16 tabs open about starting a podcast, 23 about passive income strategies, and 35 about "morning routines of successful people" that they read at 1 AM while eating cereal straight from the box.

The External Circumstances Blamer Attributes all failures to outside forces—bosses, economy, upbringing, planetary alignments—anything to avoid personal responsibility. Has used the phrase "the stars aren't aligned" to explain why they missed a deadline. Believes their specific industry is uniquely challenging in ways nobody else could possibly understand. Has blamed traffic for being late 37 times this year while never once considering leaving earlier.

The Reorganization Specialist Substitutes sorting for accomplishment. Color-coded bookshelves, elaborate file systems, and alphabetized spice racks take priority over actual deadlines. "I work better in an organized environment" justifies productive procrastination. Has reorganized their desk three times this week but hasn't started the project due tomorrow. Their desk has perfectly labeled containers for every paper clip size containing a total of two actual documents.

The more of these that make you shift uncomfortably in your seat, the deeper your head is lodged. This isn't about judgment. It's about honest recognition. Because you can't extract what you won't acknowledge is stuck.

Let's call this what it is: sophisticated bullshit protecting your ego while your dreams die.

Growth happens outside your comfort zone. Comfort is where dreams die.

Someone spends six months "researching" how to start a business instead of actually starting it. They reorganize notes three times, watch countless YouTube videos, and create a beautiful multi-tabbed project plan that absolutely nobody gives a shit about. Meanwhile, their neighbor with half their education has already launched, failed twice, pivoted, and is now making actual money.

The difference? One head is pointed toward reality while the other is enjoying the scenic tour of its own colon.

Or maybe they're "writing a book." And by writing, they mean talking about writing, thinking about writing, reading books about writing, and doing literally every possible writing-adjacent activity except actually putting words on a fucking page.

This was me while writing this book, and if you're reading this, I finally got my head out my ass and completed the book.

PART 3: THE TAXONOMY OF SELF-DECEPTION

Everybody lies. But the most dangerous lies aren't the ones people tell others - they're the ones they tell themselves. And holy shit, are most people GOOD at it. They build impressive arsenals of self-deceptions that they deploy instinctively to avoid discomfort, responsibility, and actual work.

The truly terrifying part? These lies sound completely reasonable. They make perfect sense. They feel TRUE. That's what makes them so deadly - people fall for their own con. This isn't about managing emotions—it's about stopping the lies that prevent action.

I've categorized these self-deceptions into a taxonomy after studying thousands of excuses—both from clients and, painfully, from my own arsenal of bullshit. Each category represents a different psychological defense mechanism designed to protect us from the discomfort of reality.

1. **The Temporal Illusions**

   Overthinking feels productive but creates nothing.

   These are lies about time—when we'll start, how much time we have, and why now isn't right.

   The Monday Myth: "I'll start on Monday" - the official slogan tattooed on the ass of every person who never starts anything. This lie combines the illusion of a specific plan with the emotional comfort of delay. It feels concrete. It sounds reasonable.

   Except Monday comes, and suddenly Tuesday seems like a better option. Then it's "after this project." Then "when things calm down." Then "in the new year." People have been "starting on Monday" since flip phones were cutting-edge technology. Monday is just the fictional land where all good intentions go to die.

Procrastination costs you the life you could've lived.

Take Mozart as an example. He died at 35 after creating over 600 musical works. SIX HUNDRED. Meanwhile, most people can't find 20 minutes for their side hustle because they're watching YouTube videos called "How to Be Super Productive" while simultaneously scrolling Instagram. Mozart wrote entire symphonies while many can't even write a simple email without checking TikTok three times.

I once tracked my own time for a week and discovered I was spending 14 hours weekly on "research" (read: mindless internet browsing while claiming I "couldn't find time" to write. The data didn't lie—I was lying to myself.

This is your brain's bullshit-justification system in action— we'll reference this mechanism throughout the book. Cognitive dissonance is the mental gymnastics your brain performs when your actions don't match your self-image. It's the psychological equivalent of Photoshopping reality to protect your ego.

2. **The Uniqueness Fallacies** These are lies about how special our circumstances are and why normal rules don't apply to us.
   "Well that guy had connections..." "She probably had money to start with..." "They don't have kids like I do..." "My metabolism is different..." Blah blah fucking blah.
   The cold truth? Most people's obstacles might be real, but they're about as unique as a Starbucks order. For every barrier someone uses as an excuse, someone else with more disadvantages, fewer resources, and worse circumstances has already overcome that exact same thing - and they did it without creating a PowerPoint presentation about why their situation is so special.

3. **The Readiness Myths** These are lies about preparation, perfectionism, and why we can't start yet.

The truth is way more uncomfortable: nobody will ever feel completely ready for anything worth doing. EVER. Not the first time they have sex. Not when they have a kid. Not when they start a business. The significant stuff always feels like jumping off a cliff with half a parachute. **That's not a bug - it's a feature.**

Learning happens through action and failure, not through endless preparation. While some people are "getting ready," others are learning by doing, falling on their faces, and getting better while the preparers are still color-coding their plan for the seventeenth time.

TRUTH BOMB: These self-deceptions aren't random —they form patterns unique to each person. Your particular combination of these lies creates your personal "bullshit fingerprint" that shows up across different areas of your life.

"Your strongest self already exists. Stop making excuses and become it."

PART 4: THE FOUR STAGES OF SELF-DECEPTION

The Delusion Progression: How Deep Is Your Head?

This level of bullshit doesn't develop overnight. People work on it for years, perfecting it, upgrading it from amateur hour to professional-grade delusion. It's like watching someone transform from casual drinker to full-blown alcoholic - there are distinct stages, and most people are in one of them right now.

I've mapped this progression through years of coaching and, embarrassingly, through my own journey of head-up-ass thinking. Each stage has psychological mechanisms and behavioral patterns that create a predictable downward spiral.

Stage 1: The Innocent Postponement This is the gateway drug to full-blown delusion. People genuinely intend to do the thing but decide to wait for a "better time." Maybe after this busy period at work. Or once the kids are back in school. Or when Mercury isn't in whatever the fuck retrograde is.

They still believe they're going to do it. And technically, they haven't failed yet because they haven't really started. It's the perfect crime.

What's really happening: They're creating a fantasy Future Self who will somehow have more discipline, motivation, energy, and free time than Current Self, despite being the same exact person. It's like expecting to wake up tomorrow with six-pack abs after years of Doritos for dinner.

Stage 2: The Sophisticated Procrastination Now we're getting serious. They're not just putting things off anymore—they're putting them off while feeling productive. They're "preparing," "researching," "strategizing," or "building a foundation."

Their procrastination has dressed up in a business suit and is carrying a briefcase full of important-looking but ultimately useless activities. They've got spreadsheets, planners, and seventeen browser tabs of research. They're "almost ready" to start. Just need to watch three more YouTube tutorials.

What's really happening: All these preparation activities give them the dopamine hit of accomplishment without the risk of failure that comes with actual execution. It's like intellectual masturbation - feels good, produces nothing.

Stage 3: The Identity Without Evidence Congratulations on the promotion to advanced bullshitter! Now people graduate to actually identifying as the thing they're not doing. They call themselves entrepreneurs who haven't launched, writers who don't write, or fitness enthusiasts whose most strenuous activity is opening the packaging on workout clothes. They build entire self-images around activities rarely performed. They talk about "their writing" at parties. They have business cards for businesses that don't exist. Their Instagram bios say "fitness junkie" but their fitness trackers think they died three months ago.

What's really happening: They're getting the social rewards of an identity without doing the work that actually creates that identity. It's like wearing a police uniform to get free coffee at Dunkin' Donuts when not even being a cop.

Stage 4: The Delusional Fortress The final boss level. By this stage, people have built impenetrable fortresses of excuses, justifications, and elaborate explanations for why their lack of progress isn't their fault. Their delusion has developed its own immune system that attacks any reality that threatens it.

Someone points out that they've been "about to launch" their podcast for three years? That person clearly doesn't understand how competitive the space is. Friend mentions they haven't written anything in months despite calling themselves a writer? That friend is just jealous of their creativity. Partner suggests maybe they're not actually a fitness person? That partner is being unsupportive and toxic.

What's really happening: They've invested so much in their excuses that admitting the truth would be too painful. Their delusion is no longer just a postponement strategy—it's a core part of their identity that they're defending like it's the last water in a desert.

REALITY CHECK: Most people oscillate between stages 2 and 3, with occasional visits to stage 4 when directly challenged. The deeper you go, the harder extraction becomes—but it's never impossible.

PART 5: WHY DELUSIONS FEEL SO GOOD AND DESTROY RELATIONSHIPS

The Delusion Economy: Where People Go Bankrupt Without Knowing It

Self-deception is basically its own little fucked-up economy inside people's heads. Let's break down this mental Ponzi scheme they're running:

What You Think You're Getting (The Short-Term Payoffs):

That sweet, sweet comfort of never having to face limitations. It's like emotional novocaine—numbing the pain of realizing they might not be as talented, disciplined, or exceptional as they thought. Why feel the sting of reality when they can wrap themselves in the warm blanket of "I could totally do it if circumstances were different"?

Their ego gets to stay inflated like a bounce house at a kid's birthday party. Their self-image remains pristine and untarnished by the dirty fingerprints of actual evidence. They get to keep thinking they're genius entrepreneurs who just haven't had their big break yet, rather than people who start things and abandon them when they get difficult.

You've got pre-packaged explanations for every failure that conveniently place the blame anywhere but on you. It's like having a 24/7 PR team dedicated to spinning your life story. "I would have succeeded if my boss wasn't such a micromanager" sounds so much better than "I consistently miss deadlines and produce subpar work."

The illusion of control is perhaps the most intoxicating benefit "I could succeed if I wanted to" is the ultimate get-out-of-jail-free card. It preserves the fantasy that your potential is limitless— you're just choosing not to tap into it right now.

And let's not forget the dopamine hit of potential without the risk of action. Talking about writing a book gives you 80% of the social validation of actually writing one, with 0% of the work. It's like nutritional fraud—all the taste of accomplishment with none of the calories burned.

What You're Actually Paying (The Long-Term Costs):

Your self-perception and reality are diverging like a bad marriage, creating an ocean-sized gap that gets harder to bridge with each passing day. Eventually, you're living in a parallel universe that exists only in your head.

You're preventing the very growth you claim to want. Real learning happens through failure and adjustment, but you've bubble-wrapped yourself against the educational value of falling on your face. It's like wanting muscles while avoiding the gym because lifting is uncomfortable. Fucking ridiculous.

Your relationships are taking a hit as people gradually realize they can't trust what you say. They've noticed that your "almost finished novel" has been "almost finished" for three years. Your credibility is eroding faster than a sandcastle at high tide.

You're creating a self-imposed isolation as you increasingly avoid anyone who might challenge your carefully constructed narrative. Your social circle slowly filters down to yes-men and enablers who won't call you on your bullshit, creating an echo chamber of mediocrity.

And the final bill comes due in the form of profound regret. That moment—usually around middle age—when you realize how much time you've wasted on potential rather than action. When you understand that all those "somedays" have turned into "never" and the window of opportunity is closing. That's when the true cost of your delusion hits you like a freight train of regret.

The most dangerous aspect of delusion is how gradually it disconnects you from reality. Like the proverbial frog in slowly boiling water, you don't notice the increasing temperature of bullshit until you're fully cooked in it.

REALITY CHECK: The comfort of delusion is a short-term loan with crushing interest rates. Every day you spend in self-deception, you're accumulating psychological debt that will eventually come due—often at the least convenient moment. This isn't just a solo disaster movie playing in your head. The comfort you get from your delusions comes at a direct cost to everyone around you. Your self-deception is essentially a relationship tax that others are forced to pay against their will.

This is how self-deception transitions from a personal comfort mechanism to a relationship wrecking ball—which brings us to the next phase of extraction surgery.

Relationship Destruction 101

Relationship Wreckage: How Self-Deception Ruins Your Connections

Your self-deception isn't just a personal problem—it's relationship napalm. The lies you tell yourself inevitably become lies you tell others, creating a widening credibility gap that no relationship can survive indefinitely.

The Relationship Wrecking Ball: How Your Bullshit Demolishes Connections

In Romantic Relationships:

"The Competence Con"—promising "I'll handle it" for everything from bills to home repairs, but consistently failing to follow through. Your partner knows your promises require multiple reminders and often end with them doing the task themselves while you act annoyed at their lack of trust.

"The Effort Illusion"—believing you're giving your all while delivering the bare minimum. A single romantic gesture from years ago becomes your evidence of effort while your partner slowly withers from emotional neglect.

"The Change Mirage"—perpetually claiming you're "working on" issues while making zero actual changes. Your promises to improve have anniversaries now, and your predictable patterns have become a relationship calendar.

In Friendships:

"The Flake Justification"—canceling plans with elaborate excuses while being mysteriously available when you need something. Your "something came up" texts arrive with such regularity that friends plan for your absence.

"The Support Imbalance"—taking far more emotional support than you give. Friends' problems receive token acknowledgment before conversation redirects to your ongoing drama that somehow requires hours of their emotional labor.

"The Listening Pretense"—believing you're attentive while simply waiting for your turn to speak. Friends could announce life-changing news and you'd immediately relate it back to your own experience.

In Work Relationships:

"The Competence Facade"—projecting expertise while avoiding asking for help. Your knowing nods in meetings mask complete confusion, preventing the support you actually need.

"The Responsibility Dodge"—crafting elaborate explanations for missed deadlines that rival fiction. Your "spam folder" apparently consumes important emails that everyone else manages to receive.

"The False Progress Report"—claiming projects are "90% complete" when they're barely started. Colleagues mentally recalibrate your progress reports, subtracting significant percentages from whatever figure you claim.

The ultimate toxic dynamic? Your self-deception forces others to either validate your delusions or get pushed out of your life, creating an echo chamber where truth becomes unwelcome and reality checks are seen as personal attacks.

TRUTH BOMB: The most reliable predictor of relationship failure isn't conflict—it's self-deception. Couples with a realistic view of each other and themselves have significantly higher relationship satisfaction and longevity than those who maintain comfortable delusions.

PART 6: RECOGNIZING YOUR BULLSHIT PATTERNS

Finding your personal flavor of bullshit matters because generic advice is useless here - it's like trying to open your apartment with your neighbor's key. Ain't gonna work. It's like trying to cure a specific infection with random antibiotics—you might get lucky, but more likely you'll just create resistance while the original problem flourishes.

The Bullshit Personality Types: Which One Are You?

Everyone has their signature flavor of self-deception. Here are the main characters in this psychological circus, presented as a field guide to the wild beasts of self-deception. Learn to recognize these creatures in their natural habitat—your mind.

🎓 The Infinite Preparer

Forever "getting ready to start." Believes one more book, course, or research session is needed before taking action. Has read every resource, owns all the right tools, and discusses advanced concepts fluently—but produces zero actual results. A theoretical expert with impressive knowledge and nonexistent output.

The Infinite Preparer's mind is like a hoarder's house—crammed with valuable information that's become useless because there's so much of it they can't find anything when needed, and no room left to actually do the work.

⏰ The Someday Specialist

Identifying Call: "After the holidays, I'm really going to focus on this..." Lives exclusively in future tense. "After the holidays" has been their mantra through multiple abandoned goals and forgotten resolutions. Creates detailed success fantasies

("When my podcast takes off..." with implementation plans written in invisible ink. Friends can recite their future plans from memory while their present consists mainly of talking about "someday."

The Someday Specialist treats their goals like an imaginary friend—talks about them constantly, has elaborate stories involving them, but deep down knows they aren't real.

📖 **The Excuse Encyclopedist Natural Habitat:** Comment sections and complaint circles Identifying Call: "You don't understand how hard it is for me specifically..." Has developed a scholarly collection of reasons why nothing is their fault. Can instantly identify why any suggestion won't work for their 'special circumstances.' Has an excuse ready faster than Google can search, ranging from time constraints to energy levels to 'the algorithm is against me.' Genuinely believes their obstacles are uniquely challenging, as if the universe has a special task force dedicated to their personal downfall.

The Excuse Encyclopedist's mind is like a high-powered defense attorney that never loses a case—because the client (their ego pays in the valuable currency of never having to change or grow.

🎭 **The Identity Investor Natural Habitat:** Social media bios and networking events Identifying Call: "As a writer/entrepreneur/athlete, I believe..."

The Identity Investor is like someone who buys expensive cooking equipment, follows chef influencers, and talks about cuisine—but orders takeout every night because actually cooking is too much work.

👀 **The Comparative Comforter Natural Habitat:** Social media and gossip sessions Identifying Call: "Well, she only succeeded because..."

Specializes in consuming others' failures for emotional comfort. Minimizes others' achievements by identifying advantages: "She wrote a bestseller, but her cousin works in publishing."

Feels relief when peers struggle in areas where they've made no progress—collecting permission slips to keep underachieving.

The Comparative Comforter's mind operates like a biased sports commentator who can explain away why every win by the opposing team doesn't really count, while every loss by their team was due to unfair circumstances.

I've personally been every single one of these types at different points in my life. My specialty was the infinite preparer, that would watch endless YouTube tutorials until I was exhausted and didn't have energy to act. The someday specialist where I would always push back what I could do that day to a future day. Excuse encyclopedist by saying I don't have enough money to start this app, release this project, or do anything. Comparative comforter while saying everyone else had it easier than me for any reason I could make up that day.

YOUR SIGNATURE FLAVOR: Which character makes you uncomfortable? That's your primary delusion pattern —your escape route when facing potential failure. This isn't about judgment but recognition. You can't change what you refuse to identify.

Catching Yourself in the Act

The Verbal Bullshit: Phrases That Should Set Off Your Internal Alarm

Your mouth is basically a bullshit factory producing these classic hits on repeat. If you catch yourself saying any of these, your delusion alarm should be blaring louder than a car alarm at 3 AM:

▶ **The Time-Shifting Phrases** "I'll start on Monday/next week/after this project/in the new year" – The classic postponement anthem. Monday is the fictional land where all your good intentions live but never actually materialize. It's like promising to visit a friend who lives in another country—sounds nice, probably

43

won't happen. "This is just a temporary situation" – Said about a "temporary" situation that's outlasted multiple of your romantic relationships. Your "temporary" job has become your career, your "temporary" apartment has become your long-term home, and your "temporary" weight gain is now your permanent body type.

▶ **The Potential-Preserving Phrases** "I could if I really wanted to" – The ultimate self-delusion power move. It preserves your ego while requiring zero evidence. It's like claiming you could totally win a major industry award if you felt like training, but you just don't feel like it right now. "I'm almost ready to..." – The perpetual state of almost-ness. You've been "almost ready" to launch that website since Bitcoin was worth $1. "Almost" is the comfort zone where nothing actually happens but you get to feel like it might.

▶ **The Prerequisite Phrases** "I just need one more thing before I can..." – The endless prerequisite game. There's always one more book to read, one more course to take, one more tool to buy. It's like saying you need to understand quantum physics before you can make a sandwich. "I'm waiting for the right opportunity" – As if opportunity is supposed to kick down your door, introduce itself formally, and present its credentials for your approval. Meanwhile, actual opportunities are passing by like taxis in the rain while you wait for a limousine.

▶ **The False Activity Phrases** "I'm working on it" – The classic when you haven't touched the project since Game of Thrones was still good. This phrase should come with a timestamp of when you last actually worked on it. "I'm working on it (last active: 267 days ago)."

I caught myself using the "I'm almost ready" line about this book for months. I had outlines, research, and concepts—everything except actual written pages. When I finally admitted this pattern, I set a timer for 30 minutes and just started typing. The result? Eight pages of usable content that became the foundation for this chapter. I'd been lying to myself for months about "preparation" when I just needed to put my ass in the chair and write.

The Behavioral Bullshit: Actions That Reveal Your Delusions

Your body language and behaviors are snitching on your delusions even when your mouth is shut. These physica tells are like poker "tells" that reveal when you're bluffing—not just to others, but to yourself:

▶ **The Defense Mechanisms** You get more defensive than a medieval castle when someone asks about progress on goals you claim are important. Simple questions like "How's that book coming along?" trigger fight-or-flight responses normally reserved for bear encounters. You change the subject faster than a politician caught in a scandal when certain topics arise. Your conversational pivots are so smooth they could qualify for Olympic gymnastics.

▶ **The Narrative Creations** You have elaborate explanations for your lack of progress that are more detailed and creative than your actual projects. Your excuse narratives have better character development and plot structure than most Netflix originals. You spend more time talking about future plans than a sci-fi writer, while your present actions consist mainly of scrolling through Instagram. Your future self is apparently going to be incredibly productive, while your present self is mainly focused on perfecting the art of procrastination.

▶ **The Avoidance Patterns** You avoid people who ask direct questions about your progress like they're carrying a contagious disease. Your social circle has gradually filtered down to only those who don't challenge your comfortable delusions. You have more abandoned projects than a neglectful parent, yet still tell people you're "working on them" as if they're all active ventures. Your graveyard of half-started ideas could fill a museum of good intentions.

SELF-ASSESSMENT: Think about the last three times you felt a flicker of discomfort or defensiveness when someone asked about your progress on something. This discomfort is your built-in delusion detector trying to alert you to the gap between your self-image and reality. It's like the check engine light on your car—ignore it at your peril.

Truth Triggers: When Your Bullshit Generator Goes Into Overdrive

The Success of Others (AKA The "They Got Lucky" Reflex) This is probably the most common pattern. When you see someone succeeding where you're struggling, your brain doesn't just get a little jealous - it launches a full-blown search-and-destroy mission against their achievement. It's like having your own personal investigation team dedicated to finding any reason why their success doesn't count.

"She only got that book deal because of connections." (Not because she actually wrote the damn book while you were thinking about writing one.

"He only lost weight because he has good genetics." (Nothing to do with the fact that he's at the gym while you're on the couch theorizing about genetics.

"They only built that successful business because they had startup capital." (Meanwhile your "business idea" hasn't even made it out of your Notes app.

Your mind becomes a fucking prosecutor building a case against their success to protect your fragile ego from asking the one question that might actually help you: "What if I'm not doing what it takes to succeed?" Easier to dismiss others' accomplishments than examine your own lack of effort, right?

Feedback From Others (AKA The "You Don't Understand" Defense) When someone offers constructive criticism, your brain treats it like a biological attack. Before they've even finished speaking, you've already generated seventeen reasons why their feedback is invalid, biased, or uninformed. "You don't understand my unique situation." "You're just jealous." "You've always been negative." Your mental immune system attacks the feedback before it can infect you with the dangerous virus of self-awareness.

Time Passing (AKA The "I'm Still Young" Delusion) Birthdays. New Year's. Class reunions. Facebook posts about your high school classmate's third book deal. These timeline markers don't just make you uncomfortable - they activate your brain's excuse-generating machinery like someone hit the emergency button at a bullshit factory.

Suddenly, you're manufacturing explanations so elaborate they deserve their own Netflix documentary series:

"I'm taking a different path." (Translation: I have no fucking idea where I'm going but I'm pretending it's intentional.)

"Success isn't linear." (Translation: I've made zero progress in five years but read this quote on Instagram once.)

"I'm still figuring things out." (Translation: I've been "figuring things out" since the iPhone 4 was cutting-edge technology.)

"The traditional markers of success are just social constructs anyway." (Translation: I'm terrified I'm falling behind so I'll pretend the race doesn't exist.)

Meanwhile, the clock keeps ticking. You keep getting older. Time - that non-renewable resource - keeps vanishing while your excuses get increasingly creative and your results stay exactly the same. Of course, you're "about to figure it all out" any day now. Just like you've been saying since 2011.

Identity Challenges (AKA The "That's Not Who I Am" Panic) When something threatens how you see yourself—like evidence that you're not as hardworking, talented, or ethical as you believe—your brain creates reality distortions that would impress a sci-fi writer. If you think of yourself as generous yet evidence suggests otherwise, you'll create an entire alternative reality where your stinginess doesn't exist or is actually a form of prudence. Your self-concept is the fortress of your psyche—heavily defended against any attack on its walls.

Relationship Mirrors (AKA The "You're Projecting" Reversal) When someone close to you reflects behaviors you don't want to acknowledge in yourself, your brain performs professional-level mental contortions to avoid recognition. Your partner points out that you're being controlling—just like you complain someone else in your life is—and suddenly you're explaining why these situations are COMPLETELY different. The closer someone is to you, the more likely they are to reflect your own issues back to you, the harder your delusion machine works to reject the reflection.

The solution isn't complicated, though it's about as comfortable as sleeping on a bed of nails: when you feel that defensive discomfort rising, that's your cue to lean in, not away. The discomfort functions like a neon sign pointing to exactly where your growth is hiding. It shows you where to look, not where to look away. The moment you feel yourself getting defensive is precisely when you should be getting curious.

PART 7: GETTING YOUR HEAD OUT OF YOUR ASS

The secret to breaking free from your mental prison: You need something solid to grab onto while you're pulling. Think of these as your personal bullshit circuit breakers—the emergency shut-off switches when your delusion generator goes into overdrive. Find yours and follow it like your life depends on it. Because your actual life - the one you could be living instead of this sad pretend version - absolutely does.

For The Infinite Preparer: The "Shut Up And Do It Already" Protocol Let's not sugarcoat this: your brain is a straight-up research junkie. You're constantly chasing the next information high while avoiding the withdrawal symptoms of actually DOING something. You've got more saved articles than the Library of

Congress. Your Kindle is so full of unread books it's practically begging for mercy.

So here's your new rule, and it's brutally simple: For every hour spent consuming information, you must spend at least THREE HOURS implementing what you already know. No exceptions. No negotiations. No "but this one is different."

That productivity podcast you're about to download? Not happening until you've applied the concepts from the last seven you listened to. That business book that just came out? It can wait until you've actually used the strategies from the dozen already on your shelf collecting dust.

Your brain will fight this like a toddler fights bedtime - tantrums, negotiations, promises, threats - the works. Don't give in. You already know enough to start. Honestly, you probably knew enough six months ago. The rest of this "research" is just procrastination wearing a tweed jacket and pretending to be education. This represents fear in a fancy disguise.

For The Someday Specialist: The "There Is No Tomorrow" Intervention Your fantasy future self is the most productive person who's never existed. Meanwhile, your actual self keeps pushing everything important into a tomorrow that never arrives. Your new reality check is the "Today Only" list: Write down 1-3 small, specific actions that you will complete TODAY as if tomorrow doesn't exist.

Ban the phrases "I'll start when..." and "After I..." from your vocabulary—they're just your brain's way of writing checks it has no intention of cashing. When you catch yourself saying "I'll do it after the holidays," stop and ask, "What's the smallest piece of this I could do in the next 3 hours?" Then do that piece immediately. Your future self is a myth; only your present self gets things done.

For The Excuse Encyclopedist: The "Control Freak" Therapy Your brain is a master prosecutor, building airtight cases for why nothing is your fault and everything is conspiring against you. Your new practice is the Control Inventory: For any situation you're facing, create three honest categories: "Within My Control," "Within My Influence," and "Outside My Control."

The trick? You're only allowed to think about, talk about, or act on items in the first two categories. The third category exists only for acknowledgment, then immediate dismissal. Your brain will desperately try to expand the "Outside My Control" list because it's your get-out-of-responsibility-free card. Fight this tendency like your life depends on it—because your results absolutely do.

For The Identity Investor: The "Poser Tax" System You've been collecting identities like they're Pokemon cards—claiming to be things you rarely actually do. Your new reality check is the Identity Audit: List every identity you claim (entrepreneur, writer, athlete, etc.), then track the actual hours spent on core activities versus peripheral activities for each one.

Core activities directly produce results: writing words, making sales, exercising. Peripheral activities feel related but produce no output: organizing your writing space, researching business tools, buying workout clothes. Your new rule: Maintain a minimum 5:1 ratio of core to peripheral activities, or surrender the identity. No more calling yourself a writer if you spend 10 hours reading about writing for every 1 hour of actual writing. The poser tax is paid in real output or the identity label gets revoked.

For The Comparative Comforter: The "Stay In Your Own Lane" Discipline Your brain is constantly rubbernecking at other people's journeys, either to feel better about your lack of progress or to explain away their success. Your new practice is the Advantage Inventory: Create a comprehensive list of YOUR specific advantages (education, health, time, skills, connections, etc.).

When you catch yourself comparing, immediately redirect to your own inventory and trajectory. Study successful people exclusively for strategies you can implement, not for advantages you can envy or use as excuses. Your new mantra: "Their journey is irrelevant to mine except for what I can learn and apply." This isn't about ignoring systemic issues—it's about focusing your limited energy where it can actually create change.

Choose the Reality Anchor that matches your highest-scoring delusion pattern and implement it RIGHT NOW. Not after you finish reading this chapter. Not tomorrow morning when you're "fresh." NOW. Because if you're thinking "I'll start this tomorrow," you've already proven you need it today.

PART 8: TAKING ACTION NOW

From Self-Deception to Self-Direction: Your Immediate Next Step

Escaping your self-created maze is entirely possible and surprisingly simple (though not easy). It starts with one small action that breaks the cycle of delusion. Not tomorrow. Not when you "feel ready." Now.

The No-More-Bullshit Blueprint:

Stop reading for a minute. Seriously. This isn't the part where you nod along thinking "good advice" while continuing to do absolutely nothing different. This is the part where you actually do something.

Step 1: Name Your Poison Which flavor of self-deception is your personal favorite? Be honest—which of the five bullshit patterns made you wince with recognition? That's your starting point. Not the one you think sounds smartest or is easiest to fix—the one that actually describes your life. Write it down. Say it out loud. "I am a [your pattern here]." Feel uncomfortable? Good. That's the feeling of reality making first contact with your bubble of delusion.

Step 2: Grab Your Reality Lifeline Take the corresponding Reality Anchor for your pattern and implement it right now. Not after you finish this book. Not tomorrow when you're "fresh." RIGHT NOW. Set a timer on your phone. Create the spreadsheet. Make the list. The longer you wait, the more likely your brain will generate a sophisticated reason why "now isn't the best time." There is no perfect time to start being honest with yourself—there's just now or never.

Step 3: Do One Ridiculously Small Thing Identify the tiniest possible action you can take toward a goal you've been delaying, and do it within the next 60 minutes. Not planning it. Not researching it. Not organizing your workspace for it. DOING it. Write one paragraph. Send one email. Make one sales call. Do one pushup. The action should be so small it feels almost stupid— that's how you know it's right. Your brain wants grand gestures because they're easy to postpone. Tiny actions can happen immediately, and that's what breaks the spell of delusion.

The difference between people with their heads up their asses and people making real progress isn't intelligence, resources, or luck. It's the willingness to face reality and take consistent action despite discomfort. The good news? Reality is waiting patiently for you to rejoin it. And trust me—the view is much better out here.

The Head Extraction Summary

Stepping out of your own shadow isn't random—it's a carefully choreographed dance of bullshit that follows predictable patterns. Once you recognize your signature moves, you can interrupt the routine before you complete another lap around the delusion dance floor.

Every lie you tell yourself can be flipped into its opposite truth. "I don't have time" becomes "I'm not making this a priority." "I'll start when I'm ready" becomes "I'll never feel ready, so I might as well start now." "My situation is different" becomes "My excuses are the same as everyone else's."

All that mental energy you're spending maintaining your elaborate fantasy world? It's like using a Ferrari to deliver newspapers—a catastrophic waste of high-performance equipment. Redirect that brainpower toward actual progress and watch how quickly your reality transforms.

Your self-deception isn't just screwing you over—it's contaminating every relationship in your life. Your partner, friends, and colleagues can all smell your bullshit, even when you can't. They're just too polite (or too tired) to call you on it anymore.

When you finally extract your head from your ass, the world doesn't just look different—it IS different. Opportunities you couldn't see before suddenly appear. Resources you thought weren't available materialize. And most importantly, you stop being your own biggest obstacle to the life you claim to want.

CHAPTER CONNECTION: THE BRIDGE TO EMOTIONAL RESILIENCE

Now that you've broken free from your mental prison and can see reality clearly, it's time for the next crucial step: actually DOING something with that newfound clarity. This is the natural progression of your transformation journey:

1. Chapter 1: You stopped poisoning your environment with complaints, creating space for honest self-reflection.
2. Chapter 2: You confronted the comfortable lies that kept you stuck, giving you an accurate map of reality.
3. Chapter 3: You'll develop the emotional backbone needed to act on this clarity despite discomfort. For a deeper dive into how fairness obsession creates the ultimate victim trap, see Chapter 4.

Here's the truth that most self-help books won't tell you: clarity without action is just another form of sophisticated procrastination. It's like having a perfect map but refusing to start the journey. You can see exactly where you need to go, but your feet won't move.

Why? Because even with your newfound self-awareness, you'll still face resistance when trying to change. Your brain will fight you every step of the way. It will create new, more sophisticated excuses. It will manufacture fear, doubt, and uncertainty. It will try to convince you that "knowing is enough" and that you deserve a break before taking action.

This brings us to our next chapter: Building An Emotional Backbone—where you'll develop the resilience needed to face discomfort and keep moving forward when things get tough. The self-awareness you've gained here isn't the end goal—it's the essential foundation for the emotional strength you'll build next.

Without this emotional backbone, your clarity becomes just another exhibit in your personal museum of good intentions. With it, you'll finally transform knowledge into action, and action into the life you've been bullshitting yourself about wanting.

CHAPTER 3: BUILDING AN EMOTIONAL BACKBONE (SO LIFE CAN'T BEND YOU UNTIL YOU BREAK)

"EMOTIONAL STRENGTH ISN'T ABOUT BEING UNSHAKABLE—IT'S ABOUT BEING THE PERSON WHO GETS KNOCKED DOWN SEVEN TIMES BUT STANDS UP EIGHT, WITH A MIDDLE FINGER RAISED TO LIFE'S BULLSHIT."

PART 1: EMOTIONAL WEAKLINGS VS. MENTAL TITANS

IMAGINE THIS: You can spot the emotional weaklings from a mile away. They're melting down over minor inconveniences, treating feedback like assassination attempts, and turning simple setbacks into personal apocalypses. Meanwhile, some people face genuine catastrophes—job loss, health crises, relationship implosions—without breaking stride. The difference isn't luck or genetics. It's emotional backbone, and it's time to build yours.

Now that you recognize your own bullshit from Chapter 2, you need emotional capacity to face uncomfortable truths without crumbling. Self-awareness without emotional backbone is a recipe for paralysis—seeing problems clearly but lacking capacity to address them. Those self-deception patterns you identified will trigger emotional resistance when you try changing them. That's where emotional backbone becomes essential.

The Ultimate Psychological Upgrade: From Emotional Jellyfish to Steel Spine

> "Most people's emotional stability is built like a house of cards—impressive until someone breathes too hard in its general direction."

Building emotional resilience is essential to make changes stick. Without this foundation, self-awareness will just become another thing to feel crappy about.

Ever seen someone completely lose it at the first sign of trouble? One moment they're fine, the next they're having a total meltdown because their latte came with whole milk instead of oat milk. Meanwhile, someone else is dealing with actual life disasters without missing a beat. I once watched my friend maintain perfect composure when she lost her job, apartment, and relationship in the same week—while another acquaintance had a breakdown because someone criticized her Instagram post. The difference? Emotional backbone—the mental infrastructure that separates the truly strong from those who just pretend to have their shit together.

For instance, consider two people getting negative feedback on a project. The emotionally fragile person immediately thinks 'I'm a failure' and spends the weekend in a spiral of self-doubt, while the emotionally resilient person thinks 'This specific aspect needs improvement' and uses Sunday afternoon to revise their approach. Same external event, completely different internal experience and outcome.

You can spot the emotionally fragile from a mile away: they're the ones whose entire day gets destroyed because someone forgot to put "Best Regards" at the end of an email. These people aren't just missing a backbone—they're walking around without any internal support at all, like emotional water balloons just waiting for the slightest pinprick to burst.

The good news? Building an emotional backbone is a learnable skill, not an inborn trait. If the world's most fragile people can develop psychological fortitude, anyone can—including you.

PART 2: THE DOORMAT SYNDROME

"You doubt yourself while others fear your potential. Think about that."

The Silent Surrender: When Criticism Turns You Into a Human Doormat

"You've practiced saying 'You're right, I'm sorry' more than you've practiced saying 'Actually, here's what I think.' No wonder your self-respect has the structural integrity of wet toilet paper."

The opening scene of emotional fragility looks exactly like this: That moment when someone offers even the mildest criticism of a person's work, ideas, or choices. Your throat tightens, your chest constricts, and your mind goes completely blank. Instead of standing your ground, you immediately swallow your words, nod like a dashboard bobblehead, and then spend the next three days obsessively replaying the scenario in your head while crafting perfect comebacks you'll never actually have the guts to use. Your stomach churns every time you remember it.

Imagine you're at a restaurant and your order arrives completely wrong. The emotionally fragile person will eat the incorrect meal rather than 'cause trouble,' then complain about it later to friends. The person with emotional backbone will politely but firmly say, 'I actually ordered the chicken, not the fish,' addressing the issue directly without drama or apology.

It's like watching someone fold a royal flush because someone else at the table raised an eyebrow.

So what's really happening here? They're picking the temporary comfort of shutting up over actually standing for something. They're choosing the quick hit of avoiding conflict instead of the lasting strength that comes from speaking their damn truth. They're basically telling themselves, "My thoughts and feelings are less important than avoiding two seconds of awkwardness with this person who probably doesn't even remember the conversation by dinner time."

The worst part? Most people think they're being "nice" or "keeping the peace" or "choosing their battles." Let's be real though—they're not strategically deciding which conflicts matter. They're avoiding ALL potential friction because they're scared shitless of feeling uncomfortable for even ten seconds. It's not a strategy; it's emotional cowardice masquerading as social grace.

This isn't diplomacy; it's surrender. And the territory being surrendered is self-respect, authentic voice, and ultimately, the power to shape one's own life. The world doesn't reward this kind of emotional capitulation—it simply learns that these people's boundaries are more like suggestions, their opinions are negotiable, and their needs are optional. It's like putting up a "Please Rob Me" sign on your emotional house and then wondering why people keep taking your stuff.

EMOTIONAL REALITY CHECK: People treat you how you teach them to treat you. Every time you silently surrender to avoid conflict, you're hanging up a giant billboard that says "MY COMFORT IS LESS IMPORTANT THAN YOURS."

PART 3: YOUR BRAIN ON EMOTIONS: WHY YOU REACT THE WAY YOU DO

The Science of Emotional Fragility: Your Brain on Bullshit

> "Your brain is running software from the Stone Age in modern life. It's like trying to play Fortnite on a Windows 98 computer."

Understanding how your brain builds resilience is like getting the blueprint for emotional strength.

Your Brain's Emotional Command Center: Why You React The Way You Do

Consider this your brain's user manual—we'll reference these structures throughout the book. First up, meet your brain's resident drama queen: your emotional alarm system. Picture a tiny watchdog that thinks literally everything is trying to kill you, steal your lunch money, and embarrass you in front of your high school crush—all at the same damn time. This little drama factory is like that friend who turns "they didn't text back immediately" into "they're definitely dead or hate me or both." The real problem is it can't tell the difference between an actual charging lion and your coworker saying your homemade lasagna was "interesting."

Think about checking your bank account and seeing a much lower balance than expected. Your emotional alarm system immediately fires: heart racing, stomach dropping, mind racing through worst-case scenarios like identity theft or job loss. Only later does your thinking brain show up to methodically check recent transactions and realize it was just the annual car insurance payment you'd forgotten about.

Think about what happens when you get that vague text from your boss's name, and your emotional alarm system immediately loses its shit: DANGER! DANGER! Your heart races like you just chugged three Red Bulls, your palms get sweatier than a teenager on a first date, your stomach drops like you're on a roller coaster, and your mind spirals through every worst-case scenario from getting fired to the company closing to having to live in your car. Your body dumps stress hormones into your bloodstream like you've spotted a damn saber-toothed tiger hanging out by the water cooler asking about your quarterly reports.

Then there's your thinking center (the front part of your brain)— the part that's supposed to be the adult in the room. Here's the problem though: your emotional systems fire way faster than your logical ones. Like, WAY faster. By the time your thinking brain shows up, your emotions have already thrown a party, trashed the place, puked in the plants, and passed out on the couch with their shoes still on.

Your brain has an emotional control system that makes NASA's Mission Control look like a Fisher-Price toy, yet most people operate it like a drunk toddler playing with a TV remote. Let's tour the control panel they've been ignoring:

The Thinking Center: Your Brain's "Shut The Hell Up" Button Located right behind your forehead, this is the neurological equivalent of that friend who takes your phone away when you're drunk-texting your ex. It's the part responsible for stopping people from telling their boss exactly what they think after their third tequila shot or preventing them from buying those leather pants that looked "totally wearable" at 2 AM. When this system is weak, they're essentially driving a Ferrari with no brakes— impressive speed, catastrophic endings.

The Priority Filter: Your "Is This Actually Important?" System Think of this as your brain's bouncer, deciding which emotional guests get into the club of your awareness. When emotionally strong people get overwhelmed, this system helps them focus on what matters and ignore what doesn't. Most people's priority filter, however, is like a club bouncer who's also the owner's nephew - completely useless at its job, letting in every drunk, belligerent thought that wants to crash the mental party. "That stranger looked at me funny" gets the same VIP treatment as "I might lose my job."

> "Your triggers aren't about others—they're about what's unhealed in you."

The Feeling Detector: Your Internal Weather App This part integrates body sensations with emotional experience, like a sophisticated early warning system. People with well-developed body awareness can detect emotional storms brewing and take shelter before getting drenched. Your body awareness system, meanwhile, is like a weather app that only sends notifications after you're already soaking wet in a thunderstorm. "Oh, you're having a full meltdown in a work meeting? NOW I'll let you know you were getting anxious!"

The Emotional Filing Cabinet: Your Memory System That Needs Serious Reorganization This system contextualizes emotional memories, determining whether they're filed under "Useful Life Lessons" or "Traumatic Events That Define My Entire Identity." It's the difference between "I had a bad experience with public speaking once" and "I'm permanently traumatized and can never speak in public again because that one time in 7th grade when I forgot my lines in the school play clearly indicates I'm fundamentally defective as a human being." Your emotional filing system needs serious organizational help.

Your Brain's Ability to Change: Your Secret Weapon for Building Emotional Strength

REALITY CHECK: The good news? Your brain's emotional regulation system isn't fixed; it's trainable. It's like a psychological gym where you can transform from an emotional couch potato to a resilience athlete.

> "Your brain isn't hardwired—it's more like emotional Play-Doh waiting for you to stop making the same misshapen lump of anxiety over and over again."

Your brain can change throughout your life, which is why you're not permanently stuck with your current emotional limitations. The science is clear: your brain physically changes based on how you use it. No crystals, manifesting, or bullshit required— just consistent practice and deliberate effort. This flexibility is your personal escape hatch from emotional fragility. For a complete guide to how your environment shapes your emotional state, see Chapter 7.

You're not permanently "wired" any specific way—the paths in your brain are more like trails in a forest than copper cables in a wall. The paths you use often become wider and easier to follow, while unused trails gradually disappear. Right now, most people have a superhighway to Anxiety Town with express lanes to Overreaction City. Meanwhile, the road to Emotional Stability is a barely visible deer path covered in thorns. The good news? You get to be your own department of transportation—you decide which roads get developed and which ones return to wilderness.

Your Brain's Extreme Makeover: What Actually Happens When You Train Your Emotional System

When you practice emotional resilience regularly, your brain physically changes—and not in some woo-woo 'universe responds to your vibes' way. We're talking real, measurable changes, like giving your mental muscles a gym membership you actually use instead of just paying monthly while avoiding the building.

The Thinking Center Gets Stronger: Regular mindfulness practice increases the density and thickness of your brain's thinking center (prefrontal cortex), making it better at putting the brakes on runaway emotions. It's like upgrading from bicycle brakes to Formula 1 stopping power.

The Emotion and Thinking Centers Connect Better: With practice, the emotional and rational parts of your brain build more roads between them, so they can talk to each other instead of the emotional brain doing whatever the hell it wants while the rational brain sits there helplessly like a parent watching a toddler flush car keys down the toilet.

The Stress Response Calms Down: Regular resilience practice actually shrinks your brain's alarm center, making it less trigger-happy. It's like training an overeager guard dog to stop barking at leaves blowing across the yard.

I'm not making this up—the brain literally changes shape based on what people repeatedly do. Their brain gets sculpted by their habits every day, whether those habits are freaking out over nothing or staying cool under pressure.

PART 4: THE THREE PHASES OF EMOTIONAL TRANSFORMATION

Building emotional backbone isn't a smooth, comfortable journey. It's more like renovating a house while you're still living in it—messy, uncomfortable, and occasionally makes you question all your life choices. But understanding the predictable phases helps you stick with it when things get weird.

Phase 1: The Awkward Awareness Phase (Initial Stage)

This first phase sucks. You're suddenly aware of how emotionally reactive you are, like someone turned on the lights in a dirty kitchen you've been cooking in for years. You'll notice yourself getting triggered by things you previously didn't even register: subtle disapproval, minor rejections, the barely perceptible raising of someone's eyebrow. You'll think, "What the hell? I'm becoming MORE sensitive, not less!" Nope. You're just finally paying attention to what was always happening.

This is the phase where most people quit because they mistake awareness for regression. They think, "This emotional resilience stuff is making me MORE emotional!" and give up. But increased awareness is evidence of progress, not failure. You can't fix what you don't notice.

Phase 2: The Messy Middle (Intermediate Stage)

This phase is a roller coaster. Some days you'll handle complex emotional situations with surprising ease, like a zen master who's seen it all. Other days, you'll lose your shit over someone taking too long at the coffee machine. Two steps forward, one step back. The difference is you'll recover faster and learn from each overreaction instead of just repeating it blindly.

In this phase, you'll experience increasing moments of what psychologists call "the pause"—that magical space between stimulus and response where you actually have a choice about how to react. At first, these pauses are brief and rare, but they gradually expand and become more frequent, like small islands of sanity in a sea of reactivity.

Phase 3: The New Normal (Advanced Stage)

Eventually, emotional resilience becomes your default setting. You'll still feel everything—anger, hurt, frustration, disappointment—but these emotions will move through you instead of getting stuck. You'll bounce back faster from setbacks that previously would have derailed you for days.

The biggest sign you've reached this phase? You start handling situations so differently that people notice and comment on it. "You seem different." "You used to get so upset about this stuff." "How are you so calm right now?" This external validation is a nice bonus, but the real reward is internal: the sense of emotional freedom that comes from no longer being held hostage by your reactions.

REALITY CHECK: Most people quit during Phase 1 because they mistake temporary increased emotional awareness for permanent increased emotional fragility. Push through this phase—it's the price of admission to emotional strength.

PART 5: THE E.M.P.A.T.H.Y. FRAMEWORK: BRAIN-CHANGING PRACTICES THAT ACTUALLY WORK

> "Your emotions are messengers. Anger shows boundary issues. Jealousy shows desires. Boredom shows where you need challenge."

E -**Emotional awareness:** Recognizing your feelings
M-**Mindful observation:** Watching without judgment
P-**Physical regulation:** Managing bodily responses
A-**Acceptance:** Embracing reality as it is
T - **Thought management:** Directing mental focus

H - Healing practices: Activities that restore balance

Y - Yielding to process: Allowing emotions to flow naturally

For example, when your boss criticizes your work, instead of immediately reacting defensively: - Emotional awareness: Notice the sting of embarrassment and flash of anger - Mindful observation: Watch these feelings without immediately acting on them - Physical regulation: Take three deep breaths to calm your racing heart - Acceptance: Acknowledge that criticism is part of professional growth - Thought management: Shift from 'I'm being attacked' to 'This is feedback I can use' - Healing practices: Take a short walk after the meeting to reset - Yielding to process: Allow yourself to feel disappointed initially, then move toward constructive response

Five Brain-Changing Practices That Actually Work

These specific practices work and create real changes in the parts of your brain that handle emotional resilience:

Let's say you're giving a presentation and someone interrupts with a challenging question that makes you look unprepared. You feel your face flush and your voice start to shake. Instead of panicking or getting defensive, you:

1) Recognize the trigger - 'My body is reacting to feeling embarrassed'
2) Name the emotion - 'I'm feeling a mix of embarrassment and anxiety about looking incompetent'
3) Physical reset - Take a deliberate breath and plant your feet firmly
4) Choose your response - 'That's a great question. I don't have that specific data right now, but I'll find it and follow up with everyone by email tomorrow.'

This approach transforms a potential meltdown into a professional response that actually builds credibility.

1. **The Emotional Detective:** Name That Feeling When you're emotionally triggered, stop playing emotional charades and get specific. Not just "I feel bad" (which is about as useful as saying "I'm somewhere on Earth" when someone asks your location), but "I'm experiencing disappointment with a hint of embarrassment and a dash of resentment."

   This isn't just semantic nitpicking—it's like giving your brain GPS coordinates instead of vague directions. When you precisely name your emotions, you activate the regulatory networks in your brain that help you manage them. It's like the difference between telling a taxi driver "take me somewhere nice" versus giving an exact address. One leads to confusion; the other gets you where you need to go.

   Try it right now: What are you actually feeling? Not just "fine" or "stressed"—get granular. Are you anxious-excited or anxious-dreadful? Are you irritated-tired or irritated-threatened? Your emotional vocabulary should have at least as many options as a Starbucks menu. Most people's emotional vocabulary is like trying to paint a masterpiece with only three colors - technically possible but missing all the nuance and depth.

2. **Emotional Weightlifting:** Neuroplastic Meditation Forget sitting cross-legged chanting "om" while secretly making your grocery list in your head. Neuroplastic meditation is more like emotional CrossFit—intentionally challenging and specifically targeted.

   Here's how it works: First, deliberately recall something mildly annoying (like that person who keeps using "literally" incorrectly or the coworker who microwaves fish). Notice what happens in your body—maybe your jaw tightens or your breathing changes. Don't try to fix it; just observe it like you're watching a mildly interesting nature documentary.

Then, without forcing anything, shift your focus to something that makes you feel centered (your breath, a mental image, whatever works). The key is maintaining awareness of both states—the triggered and the regulated—and noticing the transition between them. It's like watching yourself shift gears in a car instead of just driving on autopilot.

Do this for five minutes daily, and you're essentially teaching your brain "this is the path from triggered to calm." Your brain gradually strengthens these new neural pathways with practice.

3. **The Brain Balancer: Cross-Hemisphere Integration** Your brain has two hemispheres that often act like divorced parents who refuse to communicate directly. This technique is like forced family therapy for your brain halves.

    Try alternate-nostril breathing: Close your right nostril with your thumb and inhale through your left nostril. Then close your left nostril with your ring finger, release your thumb, and exhale through your right nostril. Continue alternating for a few minutes. Yes, you'll look ridiculous. No, your roommate will never understand what they just walked in on. But your brain hemispheres will start communicating better.

    Or write with your non-dominant hand for five minutes daily. It'll look like a ransom note written by a drunk toddler, but it forces communication between brain regions that don't usually talk to each other. You can also try cross-lateral movements: touch your right hand to your left knee, then left hand to right knee, alternating for 30 seconds.

    These aren't just weird exercises—they're creating new neural pathways between brain regions that typically operate in isolation, like building bridges between islands that previously couldn't communicate.

4. **The Memory Hacker:** Reconsolidation Protocol This technique is like editing a movie while it's still being filmed. Every time you recall a memory, it becomes temporarily malleable before being stored again—a process called reconsolidation.

   Pick a specific emotional trigger (like public speaking anxiety or that one comment your mother-in-law made three Thanksgivings ago that still makes your eye twitch). Briefly recall it—just enough to activate the memory without fully reliving the emotional tsunami. Then immediately introduce something that contradicts your usual response pattern. If you normally catastrophize, introduce humor. If you normally freeze, imagine taking decisive action.

   Then create a new, preferred response to the same trigger. Visualize yourself handling the situation with the emotional backbone of someone who has their shit together. Repeat this sequence 3-5 times in one sitting. You're essentially telling your brain, "We're rewriting this scene." With repetition, your brain starts to accept the new version as the default response. It's like training your dog to sit instead of jump when visitors arrive—with enough practice, the new response becomes automatic.

5. **The Nervous System Whisperer:** Autonomic Reset Training Your nervous system has two main gears: sympathetic (fight/flight/freak out) and parasympathetic (rest/digest/chill the hell out). Most emotionally fragile people are stuck in sympathetic dominance, like a car permanently revving in first gear.

   Extended exhale breathing is your emergency brake: Breathe in for 4 counts, then out for 8 counts. The extended exhale literally switches your nervous system from panic mode to calm mode. Cold exposure is your system reboot button: 30 seconds of cold water on your face or hands triggers the mammalian dive reflex (the automatic response that slows heart rate when your face contacts cold water), instantly downshifting your nervous system. It's like force-quitting all the applications running in the background of your mental computer.

Humming or singing at specific frequencies stimulates your vagus nerve through vibration. That's why singing in the shower actually makes you feel better (even if it makes everyone else feel worse). Deep pressure, like a weighted blanket or firm self-massage, tells your nervous system "you're safe" in a language more primitive than words.

REALITY CHECK: These techniques aren't mystical woo-woo or instant fixes—they're biological tools that work at the cellular level of your brain. But they only work if you actually do them, with the same consistency you'd apply to physical exercise. Your brain doesn't care about your good intentions any more than your abs care about that gym membership you never use.

The Emotional Reset Protocol: A Step-by-Step Guide

Here's a clear, step-by-step emotional reset protocol that works in real-world situations:

1. **Spot the Trigger** - Notice when your body's alarm goes off. Your heart races, breathing changes, muscles tense. This is your first warning.

2. **Name the Emotion** - Label exactly what you're feeling with precision: "I'm feeling embarrassed with a side of anger and fear of judgment." Not just "I feel bad."

3. **Physical Reset** - Immediately use a physiological circuit breaker:

   - Take 3 breaths with a 4-count inhale, 8-count exhale
   - Splash cold water on your face or wrists
   - Press your feet firmly into the ground and feel the sensation

4. **Choose Your Response** - With your system partially reset, select from at least three possible responses rather than defaulting to your automatic reaction.

PART 6: THE A.D.U.L.T. SYSTEM: FIND YOUR EMOTIONAL PERSONALITY TYPE

A - Awareness: Recognizing your emotional patterns

D - Deliberate response: Choosing reactions consciously

U - Understanding triggers: Identifying what sets you off

L - Learning from feedback: Using emotions as information

T - Transforming patterns: Creating new emotional habits

For example, when someone cuts you off in traffic: - Awareness: Notice your immediate anger and urge to honk or tailgate - Deliberate response: Choose to take a deep breath instead of reacting aggressively - Understanding triggers: Recognize that feeling disrespected is your specific trigger - Learning from feedback: Use your anger as information that your boundaries feel violated - Transforming patterns: Practice responding calmly to minor frustrations to build a new habit

7-Day Emotional Backbone Starter Kit:

Day 1: Emotion Naming Challenge - Set three alarms on your phone. When each goes off, identify and write down exactly what you're feeling with as much detail as possible.

Day 2: Discomfort Practice - Take a 30-second cold shower. Notice your initial resistance, the physical sensations, and how quickly your body adapts.

Day 3: Boundary Setting - Say 'no' to one small request without apologizing or explaining. Just a simple, 'I can't do that.'

Day 4: Criticism Reception - Ask someone you trust for honest feedback about an area you're working on. Practice listening without defending.

Day 5: Emotional Reset - Next time you feel triggered, use the 4-count inhale, 8-count exhale breathing pattern for 1 minute before responding.

Day 6: Pattern Breaking - Identify one emotional reaction that doesn't serve you (like getting defensive when questioned) and consciously choose a different response when it happens.

Day 7: Reflection - Review the week and note which exercises were most challenging. These highlight your growth opportunities.

Emotional Personality Types: Find Your Brain's Factory Settings

> "Your brain isn't a one-size-fits-all organ, and what works for someone else's emotional regulation might be like trying to put diesel in a gasoline engine for you."

Everyone's emotional operating system comes with different factory settings. Understanding your emotional processing type isn't about excusing bad behavior—it's about knowing which tools will actually work for your specific brain configuration.

The Five Emotional Types: Know Your Factory Settings

It's like knowing whether you're running Windows, Mac, or Linux—different systems need different commands. Each emotional personality type requires specific approaches to function optimally.

Type 1: The Human Smoke Detector (Anxious/Sensitive Types) Who You Are: You're basically a walking anxiety antenna, picking up trouble signals that nobody else can detect. You notice every subtle shift in tone, facial expression, and room energy like you've got emotional sonar. While others are obliviously enjoying the party, you're analyzing whether that slightly weird comment your boss made five weeks ago was actually a hidden message about your job performance. Your friends call you "perceptive" to your face and "overthinks everything" behind your back.

How To Work With Your Wiring: Don't start with your thoughts —they're already running a marathon. Start with your body. Your nervous system needs physical regulation before your mind can calm down. Slow exhale-focused breathing (longer out than in), progressive muscle relaxation (tense and release each muscle group), or cold water on your face (activates the mammalian dive reflex) are your emergency brakes. These aren't just cute wellness tips; they're physiological circuit breakers for your overactive nervous system. Set a timer for exactly 2 minutes and focus solely on extending your exhales until the timer goes off.

Structure isn't just helpful for you—it's essential. Your brain is like a border collie—smart, sensitive, and absolutely needs a job to do or it will create chaos. Establish consistent daily routines that your nervous system can predict. Use preparation checklists for anxiety-triggering events. Mentally rehearse upcoming situations with contingency plans. Your brain loves knowing there's a plan for when things go sideways.

Build recovery time into your schedule like it's non-negotiable, because for you, it isn't. Your sensitive system processes more information than others, which means you need more downtime to integrate it. Schedule short decompression breaks throughout your day. Create clear transitions between activities—don't jump from one thing to another without a buffer. Your emotional system needs time to shift gears, not crash them.

Type 2: The Emotional Loudspeaker (Expressive/ Passionate Types)

Who You Are: Your emotions don't just show up—they make an entrance like they're hosting the Oscars. When you're happy, the whole room knows it. When you're upset, the whole building knows it. Your feelings come with their own sound system, light show, and possibly backup dancers. You've been described as "passionate," "dramatic," or "a lot" (and those are just the polite terms). You don't have an indoor voice for your emotions—it's all stadium rock concert, all the time.

How To Work With Your Wiring:

Channel your emotions, don't try to block them—that's like putting a lid on a pressure cooker and being surprised when your kitchen ceiling wears your dinner. Create private expression outlets where you can let it all out without collateral damage: scream in your car, have a dance party in your living room, keep a voice memo app to verbally process. Your emotions need movement and expression like a border collie needs to run—deny that, and they'll chew up your mental furniture. Physically write down your emotional outbursts, then literally rip up the paper while saying out loud: "Released, not repressed."

Learn to catch the emotional wave earlier, before it becomes a tsunami. Check in with yourself regularly about your emotional intensity. The earlier you catch the emotional build-up, the more options you have for managing it. Waiting until you're overwhelmed is like trying to stop a freight train with a paper stop sign.

Develop sensory circuit breakers that can interrupt the emotional cascade. The 5-4-3-2-1 technique (name 5 things you see, 4 you feel, 3 you hear, 2 you smell, 1 you taste) forces your brain to shift from emotional flooding to sensory processing. Keep different textures nearby to interact with—smooth stones, rough fabric, squishy stress balls. Use specific scents as reset buttons (certain essential oils or even a distinctive lip balm). These aren't just distractions; they're pattern interruptions for your runaway emotional train.

Type 3: The Emotional Analyst (Rational/Detached Types)
Who You Are: You're the person everyone describes as "so logical" or "always calm," which is both a compliment and a potential problem. In crisis moments, you're the one methodically making

plans while everyone else is freaking out. You pride yourself on being reasonable, rational, and collected. The issue? You're often so disconnected from your emotions that they have to stage a full-scale rebellion (usually in the form of physical symptoms or unexpected outbursts) to get your attention.

How To Work With Your Wiring: You need emotion detection training like a colorblind person needs to learn traffic light positions. Your emotional awareness is like a 1990s flip phone in a 5G world—technically functional but missing most of the data. Practice regular body scans to notice physical sensations (tension, energy shifts, temperature changes) that signal emotions you're not consciously registering. Create your own personal emotional dictionary connecting bodily sensations to feelings: "Tight chest often means anxiety," "Jaw tension usually signals frustration." When that critical voice starts, say: "I notice I'm being hard on myself. This is my brain's default setting, not reality."

Build bridges between your thinking and feeling systems, which currently operate like separate countries with closed borders. When making decisions, explicitly consider both factual and emotional factors—write them down in separate columns if needed. Ask yourself not just "What makes logical sense?" but also "How do I feel about this?" and "How might others feel about this?" Your logical analysis is a strength, but it's only half the information available.

Schedule emotional processing like you'd schedule a meeting —it needs to be on the calendar or it won't happen. Set regular times to process feelings with trusted people who can help you identify and articulate emotions you might miss. Create structured formats for emotional expression that feel safe and contained, like journaling with specific prompts or therapy with a professional who can help translate your internal experience.

Type 4: The Emotional Time Traveler (Ruminating/Overthinking Types) Who You Are: Your mind doesn't just visit the past or future—it sets up permanent residency there, complete with furniture and a change of address form. You're still replaying conversations from three years ago, analyzing what you should have said differently. Or you're living in an imagined future, rehearsing all the ways things could go wrong. Meanwhile, the present moment is trying to get your attention like a neglected pet. Your brain doesn't just think—it overthinks, then thinks about its overthinking, then analyzes its analysis of its overthinking.

How To Work With Your Wiring:

Pattern interruption is your best friend—your thought loops are like a record with a scratch, and you need to physically move the needle. Set literal timers for worry or analysis sessions: "I can ruminate about this for exactly 10 minutes, then I'm done." Use physical pattern breaks like standing up, changing rooms, or splashing water on your face when you catch yourself spiraling. Implement the "worry tree" decision system: "Is this something I can act on right now? If yes, do it. If no, schedule a specific time to address it or deliberately let it go." It feels stupid at first—like a cheesy self-help infomercial—but it works better than fancy techniques with scientific names.

Develop mental containment practices to give your busy mind clear boundaries. Establish specific "worry time" with firm start and end times—your worries can have an appointment, not an open invitation. Create physical representations of thought containers: write worries on paper and put them in an actual box, or visualize placing thoughts on leaves floating down a stream. Your thoughts need to know they have a time and place, but don't get to dominate your entire mental landscape.

Master thought defusion methods to create distance between you and your thoughts. Try narrating your thoughts in the third person or in silly voices—"There goes Sarah, thinking she ruined everything again" or saying your worries in a Mickey Mouse voice. Label thoughts as "just thinking" rather than facts: "I'm having the thought that I'll fail" instead of "I'm going to fail." These techniques help you see thoughts as mental events passing through your awareness, not absolute truths defining your reality.

PART 7: THE R.E.A.C.T. METHOD: YOUR EMOTIONAL TRANSFORMATION GAME PLAN

R - **Recognize triggers**: Identify what sets off your emotional reactions

E - **Evaluate your response options:** Consider multiple ways to respond

A - **Accept reality as it is:** Acknowledge what you can and cannot control

C - **Choose your response deliberately:** Act from intention, not reaction

T - **Track and adjust:** Monitor your progress and refine your approach

For example, when your partner forgets an important date or event: - Recognize triggers: Notice that feeling forgotten activates your fear of not being valued - Evaluate options: Consider expressing your feelings calmly, silently seething, or passive-aggressive hints - Accept reality: Acknowledge you can't control their memory, only how you communicate your needs - Choose deliberately: Decide to have a direct conversation about why the date matters to you - Track and adjust: Notice which communication approaches strengthen your relationship and which create distance

Emotional Backbone in Action: Everyday Applications

At Work: When your idea gets shot down in a meeting, instead of taking it personally and withdrawing, you say, 'I understand your concerns. Can we explore which parts might still be valuable?' You separate your idea from your identity.

In Relationships: When your partner says something hurtful, instead of immediately lashing out or shutting down, you say, 'That comment felt dismissive. Can we talk about what's really going on here?' You address the issue directly without escalating.

With Family: When relatives push your buttons with the same old patterns, instead of falling into the familiar argument, you notice the trigger, take a breath, and choose a new response: ' see this conversation is heading where it always does. I'd like to try something different this time.'

In Public: When you make an embarrassing mistake in front of others, instead of dwelling on it for days, you acknowledge it ('Yep, I totally messed that up!'), maybe use humor, and move on without letting it define you.

With Yourself: When you fail at something important, instead of the usual self-criticism spiral, you talk to yourself with the same compassion you'd offer a good friend: 'This is really disappointing, but it doesn't define your worth or future potential.'

These real-world applications show how emotional backbone transforms everyday situations from potential meltdowns into opportunities for growth and connection. The difference isn't in what happens to you, but in how you respond to what happens.

Remember: emotional backbone isn't about never feeling negative emotions - it's about having the capacity to feel them fully without being controlled by them.

From Fragile to Fierce: Your Step-by-Step Emotional Upgrade

The Five Habits That Build Emotional Strength

Emotionally resilient people aren't born that way— they've developed specific practices that transform their relationship with discomfort, emotions, and challenges. These aren't vague suggestions like "practice self-care" or "be mindful." These are concrete, actionable habits that literally rewire your emotional operating system.

1. The Discomfort Gym: Intentional Exposure Training

Emotionally resilient people don't avoid discomfort—they strategically expose themselves to it in controlled doses, like building immunity through vaccination rather than trying to live in a bubble. They understand that comfort is the enemy of growth, and that avoiding discomfort is like avoiding the weights at the gym and wondering why you're not getting stronger. They treat discomfort like a spice - not the whole meal, but the thing that gives life flavor and makes experiences memorable. That feeling when you see typing indicators appear and disappear in a text conversation? Your amygdala having a field day with uncertainty.

The Actual Practice (Not Just Theory): Choose one small discomfort to voluntarily experience each day. Not huge, traumatic challenges—just small, manageable discomforts that stretch your tolerance without breaking it. Think of it as emotional weight training: you don't start with 300 pounds; you start with what you can handle and gradually increase.

Your Weekly Discomfort Workout Plan:

Monday: Make that difficult phone call you've been avoiding. Yes, that one. The one you just thought of and immediately tried to justify postponing again.

Tuesday: Speak up in a meeting with a prepared point. Not when you're 100% certain, but when you're about 70% sure— that sweet spot where growth happens.

Wednesday: Take a 30-second cold shower. Your future self will thank you while your present self curses my name. The physical discomfort builds your general distress tolerance.

Thursday: Ask for specific feedback on something you created. Not fishing for compliments—actual, potentially uncomfortable feedback from someone whose opinion matters.

Friday: Have that difficult conversation you've been postponing. You know the one. The issue isn't going away; it's just growing interest like a high-rate credit card of emotional debt.

Weekend: Review what you learned from each discomfort and plan next week's challenges. What triggered you most? What was easier than expected? Where did you bail out? No judgment, just data collection for your emotional training program.

2. Emotional GPS: Precision in Feeling Navigation

Emotionally strong people can name exactly what they're feeling with nuance and specificity. They don't just feel "bad"—they recognize when they're feeling disappointed, frustrated, embarrassed, or insecure. It's like the difference between saying "I'm somewhere in North America" versus giving exact GPS coordinates. Their emotional awareness is like having a high-definition emotional map while most people are navigating with a crayon drawing on a napkin.

The Actual Practice (Not Just Theory): Expand your emotional vocabulary beyond the basic happy/sad/angry/scared categories that most adults are still using like emotional toddlers. When you feel triggered, force yourself to identify the specific emotions involved with maximal granularity. It's like being a wine taster for feelings—"I detect notes of disappointment, with undertones of embarrassment and a hint of relief."

Your Emotional Accuracy Training Program: First, get an emotion wheel with 100+ specific emotions. Yes, there are that many. No, "fine" is not one of them. Set three daily emotion check-ins on your phone—morning, midday, and evening. When the alarm goes off, name what you're feeling with specificity.

For each significant emotional event in your day, name at least three specific emotions involved. Not just "I was upset" but "I felt embarrassed, then defensive, then resigned." Record patterns in an emotion journal to identify your common triggers. You'll start seeing that certain situations reliably trigger specific emotional cocktails.

This isn't just navel-gazing—it's developing the emotional equivalent of 20/20 vision instead of stumbling around half-blind. You can't manage what you can't name, and most people are managing their emotions with the vocabulary of a five-year-old.

CHAPTER CONNECTION: EMOTIONAL BACKBONE AND FAIRNESS

"Be who you needed when you were younger."

Now that you've built your emotional strength, you're ready to face one of life's most challenging realities: the fact that life isn't fair. Your newfound emotional resilience is precisely what you'll need to navigate a world that doesn't distribute rewards, opportunities, and challenges evenly. For more on handling criticism constructively, see Chapter 6.

Without emotional strength, the unfairness of life becomes crushing—a reason to give up, become bitter, or retreat into victimhood. With it, unfairness becomes just another reality to navigate strategically.

In the next chapter, we'll explore how emotionally strong people don't waste energy expecting fairness or demanding it. Instead, they use their emotional backbone to:

1. Accept reality as it is, not as they wish it would be
2. Focus their energy on what they can control, not what they can't
3. Create their own advantages rather than complaining about others' head starts

Emotionally strong people have multiple ways to respond to any given situation, like a chess player who sees many possible moves. Emotionally fragile people have rigid, predictable response patterns—they're playing emotional tic-tac-toe while life is playing chess.

CHAPTER 4: LIFE ISN'T FAIR (AND WHY THAT'S ACTUALLY GOOD NEWS)

"THE MOMENT YOU STOP DEMANDING FAIRNESS IS THE MOMENT YOU START TAKING CONTROL OF YOUR LIFE."

PART 1: WELCOME TO THE UNFAIR UNIVERSE

The Cosmic Injustice: When Life Deals You a Shit Hand

> "Life deals cards so random that Vegas would get shut down for running the same odds. Some people get a royal flush while you're playing Go Fish with half a deck."

The universe doesn't give a damn about fairness. Not one single fuck. Understanding this reality connects your emotional strength to a world you can't control but can navigate.

Fairness complaints are premium versions of the bitching you eliminated in Chapter 1—more legitimate-sounding but equally wasteful. Just as complaining drains energy from action, fairness obsession drains energy from strategic thinking. Instead of "my job sucks," you've upgraded to "my job is unfair"—still not solving anything. Fairness complaints create the same addiction cycle as general complaints, with added self-righteousness.

How people deal with fairness basically determines if they'll spend their lives bitter on the sidelines or actually getting shit done. Most people waste about 70% of their emotional energy obsessing over unfair situations they can't control, leaving just 30% for making actual progress. Think about what someone could accomplish if they redirected all that wasted energy toward doing something useful instead of just whining about how unfair everything is while scrolling through Instagram looking at people who have it better than them. It's like driving a car with the parking brake on and wondering why you're not getting anywhere fast.

Just look around you. Some people are born with trust funds while others start with nothing but debt and dysfunction. Some people have natural talents that come easier than breathing while others have to fight and claw for every tiny bit of progress. Some idiots make absolutely terrible decisions and face zero consequences while good people pay a massive price for tiny mistakes. The world doesn't run on fairness—it runs on a messy, chaotic mix of random luck, circumstance, privilege, timing, who your parents were, and countless other factors that don't give even half a shit about what you or anyone else "deserves."

Yet we hang onto this fairness fantasy like it's the last life raft on a sinking ship. We rage against injustice thinking our outrage will somehow magically balance everything out. We obsess over other people's success, analyzing whether they really "earned it" based on our personal fairness rules. We keep detailed mental lists of every slight, every disadvantage, every time someone overlooked us, basically creating giant fairness spreadsheets in our heads that do nothing except make us miserable.

Here's the truth nobody wants to hear but everyone needs to understand: The world doesn't owe you fairness. It never signed a contract promising equal outcomes or opportunities. Nobody guaranteed that hard work would equal success or that being a good person would get you ahead. Those are just ideas we made up to feel better about a universe that honestly doesn't care. The sooner you accept this reality, the quicker you can stop being a professional victim and start actually doing something with your life. Harsh? Yes. True? Absolutely fucking true.

One hour daily on this pity party equals 365 hours yearly—NINE workweeks—documenting why you can't succeed instead of taking action. That's a part-time job dedicated to making yourself miserable. Your chest tightens, jaw clenches, a mix of envy and resentment floods your system—a biological response using the wrong tools for the job. While building fairness spreadsheets in your head about missed promotions, you invest zero minutes in skills for the next one.

Every single minute you spend whining about unfairness is a minute you're not using to solve your problems. Ask yourself: "Is my righteous outrage actually improving anything, or am I just making myself feel better while staying exactly where I am?"

PART 2: THE FAIRNESS FANTASY

The Fairness Fantasy: What We're Really Looking For

> "Your fairness detector is like a smoke alarm that goes off whenever someone else gets ice cream. It's not protecting you; it's making you miserable. And unlike a real alarm, it never runs out of batteries."

Our fairness obsession isn't really about fairness at all. It's about three deeper psychological needs that fairness seems to promise but never delivers:

1. **The Need for Control** At its core, fairness obsession is an attempt to impose order on a chaotic world. When we insist that things should be fair, we're really saying, "The world should operate according to rules I can understand and predict." This gives us the comforting illusion that we can control outcomes if we just follow the right rules. But here's the problem: that control is imaginary. The universe runs on physics, not fairness. Demanding fairness is like trying to negotiate with gravity—you can complain all you want about how unfair it is that you can't fly, but you'll still hit the ground when you jump off a building.

2. **The Need for Meaning Fairness** narratives give meaning to our suffering and success. If good things happen to good people and bad things happen to bad people, then

the universe makes sense. Our pain has purpose, and our efforts have guaranteed rewards.

This is why people cling so desperately to ideas like karma, meritocracy, or divine justice. These concepts promise that our experiences aren't random—they're meaningful parts of a coherent narrative where everyone eventually gets what they deserve.

The harsh reality? Meaning isn't delivered by fairness; it's created by how we respond to whatever happens, fair or not.

3. **The Need for Self-Protection Fairness expectations** serve as psychological armor. If we believe we're entitled to certain outcomes based on our efforts or inherent worth, we feel temporarily protected from the terror of randomness that characterizes much of life.

   This mental armor feels good but fails when tested against reality. Then the real damage happens—not just disappointment at the specific unfairness, but the shattering of our entire protective worldview.

   The most dangerous belief isn't that life is unfair—it's that life should be fair. This expectation creates a perpetual gap between reality and our demands, and that gap is where misery thrives.

Fairness Complaints vs. Legitimate Injustice

This is your definitive guide to escaping the victim trap—we'll reference these concepts throughout the book. But let's be clear: there's a crucial distinction between unproductive fairness complaints and legitimate injustice concerns.

Fairness Complaint	Legitimate Injustice
"My coworker got promoted before me"	"The algorithm is random"
"That influencer got famous overnight while I've been grinding for years"	"Entire groups face systematic barriers to entry in this industry"
"My friend's parents paid for college while I had to take loans"	"Educational access is systematically denied to qualified students based on income"
"My boss likes my colleague more than me"	"Harassment or discrimination is occurring in the workplace"
Focus on personal disappointment	Focus on systemic patterns affecting many
Primarily emotional reaction	Evidence-based assessment
Leads to rumination and inaction	Leads to strategic response or advocacy
Keeps you stuck	Can drive meaningful change

This isn't about ignoring genuine injustice. It's about distinguishing when fairness expectations help versus harm you. The key questions to ask yourself:

1. "Is my complaint about something I can influence, or an excuse to avoid action?"
2. "Am I focused on personal disappointment or addressing a genuine pattern?"
3. "Will my response improve the situation or just make me feel righteous?"

4. "Is this about me not getting what I want, or about a system that needs fixing?"

PART 3: THE ATTENTION ECONOMY

The Attention Economy: Why Your Mental Bandwidth Matters

> "Your mental bandwidth is the most precious resource you'll ever own. Spending it on fairness complaints is like using your last gallon of gas to drive in circles."

Let's talk about what happens in your brain when you fixate on unfairness. Your cognitive resources—your mental bandwidth—are strictly limited, like a phone with a battery that can't be replaced or upgraded. Every thought, every emotional reaction, every analysis costs power from that battery.

When you obsess over unfairness, you're allocating your premium cognitive resources to situations that typically offer zero return on investment:

The Zero-Sum Attention Game: Every moment spent dwelling on unfairness is a moment not spent on something else. This isn't just philosophical—it's neurological. Your brain has a finite capacity for conscious processing. When fairness obsession occupies that space, it literally displaces other, more productive thoughts.

The Opportunity Cost of Outrage: When you direct your attention toward unfairness, you create blind spots elsewhere. While you're mentally cataloging injustices, you're missing opportunities, overlooking solutions, and failing to notice resources that could help you advance.

The Attention Harvesting Industry: There's an entire ecosystem of media, politics, and social platforms designed to harvest your attention through fairness outrage. They're not helping you—they're farming your mental bandwidth for their benefit.

Every rage-inducing headline about unfairness is designed not to inform you, but to capture and monetize your attention.

The Decision Fatigue Factor: Constant rumination about fairness depletes your decision-making capacity. Studies show that judges give harsher sentences later in the day after their mental resources are depleted. Your ability to make good choices deteriorates when your cognitive battery runs low.

Start treating your attention like the non-renewable resource it is. Audit where your mental bandwidth goes: Are you investing it in concerns that might actually yield returns, or are you dumping it into a bottomless pit of unfairness complaints?

PART 4: ENTITLEMENT: THE MODERN DISEASE

The Entitlement Epidemic: Modern Life's Fairness Obsession

> "Your expectation of fairness is like bringing a strongly-worded letter to a tsunami. It might make you feel better, but nature doesn't have a customer service department. And there's definitely no manager you can speak to."

Our fairness obsession has turned into something even worse these days: massive entitlement. We went from the sensible idea that people should have equal rights and opportunities to the completely nuts idea that everyone deserves equal outcomes, equal treatment, and equal everything no matter what they do, how hard they work, or what reality actually allows. It's batshit crazy when you think about it. Social media has poured gasoline on this entitlement dumpster fire. We're constantly bombarded with perfectly filtered highlight reels of other people's lives, which triggers this non-stop "why not me?" comparison game. We see someone else's success and immediately wonder why we don't have the same stuff. We watch total strangers getting opportunities and instantly feel cheated, like someone else's good luck is somehow being stolen directly from our personal supply of good fortune.

The entitlement mindset has a distinctive whine to it, like a luxury car alarm that won't shut off in an upscale neighborhood. It sounds like:

"I should be making as much as my college roommate by now" – as if your bank accounts were supposed to grow in tandem like synchronized swimmers.

"That promotion was rightfully mine" – because apparently your company has a secret cosmic ledger where promotions are pre-assigned based on moral merit rather than business needs.

"People like me deserve better than this" – the rallying cry of everyone who believes their particular demographic, personality type, or zodiac sign comes with a guarantee of specific outcomes.

"After everything I've done, I should be further ahead" – as if life keeps a meticulous accounting system where every good deed and effort automatically converts to success at a fixed exchange rate.

"It's not fair that others have it easier than me" – the adult version of "but Mom, he started it!" that somehow didn't get left behind in elementary school where it belongs.

Notice the common thread? The assumption that your expectations trump reality. The belief that there's some "should" that the universe is obligated to fulfill. This is the emotional equivalent of a toddler's tantrum—demanding that reality conform to your preferences rather than adapting to reality as it exists.

The brutal truth? People aren't entitled to anything beyond basic human dignity and rights. Not success. Not comfort. Not recognition. Not wealth. Not love. Not health. Not happiness. Nothing. Zip. Zilch. Nada. Anything beyond basic rights isn't an entitlement; it's something to negotiate, earn, or encounter through the complex interplay of effort and circumstance. Expecting otherwise isn't idealism; it's delusion. It's like expecting a participation trophy for the Olympics of life - that's not how any of this works. FAIRNESS FALLACY NOTICE: Your sense of entitlement is directly proportional to your future disappointment. The more you believe the world "should" conform to your expectations of fairness, the more bitter you'll become when reality repeatedly fails to meet those expectations.

PART 5: ESCAPING THE HAPPINESS HOSTAGE SITUATION

The Freedom Protocol: Breaking Free from Fairness Demands

> "Waiting for fairness before allowing yourself to be happy is like refusing to eat until world hunger is solved. You'll starve while the problem persists. It's a hunger strike that the universe doesn't even know is happening."

When fairness becomes your prerequisite for happiness, you've created the perfect trap for yourself. Here's how to break free with the three-step Freedom Protocol:

Step 1: Identify Your Fairness Triggers

Most people have specific fairness trigger points that cause disproportionate emotional reactions. Common categories include:

Comparison Triggers: When peers or colleagues advance faster than you despite seemingly equal or lesser efforts Procedural Triggers: When rules are applied inconsistently or exceptions are made for others but not you
Outcome Triggers: When rewards don't match efforts or punishments don't match transgressions Recognition Triggers: When acknowledgment and appreciation aren't distributed according to contribution

Map your personal trigger landscape. What specific types of unfairness consistently hijack your emotional state? These are the tripwires you need to disarm.

Step 2: Create Happiness Firewalls

Develop specific mental protocols that separate your happiness from fairness conditions:

The 24-Hour Rule: Allow yourself exactly 24 hours to feel whatever emotions arise from unfairness, then deliberately redirect your focus The Triple-Question Test: For any fairness concern, ask: "Can I change this? Will obsessing help? Is this worth my limited mental bandwidth?" The Alternative Narrative: Deliberately create three alternative explanations for any situation that seems unfair, focusing on perspectives that don't require fairness

Step 3: Establish Fairness-Free Zones Designate specific areas of your life where fairness considerations are completely off-limits:

Fairness-Free Times: Certain hours of your day or week when you don't allow fairness thoughts Fairness-Free Relationships: Connections where you commit to never keeping score Fairness-Free Projects: Creative or personal endeavors where you judge solely by your own standards

The ultimate freedom comes not from achieving fairness, but from breaking the link between fairness and your emotional state. You can acknowledge unfairness without surrendering your happiness to it.

PART 6: THE FREEDOM OF ACCEPTANCE

The Freedom of Acceptance: How Embracing Unfairness Paradoxically Improves Your Life

Accepting that life isn't fair doesn't make you a passive victim —it makes you powerful. It's the emotional equivalent of finally putting down a hundred-pound pack you've been needlessly carrying up a mountain. Suddenly, you're lighter, faster, and able to direct your energy toward what actually matters instead of wasting it on useless outrage. You're free. Finally fucking free. This acceptance isn't resignation or giving up. It's not saying, "Well, everything is unfair so nothing matters." It's saying, "Life contains significant unfairness that I cannot control, so I'll focus on what I can control instead." That shift—from fighting an unwinnable battle against cosmic injustice to directing your energy toward effective action—is transformative.

Think about the staggering amount of mental and emotional energy you waste on fairness calculations—it's like running a supercomputer 24/7 to solve a problem that has no solution:

You spend hours in endless rumination about why someone else got what you "deserved," like a detective trying to solve a crime that isn't actually a crime. "Why did KAREN get that promotion when I've been here longer?" you wonder for the 47th time this week, as if repeating the question will suddenly reveal a conspiracy instead of the obvious answer: life isn't fair, Karen had skills you don't, and your boss doesn't use a seniority-based promotion system.

You create mental replays of situations where you were treated unfairly with the obsessive detail of a sports analyst breaking down a controversial play. You've replayed that one meeting from 2019 so many times you could write a frame-by-frame screenplay of it, complete with dialogue and camera angles. Meanwhile, the people who "wronged" you probably don't even remember the incident.

You craft elaborate fantasies about karmic justice eventually being served, like a vengeful screenwriter plotting the perfect comeuppance for your personal villains. You imagine your ex who cheated on you eventually being cheated on, your boss who overlooked you getting fired, or that friend who betrayed you coming crawling back for forgiveness. It's basically revenge porn for your ego, and it's taking up valuable mental real estate.

You deliver detailed explanations to others about how you've been wronged, turning casual conversations into one-person theatrical performances of "The Tragedy of Me: A Five-Act Play About Injustice." Your friends have started checking their watches and suddenly remembering urgent appointments whenever you begin a sentence with "You won't believe what happened to me..."

You perform constant evaluation of whether various situations meet your fairness standard, like you're the one-person Supreme Court of Cosmic Justice. You've appointed yourself the final arbiter of what's fair and what isn't, despite having absolutely no power to enforce your rulings on reality.

Now imagine redirecting all that energy toward actual progress in your life. Toward building skills, toward strengthening relationships, toward creating opportunities, toward focusing on solutions. The difference is like stopping a leak in a boat versus endlessly complaining about how unfair it is that boats can leak. One approach keeps you afloat. The other ensures you'll drown while feeling righteously indignant about it. The most successful people share a common trait: they don't waste time on fairness complaints. They acknowledge unfairness when they encounter it, then immediately shift to the question, "Given this reality, what's my next move?" They don't pretend the playing field is level, but they also don't use its tilt as an excuse for inaction. They simply factor it into their strategy and keep moving forward.

PART 7: YOUR BRAIN ON FAIRNESS

The Neuropsychology of Fairness: Why Your Brain Is Obsessed With Justice

> "Your brain's fairness detector is like a smoke alarm that goes off when someone else gets a bigger slice of cake. It's designed for survival, not for your happiness. And unlike a real smoke detector, you can't just take out the batteries when it's driving you crazy. Fairness obsession is carrying a 50-pound backpack of grievances while climbing life's mountain."

Your fairness obsession isn't a character flaw; it's an evolutionary feature that's now malfunctioning in modern environments. Understanding the neurological basis can help you break free from this fixation.

The Evolutionary Origins of Fairness Detection

Your brain's fairness detector is like an ancient security system installed in a modern house. It was built for small tribes where unfairness could mean not getting enough food to survive. Now it goes off when someone gets more social media likes than you. It's trying to protect you from threats that no longer exist, making you miserable over things that don't actually matter to your survival.

Your fairness detector was designed for small tribal groups of 50-150 people you personally knew and interacted with daily. It was meant for a world where you could literally see if Grok was hoarding all the mammoth meat while everyone else went hungry. Your brain expected direct, observable exchanges where you could immediately see who contributed what and who received what in return.

It evolved in an environment with immediate, visible consequences for fairness violations—if someone took more than their share, the group would collectively enforce norms through social penalties that were swift and obvious. Your ancestors lived with limited exposure to others' possessions and circumstances—they only knew about the resources and living conditions of their immediate community, not the entire planet.

But today? You're living in a world your Stone Age brain wasn't designed to process:

You have global awareness of billions of people you'll never meet, with your social media feeds showing you the top 0.1% of outcomes from all of them. Your brain is trying to compare your ordinary Tuesday to the highlight reels of literally everyone on Earth. It's like being the only person who can see their own blooper reel while everyone else appears to be starring in a perfectly edited movie.

You're navigating complex, abstract systems where cause and effect are about as clear as mud. The connection between effort and reward is filtered through layers of systems, institutions, and circumstances that make direct fairness calculations impossible. Your brain is trying to apply simple "this for that" fairness rules to situations with hundreds of variables.

You're dealing with delayed or invisible consequences for many actions, where the feedback loop between behavior and outcome might take years or decades to complete. Your fairness detector was designed for immediate feedback—"Grok took too much meat, Grok got ostracized"—not "This corporation exploited a tax loophole and might face consequences in 7-10 years if regulatory agencies decide to act." Your brain processes Instagram with circuits designed to monitor if Grok hoarded berries while others starved.

And you're subjected to constant exposure to the most fortunate outcomes of millions of people, curated and amplified by algorithms specifically designed to trigger your emotional responses. Your Instagram feed isn't showing you the average human experience; it's showing you the most envy-inducing moments from the most photogenic people on their best days in the most flattering light.

Your ancestral fairness calculator is being asked to process data it was never designed for. It's like using a calculator designed for basic arithmetic to solve quantum physics equations—the machinery simply can't handle the complexity.

Breaking the Neurological Fairness Fixation

Understanding the neuropsychology of fairness gives you powerful tools to override your brain's maladaptive fairness obsession. Think of these as neurological cheat codes for your own operating system:

When your fairness detector activates and you feel that surge of righteous indignation, pause and acknowledge: "This is my brain's ancient survival mechanism firing—the same circuit that kept my ancestors from getting screwed out of their fair share of mammoth meat. It doesn't mean this modern situation actually requires my emotional energy." This simple recognition creates a crucial gap between stimulus and response, like recognizing the false alarm before you evacuate the building.

Your fairness expectations are set to "small hunter-gatherer tribe" mode, but you're living in "global interconnected society" reality. Deliberately adjust your fairness expectations like you'd adjust the settings on a miscalibrated instrument. When you catch yourself thinking "That's not fair!" immediately counter with "Of course it's not fair—the universe never promised fairness, and my expectation of it is based on outdated neural programming."

When fairness emotions arise, create psychological distance by labeling them in the third person: "The brain is experiencing fairness violation distress" rather than "This isn't fair to me!" This linguistic shift is like watching yourself in a movie instead of being caught in the drama. "Sarah is feeling angry about the promotion decision" hits differently than "I CAN'T BELIEVE THEY

GAVE THAT PROMOTION TO BRAD INSTEAD OF ME!" One is an observation; the other is an emotional hijacking.

When fairness obsession starts spinning up like a tornado in your mind, deliberately engage in complex tasks that require your full cognitive resources—math problems, puzzles, detailed work, or physical activities requiring concentration. This is like forcing your computer to run a different program when one is stuck in an infinite loop. Your brain literally cannot maintain fairness rumination while simultaneously solving complex problems that demand full attention.

Each time you successfully redirect from fairness rumination to constructive thinking or action, you're literally carving a new neural pathway through your brain tissue. It's like creating a new trail through a forest—the first few times are difficult, but with repetition, the path becomes clearer and easier to follow. Eventually, this redirection becomes your brain's default response, and the old fairness obsession pathway grows over from disuse.

PART 8: FOCUS SHIFTING: YOUR NEW SUPERPOWER

Focus Shifting: From Fairness to Influence

You become the person everyone dreads sharing good news with. "I got a promotion!" is met with your analysis of why it should have been you instead. Your fairness obsession makes you the person who can find the cloud around any silver lining.

> "Complaining about fairness is like yelling at the weather—it might feel good for a minute, but you still end up wet if it's raining. Grab an umbrella instead. Or better yet, build a roof."

Shifting your focus from what's fair to what's within your influence is the antidote to fairness obsession. This mental reorientation doesn't deny that unfairness exists; it simply acknowledges that your energy is better spent elsewhere.

Think about your concerns as two circles: one contains everything you care about, and the other, smaller circle contains only what you can directly affect. Most fairness issues fall into the outer circle but outside the inner one. You can care about them, but you can't control them.

What does focus shifting look like in practice?

Instead of: "It's not fair that others got opportunities I didn't have." Shift to: "What opportunities can I create or pursue right now?"

Instead of: "It's not fair that my colleague got promoted before me." Shift to: "What specific skills or achievements would make me undeniable for the next promotion?"

Instead of: "It's not fair that some people are born into wealth while I had to struggle." Shift to: "Given my starting point, what's the smartest path to where I want to go?"

This isn't magical thinking or denying reality. It's strategic allocation of limited resources—specifically, your mental and emotional energy. Every minute you spend dwelling on unfairness is a minute not spent on improvement. Every hour wasted on "it's not fair" is an hour you could have used to get better, stronger, smarter, or more connected. Time doesn't give a shit about your fairness complaints. It just keeps ticking.

PART 9: UNFAIRNESS AS OPPORTUNITY

Unfairness as Opportunity: The Counterintuitive Competitive Advantage

> "The most successful people don't just accept unfairness—they leverage it as rocket fuel while everyone else is still complaining about the smell. They're not just making lemonade from lemons; they're building a lemonade empire with a global supply chain."

What if unfair situations aren't just obstacles to overcome but unique opportunities that others miss? The very unfairness you're resenting might contain hidden advantages that the fairness-obsessed will never discover. What if your "bad luck" is actually your golden ticket? The most successful people throughout history share a counterintuitive approach to unfairness—they don't just tolerate it; they actively mine it for strategic advantages and growth catalysts. They've discovered that unfair situations often contain unique opportunities precisely because most people avoid, resent, or give up when facing them.

The Innovation Advantage of Unfair Constraints

Here's a weird truth that creative geniuses understand: constraints often drive innovation more effectively than abundant resources. When NASA engineers had to figure out how to bring Apollo 13's astronauts home safely with severely limited resources, the unfairness of the situation didn't matter—only the creative solutions it forced them to develop.

Look at some of today's biggest companies. They weren't born with silver spoons in their corporate mouths—they were the scrappy underdogs who turned lemons into multi-billion-dollar lemonade stands:

Airbnb emerged when its founders were so broke they couldn't afford their San Francisco rent and decided, "Hey, maybe strangers would pay to sleep on our air mattresses." What sounds like the beginning of a horror movie became a $100+ billion company. If they'd had enough money to make rent, millions of travelers would never have discovered the joy of authentic local experiences, cultural connections, and the sense of belonging that comes from staying in real neighborhoods instead of tourist districts.

Slack was born from the ashes of a failed gaming company that was circling the startup drain. After burning through millions on a game nobody wanted to play, they pivoted to the only part of their failed product that actually worked—the internal messaging tool they'd built for their team. Their unfair circumstance (total gaming failure) forced them to recognize the actual value they'c created. If their game had been moderately successful, they'c be a forgotten footnote instead of a $27 billion communication platform.

Netflix only exists because its founder Reed Hastings got slapped with a $40 late fee for returning "Apollo 13" past its Blockbuster due date. That moment of unfairness—being financially penalized for forgetting to return a plastic box— sparked the idea for a subscription model with no late fees. If Blockbuster had been more forgiving about that DVD, they might still be in business, and we'd all still be driving to strip malls to rent physical media like cavemen.

Constraints that initially seem unfair can often lead to unexpected benefits. A tight deadline might force someone to develop a more efficient process. Without the luxury of endless revisions or perfectionism, they have to get ideas down clearly the first time. Such constraints can ultimately make work more direct and actionable than if they'd had unlimited time to overthink every detail.

In each case, unfair constraints didn't just challenge these founders—they catalyzed breakthrough thinking that wouldn't have emerged in more comfortable circumstances. If everything had been "fair," these innovations might never have happened.

The Unfair Advantage Playbook: From Victim to Opportunity Hunter

Most people treat unfairness like a dead end—they see the "Road Closed" sign and turn around, complaining about the detour. But what if that closed road is actually an exclusive pathway that only the creative and persistent get to access? What if the detour is actually a shortcut in disguise? Here's how to transform your unfair circumstances from obstacles into secret weapons:

When life hands you a steaming pile of unfairness, don't just hold your nose—grab a shovel and start digging for the valuable stuff buried within. For any unfair situation, ask yourself:

"What skills am I being forced to develop that others get to avoid?" Maybe you're learning resilience, creative problem-solving, or resourcefulness that the "lucky ones" never have to build. While they're developing the skills of having things handed to them (not particularly marketable), you're developing the skills of overcoming obstacles (incredibly valuable).

"What perspectives do I now have access to that the 'fortunate' people will never understand?" Your struggles give you insight into realities that privileged people pay consultants to explain to them. Your "unfair" background might be giving you a 3D view of a world others only see in 2D.

"What conventional wisdom am I now free to ignore?" When you're already operating outside the "normal" path, you're liberated from having to follow the standard playbook. While others are trapped in "this is how it's always been done" thinking, your unfair circumstances might be giving you permission to try approaches no one else would consider.

"What unique approach does this situation make possible that would be unavailable to someone on the 'fair' path?" Sometimes the back door, side entrance, or climbing through the window gets you to places the front door never would.

This is where you perform the magic trick of turning your specific unfair circumstances into specific strategic advantages. It's like discovering your kryptonite is actually a power source if you wire it differently:

Resource constraints don't just limit you—they force you to become ruthlessly efficient and creative. While well-funded competitors throw money at problems, you're developing the muscle of doing more with less. When the market turns (and it always does), they'll collapse under their bloated infrastructure while you'll thrive in the lean times.

Outsider status isn't just isolation—it's freedom from industry groupthink and the ability to see problems with fresh eyes. While insiders are all looking in the same direction, you're coming from an angle they never considered. Every industry disruption in history has come from someone who didn't know they were "supposed" to follow the established rules.

A difficult background isn't just hardship—it's direct insight into markets and communities that others can only theorize about. Your lived experience gives you authenticity and understanding that privileged competitors will spend millions trying to research or fake.

Health challenges aren't just limitations—they're crash courses in empathy, patience, and perspective that make you better at understanding human needs. Some of the most successful products and services were created by people solving their own health problems because existing solutions were inadequate.

Systematic barriers aren't just obstacles—they're filters that weed out the casually interested and leave only the truly determined. While insiders get complacent with their easy access, you're developing the hunger, creativity, and persistence that make for unstoppable entrepreneurs and innovators. The harder the path, the fewer the competitors. That's a fucking advantage. Every unfair advantage someone else has over you comes with blind spots and weaknesses. Every unfair disadvantage you face contains growth opportunities and perspective advantages others will never develop. The question isn't whether your situation is fair— it's whether you'll extract the unique value from your specific circumstances that others would miss.

PART 10: THE FOCUSED INFLUENCE FRAMEWORK

The Influence Matrix: Where to Invest Your Energy

> "Your attention is like your bank account—spend it on things that give you a return. Outrage about fairness has worse returns than a Nigerian Prince email scam. At least with the scam, there's a theoretical chance you might get something back."

Instead of dividing your concerns into abstract circles of control, influence, and concern, use this practical Influence Matrix to determine where your energy belongs:

Priority Zone (High Control + High Impact) These are the gold mines of personal effectiveness—areas where your direct actions create significant positive outcomes. Examples include:

Your skill development and knowledge acquisition Your daily habits and routines Your responses to challenges and setbacks Your communication choices in key relationships Your focus and attention management

This zone deserves 70-80% of your mental and physical energy. When you're not sure where to focus, default to this quadrant.

Efficiency Zone (High Control + Low Impact) These are areas where you have complete control but the immediate impact is smaller. The key is to optimize these for efficiency to free up resources for the Priority Zone:

Daily chores and maintenance tasks Low-stakes decisions (what to eat for breakfast, what to wear) Personal organization systems Administrative tasks

Systematize, delegate, or minimize these activities—they're necessary but shouldn't consume prime mental real estate.

Strategy Zone (Low Control + High Impact) These areas require indirect influence rather than direct control. Your approach must be strategic, persistent, and patient:

Career advancement in organizational structures Market trends affecting your industry Relationship dynamics with key stakeholders Community or policy issues affecting your quality of life

Allocate 15-25% of your energy here, focusing on strategic leverage points rather than brute-force control attempts.

Waste Zone (Low Control + Low Impact) This is where fairness obsessions typically live—areas where you have minimal influence and the impact on your life is relatively small:

Other people's opinions about issues unrelated to you Historical injustices you cannot remedy Celebrity behavior and distant drama Most news events that don't directly affect your sphere Random unfairness in systems you rarely interact with

Starve this quadrant of your attention. Any energy spent here is essentially thrown away.

The One-Week Influence Audit For one week, track where your mental energy goes using this matrix. At the end of each day, estimate the percentage of your attention spent in each quadrant. Most people are shocked to discover they're investing over 50% of their mental bandwidth in the Waste Zone while neglecting the Priority Zone that actually determines their outcomes.

PART 11: PRACTICAL TOOLS FOR LETTING GO

Reality Acceptance Rituals: Practical Tools for Letting Go

Reality Acceptance Rituals are specific techniques that help you release fairness expectations and redirect your energy toward constructive responses. These practices require consistent reinforcement.

The Emotional Expiration Date Technique

When life serves you a steaming platter of unfairness, don't pretend it doesn't stink—that's just denial wearing a fake mustache. Instead, give yourself exactly 48 hours to feel all the natural emotions: rage at the injustice, disappointment that reality doesn't match your expectations, frustration that you can't control the situation, even a good old-fashioned pity party if needed.

But—and this is crucial—set an actual timer. Mark your calendar. When those 48 hours are up, your emotional processing period expires like milk left on the counter. At that point, you must shift your focus entirely to the question: "Given this reality that I didn't choose and can't change, what's my next move?" No extensions, no emotional overtime, no "but this is REALLY unfair so I need more time." The universe doesn't give time extensions for extra-special unfairness.

This isn't about suppressing emotions—it's about giving them an appropriate container rather than letting them colonize your entire life. It's the difference between visiting Grieftown for the weekend versus moving there permanently and running for mayor.

The Reality Triage System

When facing any challenging situation, grab a piece of paper and create three columns labeled "Control," "Influence," and "Observe." This is your reality triage system—a method for sorting aspects of your situation into appropriate categories for treatment.

List every aspect of your current challenge, then ruthlessly sort each item into its proper column. Be brutally honest—your ego will try to put items in the "Control" column that actually belong in "Observe."

Then follow this treatment protocol: Commit to taking immediate, specific actions on everything in the "Control" column. Develop strategic, persistent approaches to items in the "Influence" column. And practice radical acceptance for everything in the "Observe" column—these items get your acknowledgment but not your emotional energy.

This practice prevents you from the common mistake of investing 80% of your energy worrying about things in your "Observe" column while neglecting the items in your "Control" column that could actually improve your situation.

The Mental Circuit Breaker

Develop a personal phrase that acts as an emergency circuit breaker for your brain when it starts spinning into fairness obsession. This isn't a magical incantation—it's a pattern interrupt that helps you switch mental tracks.

Choose something short, action-oriented, and slightly blunt: "Noted, now next." "Unfair, still moving forward." "That sucks, what now?" "Interesting, irrelevant, onward."

The key is to practice using this phrase consistently for minor fairness violations so it becomes automatic when major ones occur. It's like training a dog—you can't expect it to perform a command during a crisis if you haven't practiced it a thousand times in calm situations first.

When you catch yourself ruminating on unfairness, say your phrase out loud (yes, actually out loud—the physical act of speaking engages different neural pathways than thinking). Then immediately take one small action related to something in your Circle of Control. The phrase without the action is just a fancy form of denial.

PART 12: THE ULTIMATE LIFE CHOICE

Fairness vs. Freedom: The Ultimate Life Choice

> "Your obsession with fairness is like wearing handcuffs and complaining about limited mobility. The key has been in your pocket the whole time. You've been both the prisoner and the warden of your own mental jail."

You can have fairness or freedom, but you cannot have both. By "fairness," I mean a life where everything happens according to your sense of justice and desert. By "freedom," I mean liberation from the emotional prison created by fairness expectations.

As long as your happiness depends on the world meeting your fairness standards, you are not free. You're a hostage to conditions you cannot control. You've handed the keys to your emotional state to an indifferent universe that will inevitably disappoint you. You've chosen to make your contentment contingent on something that has never consistently existed in human history.

The alternative is freedom—the release that comes from accepting reality as it is while working strategically to create the best possible future within that reality. This freedom doesn't mean loving unfairness or ignoring injustice. It means declining to tie your emotional well-being to factors outside your control. It means choosing to direct your finite energy toward what you can change rather than what you can only complain about.

Consider two people facing identical unfair circumstances:

Person A demands that the situation change to meet their fairness standards before they can move forward. They spend their days documenting how they've been wronged, explaining to others why the situation is unjust, and waiting for the world to correct itself. They feel righteous in their anger but remain stuck in circumstances they hate.

Person B acknowledges the unfairness, allows themselves appropriate emotional processing, then asks, "Given this reality, what's my best move?" They work within the constraints they cannot change while seeking creative ways around barriers. They don't pretend the situation is fair, but they refuse to let that unfairness define their response or determine their future.

Which person would you rather be? Which approach is more likely to create a life you actually want to live?

The most successful, fulfilled people all share this trait: they've chosen freedom over fairness. They've stopped expecting the world to align with their preferences and started creating the best possible life within the world as it actually exists. They acknowledge unfairness when they encounter it, then immediately redirect their focus to what they can control.

This isn't settling or giving up. It's the opposite—it's refusing to waste your limited time and energy on an unwinnable battle against reality. It's choosing to play the game that's actually on the field rather than the one you think should be there. It's liberating yourself from the emotional purgatory of perpetual disappointment that fairness expectations inevitably create.

The choice is yours: Remain hostage to a fairness standard the world will never meet, or free yourself to create the best possible life within the imperfect, unfair, yet opportunity-filled reality that actually exists. One path leads to bitter righteousness, the other to effective action. One keeps you perpetually disappointed by what is, the other empowers you to create what could be.

Fair is where you get cotton candy, not where you get fulfillment. Choose freedom over fairness, and you choose a path that can actually lead to the life you want.

CHAPTER CONNECTION: Now that you've accepted the fundamental unfairness of life, you're ready to develop the strategic patience needed to succeed anyway. This is the natural progression of your transformation journey. In Chapter 1, you stopped poisoning your environment with complaints. In Chapter 2, you confronted the comfortable lies that kept you stuck. In Chapter 3, you developed the emotional resilience needed to face challenges without breaking. And now, in this chapter, you've accepted that life isn't fair and never will be.

Fairness obsession locks you into a short-term mindset, comparing today's outcomes rather than building toward future advantages. Stop wasting energy on fairness complaints, redirect toward long-term strategies that actually change circumstances. Letting go of fairness expectations means shifting focus to the long game, creating your own advantages instead of complaining about others'. The attribution theory we've explored here—how you explain the causes of events— directly impacts your ability to delay gratification, which we'll explore in Chapter 5.

But acceptance without strategy is just resignation. Your next challenge is developing the patience and persistence to play the long game in a world obsessed with quick fixes and instant gratification. This brings us to our next chapter: Playing the Long Game—where you'll learn to think in decades rather than days, building systems that compound over time while everyone else chases short-term wins.

CHAPTER 5: PLAYING THE LONG GAME

"THE PEOPLE WHO CHANGE THE WORLD AREN'T FASTER THAN EVERYONE ELSE—THEY JUST KEEP GOING WHEN EVERYONE ELSE HAS QUIT."

PART 1: THE MICROWAVE MINDSET

UNDERSTANDING DELAYED RETURNS

The Instant Gratification Trap

> "If patience were a cryptocurrency, most people would be too broke to buy a digital pet rock. Your commitment to long-term goals has the same half-life as a TikTok trend—about 72 hours before you're chasing the next shiny distraction."

Strategic patience is one of the most powerful skills you can develop. By understanding compound effects over time, you can create success in an unfair world through consistent long-term thinking.

This is your delayed gratification headquarters—the definitive guide to playing the long game. A person's ability to delay gratification predicts success better than almost anything else—even better than intelligence, education, or socioeconomic background. The research is clear: people who can play the long game end up making 2-3 times more money throughout their lives, have relationships that don't implode every six months, and are just generally way happier with their lives than the instant gratification crowd. But in our world of one-click purchases, streaming everything, and food delivery apps, almost nobody has this skill anymore—which makes it an even bigger advantage for those who can master it while everyone else is busy checking if their latest Instagram story got enough likes.

Most of us have started a diet only to quit after three days, set up a savings plan just to blow it on some impulse purchase, or walked away from a relationship at the first sign of trouble. We're a society of quick-fix junkies constantly chasing immediate results while wondering why nothing in our lives ever really changes. Our commitment to improvement has the structural integrity of a chocolate teapot in a sauna—looks great until the slightest heat is applied, then melts into a sticky fucking mess.

> "Just because it takes time doesn't mean it isn't happening."

In a world where success gets measured in likes, shares, and 30-second videos, being able to think past your next social media post has become weirdly rare. Everyone's chasing overnight success, six-week abs, and ten-minute enlightenment like they're Pokemon cards. We're all suffering from what I call temporal myopia—basically, we can't see past what's right in front of our face, and we're about as patient as a toddler who needs to pee at a highway rest stop that's still 20 miles away. Our attention spans have shrunk to the size of a fucking gnat on Adderall.

Most achievements worth anything take years, not weeks. That "overnight success" you're jealous of probably spent a decade grinding in total obscurity before anyone knew their name. That person with "natural talent" you envy almost certainly put in thousands of hours of practice when nobody was watching.

Hard truth time: The person who plays the long game looks like a total loser at first while everyone else seems to be crushing it. Their friends are posting vacation pics from maxed-out credit cards while they're building an emergency fund. Others are showing off fancy job titles at companies that might not exist next year while long-game players are building transferable skills. It's like being the only sober person at a casino watching everyone else hit small jackpots and high-five each other—boring as hell while you're there, but the long-game player is also the only one who drives home in their own car instead of a depressing Uber ride with nothing but regret and an empty wallet. The long game player is out there planting oak trees that take decades to grow while everyone else is arranging cute little Instagram-ready succulents that look perfect now but die if you forget to mist them for like two days.

This quick fix mentality isn't just about laziness—it's about how our brains have been rewired by modern conveniences. When you can get virtually anything delivered to your door within hours, stream any content instantly, and receive immediate validation through social media, the idea of waiting months or years for results feels like an outdated concept.

The reality? Most worthwhile achievements require consistent effort over extended periods. Consider what people want most in life—whether it's financial independence, a fulfilling career, a healthy body, meaningful relationships, or mastery of a skill. None of these come from sporadic bursts of effort followed by long stretches of neglect. They come from showing up day after day, especially when motivation is low, when no one's watching, and when results aren't immediately visible.

Consistent small efforts are what create meaningful results. Writing 500 words daily, even when you don't feel like it or have other pressing demands, eventually accumulates into a complete manuscript. There may be weeks where it feels like no progress is happening, but those consistent efforts add up. Ironically, the days when motivation is lowest often produce the most valuable insights.

This chapter isn't about improvement strategies—that's Chapter 13. This is about developing patience for compound returns. But there's a crucial distinction between strategic patience and procrastination that many people miss:

Patience	Procrastination
Working consistently before expecting results	Waiting for "the right time" to start
"I'll keep showing up daily even though results take time"	"I'll start when conditions are perfect"
Present action with delayed rewards	Present inaction with imaginary future action
Planting seeds and tending them while waiting for growth	Holding seeds while planning elaborate gardens that never get planted
Focused on process with faith in eventual outcomes	Focused on perfect outcomes while avoiding process
"I'm working on this project daily, even though no one will see it for months"	"I'll start my project when I have more time/money/ energy/inspiration"
Accepts current limitations while working within them	Uses limitations as excuses to avoid starting
Recognizes that perfect conditions never arrive	Waits for perfect conditions that never arrive

The diagnostic question to ask yourself: "Am I working while waiting for results, or just waiting to start working?"

Procrastination often disguises itself as strategic thinking. "I'll start when conditions are perfect" sounds wise but is usually just fear wearing a business suit. Patience, on the other hand, means doing the work now while accepting that results come later.

The F.U.T.U.R.E. Framework: Your Long Game Strategy System

> "Rivers cut through stones not by force but by persistence."

Most people approach long-term thinking with vague intentions, minimal strategy, and the attention span of a caffeinated squirrel. What actually works is a systematic approach that turns the abstract concept of "playing the long game" into a concrete practice.

> "The path to your goals is paved with uncomfortable decisions."

The F.U.T.U.R.E. framework is your practical system for long-term thinking in a short-term world:

Foundation First: Build systems and skills that compound over time. The most successful long-term thinkers prioritize building strong foundations. Consider Warren Buffett, who spent years developing his investment philosophy before making the moves that would eventually generate billions. While others were chasing hot stock tips and market fads, he was building a knowledge base and system that would work decade after decade.

Building a foundation isn't sexy. It doesn't make for good Instagram stories. Foundation work happens in private, with little external validation, which is precisely why so few people commit to it.

Understand Delayed Returns: Train your brain to value future rewards. Our ancestors evolved in an environment where immediate returns were crucial for survival—find food now, avoid danger now, secure shelter now. Our brains are wired to prioritize immediate rewards over future benefits, a tendency psychologists call "hyperbolic discounting." This made perfect evolutionary sense when life was short and uncertain, but it's catastrophically misaligned with modern success, which typically requires delayed gratification.

The 1-3-5-10-25 Rule for Time Horizon Decisions

For major decisions, evaluate through five timeframes: 1 day, 3 months, 5 years, 10 years, and 25 years. This simple framework forces you to consider both immediate and long-term consequences:

Example 1: That impulsive tattoo - 1 day: Exciting! Social media attention, feels rebellious and fun - 3 months: Still novel, but some regret during job interviews - 5 years: Faded, doesn't match your evolving style or identity - 10 years: Embarrassing explanation to your children - 25 years: Expensive removal or permanent reminder of a temporary feeling

Example 2: Higher-paying toxic job vs. lower-paying growth opportunity - 1 day: Toxic job wins (bigger paycheck) - 3 months: Toxic job still winning (financial comfort) - 5 years: Growth opportunity pulls ahead (skills developed, network built, opportunities multiplied) - 10 years: Growth opportunity dominating (career trajectory established) - 25 years: No contest (compound career growth vs. burnout recovery)

Time Horizons: Think in decades for what matters most. Simply understanding that long-term thinking matters isn't enough—you need a practical system to implement it. The Multi-Horizon Decision Framework allows you to navigate decisions across five distinct timeframes simultaneously, from daily execution to legacy impact.

Unsubscribe from Urgency: Distinguish between important and immediate. We live in an economy of manufactured urgency, where everything is positioned as requiring immediate attention. "Limited time offer!" "Don't miss out!" "Last chance!" This constant urgency hijacks your attention from what's truly important but not urgent.

Long-term thinkers develop the ability to distinguish between real urgency and manufactured urgency. They evaluate opportunities not by artificial deadlines but by alignment with long-term objectives. They understand that most "once-in-a-lifetime" opportunities are actually routine events dressed up in urgent packaging.

Repetition Over Intensity: Value consistent small actions over heroic efforts. The most common mistake in pursuing long-term goals is prioritizing intensity over consistency. You see this in the person who works out for three hours on Monday and then doesn't exercise again until the following week, or the entrepreneur who pulls an occasional all-nighter but doesn't maintain regular productive hours.

Intensity makes for better stories. Consistency makes for better results. The long game isn't about heroic efforts; it's about sustainable systems that can operate day after day, year after year. It's about showing up when you're tired, discouraged, and not seeing immediate results.

Environmental Design: Create surroundings that suppor: long-term thinking. Willpower is a finite and fickle resource. Trying to play the long game through sheer force of will is like trying to hold your breath underwater indefinitely—possible for a while, but ultimately doomed to failure. Instead, design your environment to make long-term decisions the path of leas: resistance.

This means creating systems that automate good decisions, removing triggers for short-term thinking, and surrounding yourself with people who reinforce your long-term values. It means designing your physical and digital spaces to reduce temptation rather than relying on constant resistance.

Applying environmental design principles might involve creating a distraction-free workspace with no internet access scheduling specific times for focused work that are non-negotiable, and communicating boundaries to friends and family. Rather than relying on willpower to avoid distractions, this approach eliminates them entirely. The system makes the desired activity the default action during those blocks, rather than something that requires constant choice over more immediately gratifying alternatives. 117

PART 2: REWIRING YOUR BRAIN: THE SCIENCE OF PATIENCE

The Neuroscience of Now vs. Later

> "Graveyards are full of people who thought they had more time."

The human brain is running on hardware that was optimized for immediate survival in a world where long-term meant "will these berries kill me in the next hour?" This is your brain's reward system headquarters—the definitive guide to how dopamine drives behavior. Your dopamine system was designed for immediate feedback - hunt food, eat food, feel good. It wasn't built for "invest in your 401(k) and maybe feel good in 30 years."

It's a fucking miracle we can plan lunch, let alone retirement.

When you're choosing between immediate and delayed gratification, you're experiencing a neural cage match between your limbic system (emotional, impulsive) and your prefrontal cortex (rational, planning). Your brain irrationally devalues future rewards compared to immediate ones—a phenomenon called hyperbolic discounting. That's why $100 now feels more valuable than $200 in a year, even though that's a 100% guaranteed return.

Modern technology has trained your brain to expect immediate rewards for minimal effort, creating a feedback loop of constant dopamine hits that make delayed gratification feel actively painful. That itch to check notifications, the anxiety of missing out, the dopamine hit from likes—these are responses to engineered addiction triggers. Your brain screams to check your phone—where a quick post gets 47 likes in 20 minutes versus working on something important nobody will see for months.

People abandon meaningful work when phones ping with notifications offering immediate validation. As we'll explore more deeply in Chapter 7, your environment shapes these neural pathways. Successful people take extreme measures like locking phones in timed safes during deep work to resist instant gratification. They understand that willpower alone is rarely enough against algorithms designed by teams of psychologists to hijack your attention.

Science-Backed Strategies for Overcoming Present Bias

"The magic isn't in the speed—it's in laying bricks nobody else sees until they form a fucking Colosseum."

Understanding the biological basis of present bias is just the first step. The real power comes from implementing research-validated techniques that work with your brain's architecture rather than fighting against it.

The Future Self-Continuity Intervention

Stanford researchers found that showing people age-progressed images of themselves led to significantly increased retirement savings. Why? Because it created emotional continuity with the future self who would benefit from those savings.

Create concrete representations of your future self—whether through aging apps, detailed written descriptions, or even regular letters to your future self. The key is making Future You feel like a real person with needs and desires, not an abstract concept.

The Pre-Commitment Protocol

Research from behavioral economics shows that we can leverage our present bias against itself through pre-commitment devices—strategies that lock in decisions for our future selves before temptation arises.

Create binding pre-commitments that remove future choice points, such as automatic savings transfers, blocking software for distractions, or public commitments with social consequences.

The Temporal Reframing Technique

Research shows that how we mentally represent time dramatically impacts our decisions. Most people think of the future in abstract terms while thinking of the present in concrete, vivid terms.

Deliberately reverse this pattern by making the future concrete and the present abstract.

Instead of thinking: - "I'm saving for retirement" (abstract) - "I'm enjoying this purchase" (concrete)

Reframe as: - "I'm securing my ability to pay my specific bills and travel to Italy at age 65" (concrete) - "I'm choosing temporary pleasure at the expense of my life goals" (abstract)

The Environmental Choice Architecture System

Behavioral science demonstrates that willpower is an inefficient resource compared to environmental design. The research is clear: your environment will usually win against your intentions.

Rather than fighting temptation, eliminate it from your environment by keeping tempting foods out of your home, working in spaces without distractions, setting up automatic transfers for financial goals, and using website blockers during focused work periods.

The key insight from the research isn't that you need superhuman willpower—it's that you need sophisticated systems that work with your brain's architecture rather than against it.

The pre-commitment protocol can be implemented by publicly announcing your schedule to friends and colleagues, creating social accountability. Pre-paying for services related to your goal creates financial incentives to follow through. These aren't just motivational tricks—they're structural supports that align present actions with future goals when motivation inevitably fluctuates.

PART 3: MONEY THAT MULTIPLIES

THE FINANCIAL LONG GAME

The Financial Long Game

> "A 401k is basically a time machine that turns small sacrifices today into a rich future self who doesn't hate your guts for spending everything on DoorDash and Amazon impulse purchases. It's the closest thing to actual magic in the financial world."

Money is where most people's long-term thinking goes to die. Everyone wants to get rich quick, but real wealth is built like a glacier - slow, steady, and unstoppable. It's not about finding the next crypto moonshot; it's about consistent, strategic decisions that compound over time.

Think about it like this: Every financial decision you make is either feeding your future self or stealing from them. That $5 coffee isn't just $5 - it's $5 plus all the compound interest it could have earned over decades. It's like taking a sledgehammer to your future self's piggy bank every time you swipe your card for some trivial bullshit you won't remember next week. The True Cost of Instant Gratification

Let's put some actual numbers on this abstract concept:

If you save $100/month starting at age 25, you'll have $335,194 at age 65. If you wait until age 35 to start, you'll have only $138,599 at age 65. The cost of waiting 10 years? A staggering $196,595.

(Assuming 8% average annual returns)

That's not just money—that's freedom, options, security, and opportunities that vanish because of a decade of prioritizing immediate desires over long-term needs.

The Financial Independence Matrix

The long game with money isn't just about being rich—it's about creating freedom:

1. Build an emergency fund foundation with 3-6 months of living expenses in high-yield savings
2. Eliminate high-interest debt before trying to invest
3. Set up systematic investments that happen before you can spend the money
4. Keep your standard of living flat when income increases
5. Know exactly what number you need to work because you want to, not because you have to

PART 4: ATTENTION & CAREER: COMPOUND INTEREST OF FOCUS

The Modern Attention Crisis

> "Attention isn't just being distracted—it's being systematically harvested like a natural resource, except nobody's making you sign a permission slip before they start drilling."

Your phone isn't just a distraction; it's the front end of a sophisticated attention-harvesting operation designed by some of the smartest people on the planet. It's basically a slot machine designed by psychology PhDs who studied addiction for a living, disguised as a communication tool. It's like having a tiny casino in your pocket that's rigged to make you lose your most precious resource—your attention—while making you think you're winning. It's the most elegant mind-fuck ever engineered. To play the long game, you first need to reclaim your most valuable resource—your focused attention. Audit your interruptions, create technology boundaries, batch similar tasks, design your environment for focus, eliminate notifications, block time for deep work, curate your information diet, focus on one important thing daily, and build in recovery periods for your brain.

Implementing a radical attention management system might involve deleting social media apps, using website blockers during focused work sessions, turning off all notifications, and even using timed lockboxes for phones. While these measures might seem extreme to others, they protect your most valuable resource—attention—when it's most needed. Many important projects simply wouldn't exist without such drastic steps to safeguard focus.

The Career Long Game

"Most people approach their careers like they're playing Frogger—desperately hopping between jobs, trying not to get squashed. Meanwhile, the people who win are playing SimCity, building entire ecosystems that generate opportunities while they sleep. They're not just collecting paychecks; they're building fucking empires."

The key isn't just about climbing the ladder - it's about building your own ladder that doesn't depend on any one company or industry. It's about developing skills, relationships, and expertise that compound over time, creating professional capital that no one can take away from you even if your entire industry gets disrupted.

To build a career that compounds over time, focus on stackable knowledge that complements what you already know, develop rare and valuable skill combinations, create intellectual property that generates value while you sleep, build systems for continuous improvement, develop relationships across industries and disciplines, and become known for specific expertise rather than general competence.

PART 5: RELATIONSHIPS, HEALTH & YOUR UNFAIR ADVANTAGE

The Relationship Long Game

> "Most people treat relationships like disposable razors—use them until they don't feel perfect anymore, then toss them out. Meanwhile, successful couples are sharpening the same blade for decades, making it work better over time, not worse. They're not just staying together; they're growing together like two trees whose roots have become so intertwined underground that they're essentially one organism with two trunks."

Real relationships are more like growing a forest than decorating a Christmas tree. You can't just throw some ornaments on and call it done. You need to plant seeds, nurture growth through all seasons (including the brutal winters when everything looks dead), and think in terms of decades rather than days.

For relationships that grow more valuable over time, create and revisit shared future aspirations, develop habits for honest communication during difficulties, regularly acknowledge and appreciate investments made, and encourage growth even when it creates temporary discomfort.

The Health and Wellness Long Game

> "The human body is like a credit card with no spending limit but very high interest rates. You can charge whatever you want to it in your twenties, but the statement always arrives in your forties—and there's no bankruptcy option. That debt gets collected one way or another, and the repo man

doesn't just take your car—he takes your mobility, your energy, and eventually your independence."

Most people treat their bodies like rental cars - they drive them hard, ignore the warning lights, and figure someone else will deal with the consequences. But your body isn't a rental; it's the only vehicle you get for this journey.

For physical resilience that compounds over time, establish non-negotiable health foundations, track key metrics to catch issues early, create systems to limit inevitable health stressors, and optimize environments for automatic healthy choices.

The Final Truth: Long-Term Thinking as Your Unfair Advantage

"In the land of microwave thinkers, the slow-cooker strategist is king. While they're snacking on instant ramen, you're preparing a feast that takes time but nourishes for years. They're getting a quick hit of sodium and carbs; you're building a fucking Michelin-star meal that will sustain you through winters."

Want to know the ultimate level of playing the long game? It's when you stop seeing it as a sacrifice and start seeing it as an advantage. It's when you understand that your willingness to think long-term is actually your greatest competitive edge in a world of short-term thinkers who are constantly starting over while you're building momentum.

When everyone else is trying to go viral, you're building something viral-proof. When they're chasing trends, you're setting them. When they're starting from scratch for the tenth time, you're benefiting from a decade of compound interest across multiple domains of your life.

The modern world hasn't just made long-term thinking harder - it's made it more valuable than ever. Every person who succumbs to short-term thinking is one less competitor in the long game. Every app that shortens attention spans makes sustained focus more powerful. Every trend that comes and goes makes lasting value more precious.

Creating substantial content like a book is a commitment to the long game. Rather than producing short-form content for quick validation and faster feedback, or churning out social media posts that might go viral, it requires investing in something more substantial that demands months of consistent effort with no immediate payoff. When such projects succeed, they become living proof that the long game works—not just in theory, but in practice.

> "In a world obsessed with the viral and immediate, the most revolutionary act is to focus on the sustainable and enduring."

So here's a wake-up call for everyone: Stop letting the modern world's addiction to instant gratification infect your thinking. Start playing the kind of game that creates lasting value, even if nobody else can see it yet. The greatest opportunities in life come from being willing to play games that most people don't have the patience for.

Your future self is waiting for your answer. And trust me, that future self would really appreciate if you'd stop stealing from them to fund your present impulses.

Now go build something that matters. Your ten-year overnight success story starts today.

CHAPTER CONNECTION: You've now completed the core transformation journey that will fundamentally change how you approach life. In Chapter 1, you stopped poisoning your environment with complaints. In Chapter 2, you confronted the comfortable lies that kept you stuck. In Chapter 3, you developed the emotional resilience needed to face challenges without breaking. In Chapter 4, you accepted that life isn't fair and never will be. And now, in this chapter, you've learned to play the long game in a world obsessed with quick fixes.

Playing the long game attracts criticism from those trapped in short-term thinking. When you commit to long-term strategies, you'll face resistance from others threatened by your patience. Friends may mock your financial discipline while they're maxing out credit cards. Colleagues may question your career choices when you prioritize skill development over quick promotions. Family members may pressure you to "live a little" when you're focused on long-term goals. In Chapter 6, you'll learn to handle criticism without abandoning your long-term strategy—a crucial skill for anyone committed to delayed gratification in an instant-results world.

This five-chapter foundation forms your complete mental operating system upgrade. Each chapter builds on the previous ones, creating a powerful psychological infrastructure that can withstand real-world challenges. The patience you've developed here in Chapter 5 will be immediately tested in Chapter 6, where you'll learn to handle the inevitable criticism and resistance that comes when you start playing a bigger game. As you move forward, you'll face new challenges that will test this framework. The remaining chapters will equip you with specific strategies for these challenges, building on the foundation you've now established.

CHAPTER 6: HOW TO HANDLE HATERS (WHILE BUILDING AN EMPIRE ON THEIR TEARS)

"PEOPLE WHO SAY IT CANNOT BE DONE SHOULD NOT INTERRUPT THOSE WHO ARE DOING IT."

PART 1: THE HATE TAX

The Inevitable Tax of Success: Why Achievement Requires a Thicker Skin

One of the most predictable problems anyone faces when starting to grow is dealing with other people trying to drag them down. When someone starts thinking long-term in our instant-gratification world, the critics inevitably come out of the woodwork.

The emotional backbone you developed in Chapter 3 is about to face its ultimate test: criticism from others. This is your criticism response headquarters—the definitive guide to processing feedback without letting it derail your progress.

How well people handle criticism will slap a hard ceiling on their success faster than almost anything else. Studies show about 67% of people completely abandon important goals specifically because other people criticized them. Think about that - two-thirds of people quit chasing their dreams because someone said something mean to them. The most successful people aren't necessarily the ones with the most talent or best connections—they're the ones who've basically developed a psychological force field against opinions that would stop everyone else dead in their tracks. This isn't some cute little bonus skill for a personal development vision board; it's the essential armor needed to protect all the progress fought for against the arrows that start flying the second someone sticks their head above the crowd.

Ever notice how the second someone starts doing something that actually matters, critics start popping up everywhere like cockroaches when the kitchen light flips on at 2 AM? It's one of life's most reliable formulas: **Success = Achievements × Haters²**. The bigger someone tries to play, the louder critics scream. The more a person accomplishes, the more they nitpick. The higher someone climbs, the more haters try to grab their ankles on the way up. And if anyone wants to do something remotely meaningful with their life instead of just existing until they die, they better get real fucking comfortable with that math because it's not changing for anyone.

Let's talk about those special people who've mastered the art of criticizing without ever creating a damn thing themselves - your haters. You know exactly who I mean: they've got way more opinions than actual achievements, more complaints than accomplishments, and they've basically turned judging others into their full-time job (with no benefits or 401k, but plenty of overtime). They're like those armchair quarterbacks sitting on their couch with Cheeto dust on their fingers who've never even touched a football since high school gym class but somehow know exactly why the professional athlete making millions is doing everything wrong. "He should have passed it!" they yell between mouthfuls of nachos, as if the NFL is desperately waiting for their coaching insights.

Here's the beautiful truth about haters - they're basically just seagulls at a beach party. The better your food, the more they circle and squawk. The tastier your success looks, the more desperately they want to steal a bite. The bigger your ambitions, the louder they screech. The higher you climb, the more they swarm around you trying to shit on everything from above. They don't actually build nests or contribute anything - they just fly around looking for other people's picnics to ruin.

And you know what? That's actually fantastic news. If you don't have any haters, you're probably not doing anything worth talking about in the first place. Nobody wastes time critiquing mediocrity—they just scroll past it. Hate is basically just attention wearing a disguise and throwing a temper tantrum.

Think about it: Has anyone ever built a statue to honor some random critic? Hell no. The world remembers the doers, the creators, the risk-takers—not the people who spent their entire lives sitting on the sidelines critiquing everyone else.

People know they're on the right track when their progress triggers other people's insecurities. When forward motion makes others uncomfortable enough to criticize, that's confirmation of growth beyond their comfort zone.

When sharing creative work, you may receive critiques from people without relevant experience. For example, someone might say "People want gentle encouragement, not direct confrontation" or "This approach is too harsh." It's important to recognize when criticism stems from someone's personal discomfort rather than genuine expertise. This realization can free you to continue in your authentic voice rather than watering down your work to avoid criticism.

PART 2: INSIDE THE HATER'S MIND

The Psychology of Professional Haters: Inside the Mind of Your Critics

Understanding the psychology of hate is half the battle when dealing with critics.

> "The loudest boos come from the cheapest seats."

First, let's understand what drives a hater's mind. Picture someone who's found the world's most pathetic addict on - getting high on other people's misery. Every time they spit venom, their brain rewards them with a little hit of satisfaction. They're literally addicted to hate, like someone who's discovered they can get drunk on their own bitterness. Their brain chemistry is like a sewage treatment plant that's been rewired to produce dopamine when processing shit instead of cleaning it.

> "Some people are too jealous to like your posts but too nosy to unfollow."

In their minds, they feel powerful, important, relevant - all the things they're desperately missing in their real lives. They're essentially emotional vampires, trying to suck the joy out of your success because they have none of their own to feed on.

The Four Core Motivations of Haters

All haters, whether online trolls or workplace saboteurs, operate from four primary psychological drivers:

Projection of Insecurity Haters aren't actually criticizing you—they're responding to what your success triggers in them. Your achievement is holding up a mirror to their lack of achievement, and they're attacking their reflection, not you.

When someone says "You're not that great," what they're really saying is "I feel inadequate when I compare myself to you, and I need to tear you down to protect my fragile self-image."

Fear of Irrelevance In a world where attention is currency, some people would rather be hated than ignored. Attacking someone successful makes them feel like they're part of the conversation, even if their only contribution is negativity.

Tribe Signaling Some hate isn't actually about you at all—it's about signaling loyalty to a particular group. By criticizing you, they're telling their tribe, "See? I'm one of you! I hate the right people!"

Misery Loves Company Some haters are simply unhappy people who can't stand seeing others thrive. They operate under the logic that if they can't be happy, no one else should be either.

Most hate isn't really about the person being criticized at all—it's about the hater's relationship with themselves. Success is just a mirror reflecting back their own perceived inadequacies.

The most liberating realization is that their criticism says infinitely more about them than it does about you. Once you truly understand this, you can listen to criticism without taking it personally, like a doctor examining symptoms of a patient's condition rather than taking their fever as a personal insult.

PART 3: YOUR BRAIN ON CRITICISM

The Neuroscience of Criticism: Why Hate Hurts and How to Hack Your Response

Let's get scientific about why criticism feels like someone's stabbing a person in the soul. This isn't just philosophical—it's neurological. As we learned in Chapter 3, criticism triggers your amygdala—your brain's alarm system—just like physical threats. The human brain literally processes social rejection using many of the same neural circuits it uses for physical pain.

When you experience criticism, your brain's anterior cingulate cortex lights up like Times Square on New Year's Eve. This is the same region that activates when you burn your hand or stub your toe. Your brain doesn't say, "Oh, that's just words." It says, "DANGER! PAIN! EMERGENCY!" and floods your system with cortisol and adrenaline. It's like having a fire alarm that can't tell the difference between a five-alarm blaze and someone making toast - it screams just as loudly either way.

This isn't some design flaw in your neural architecture—it's a feature that kept our ancestors alive. Humans evolved as tribal creatures; being rejected from the group meant certain death. Your brain treats social threats as survival threats because for most of human history, they were exactly that.

The Amygdala Hijack: Why You Can't Think Straight When Criticized

When harsh criticism hits, the amygdala (the brain's threat detection center) activates before the prefrontal cortex (the rational thinking area) can process what's happening. This "amygdala hijack" explains why the first reaction to criticism is often emotional rather than logical—the thinking brain literally hasn't had time to come online yet.

The Four Horsemen of Criticism Response

Research in affective neuroscience has identified four primary neural patterns people default to when facing criticism:

Fight Response: Characterized by defensive anger, counterattacks, and justification. The Fight Response isn't just disagreeing—it's that immediate defensive rage that makes you fire back a response you'll regret before your rational brain can intervene. Instead of addressing valid points, you attack the critic's credentials, point out typos, or bring up unrelated issues—anything to avoid the actual content. This is the most common and often most damaging response pattern.

But if you think the Fight response is bad, wait until you see what the Freeze response does to your reputation...

Freeze Response: Appears as anxiety, overthinking, and rumination. You become paralyzed, unable to respond at all while your mind races through every possible interpretation of the criticism. You obsessively reread the comment, analyze it from every angle, and imagine worst-case scenarios. Meanwhile, your silence is often interpreted as agreement or guilt by others. This response pattern can be career-killing in professional contexts where quick, confident responses are expected.

Flight Response: Manifests as withdrawal, avoidance, and disengagement. You suddenly "get busy" with other projects, stop showing up in spaces where you might face criticism, or abandon projects entirely rather than address feedback.

Fawn Response: Shows up as excessive agreement, people-pleasing, and abandoning your position. You immediately capitulate, apologize profusely (even for things you didn't do), and change your position to match the critic's—not because you actually agree, but because you're desperate to end the discomfort.

Remember the emotional labeling you practiced in Chapter 3? It becomes crucial here: "I notice I'm feeling defensive and embarrassed by this feedback, not just angry." Apply the emotional intensity scale from Chapter 3 to criticism by monitoring your reaction temperature before responding.

Most people's first reaction to criticism is pure garbage. That initial response forming in your head is almost always defensive bullshit, petty counterattacks, or pathetic justifications.

Most people have a primary default response that gets triggered automatically. Identifying this personal pattern is the first step toward developing more strategic reactions.

Neural Reprogramming: Science-Based Techniques for Criticism Resilience

Just as your brain can be hijacked by criticism, it can be reprogrammed to respond differently. Here are four neuroscience-backed techniques to hack your brain's response system:

The Cognitive Distancing Protocol When criticism hits, mentally narrate in the third person: "Sam is feeling defensive right now because he received criticism about his presentation." This simple shift activates your prefrontal cortex, bringing your rational brain back online faster.

The Emotion Regulation Delay Implement a strict 90-second rule when facing criticism. Don't respond immediately. Take a deep breath, count to ten, drink some water, or simply sit with the discomfort for 90 seconds.

The Parasympathetic Activation Technique Practice 4-7-8 breathing when facing criticism: inhale for 4 counts, hold for 7 counts, exhale for 8 counts. Repeat 3-4 times. The extended exhale is key—it signals your brain that the emergency is over.

The Pre-Criticism Mental Vaccination Before putting work out into the world, spend 5 minutes imagining specific criticism you might receive. For each potential criticism, craft a rational, non-defensive response. This isn't about becoming paranoid—it's about being prepared.

Valid vs. Toxic: The Criticism Spectrum

Not all criticism is created equal, and learning to distinguish between valid feedback and toxic attacks is essential:

Valid Criticism	Toxic Criticism
"Your argument would be stronger with more data to support point 3"	"This is garbage. You clearly don't know what you're talking about"
"I found the pace of the presentation too fast to follow the main points"	"You're a terrible presenter. I've seen high schoolers do better"
"The project missed the deadline because the requirements weren't clear"	"You always mess things up. This is just like the last project"
"The tone of your email came across as dismissive"	"You're so arrogant. No one wants to work with you"
Addresses what you did	Attacks who you are
Offers specifics	Deals in generalizations
Focuses on improvement	Focuses on tearing down
Delivered respectfully	Delivered with contempt
Can be acted upon	Leaves nowhere to go

Ask yourself: "If I set aside my emotional reaction, is there anything I could learn from this feedback?" Valid criticism addresses what you did; toxic criticism attacks who you are. Valid criticism offers specifics; toxic criticism deals in generalizations.

Notice when criticism focuses entirely on tone rather than substance—that's often a sign someone can't actually dispute your content. For more on escaping the victim mindset in general, see Chapter 4.

PART 4: THE DIGITAL HATE MACHINE

The Modern Hate Factory: How Social Media Turned Criticism into an Industry

Social media has given every keyboard warrior with a WiFi connection and an opinion their own personal hate broadcasting network, turning criticism into a cottage industry. It's like handing out free megaphones to everyone in a stadium and being surprised when it turns into a fucking cacophony of hot takes and uninformed opinions.

Platform-Specific Hate Styles: Know Your Battleground

Each social platform has developed its own unique criticism culture that you need to understand:

Twitter/X: The Snark Olympics Twitter has evolved into a competition for who can craft the most devastating takedown in the fewest characters.

Defense strategy: Remember that Twitter rewards emotion over accuracy. Most Twitter criticism is literally engineered to provoke a reaction from you that will drive more engagement to their criticism. Twitter isn't just "people sharing thoughts"—it's bloodsport where the snarkiest takedowns get the most engagement. The most effective response is often no response. If you must respond, use "acknowledge and redirect": "Appreciate the feedback. For those interested in the data behind my conclusion, check out the full article here: [link]."

Instagram: The Passive-Aggressive Paradise Instagram criticism comes wrapped in false positivity and concern-trolling.

Defense strategy: Remember that most Instagram critics are performing for their audience, not genuinely engaging with you. Their criticism says more about the image they're trying to project than about your work. Instagram criticism comes with a side of toxic positivity—"Just wondering why you look so tired in this photo? 💕 " The best response is often a simple "Thanks for your concern!" followed by no further engagement

LinkedIn: The Professional Underminer LinkedIn has perfected the art of criticism disguised as professional advice.

Defense strategy: LinkedIn criticism is all about professional posturing. Critics are often more concerned with displaying their expertise to potential employers or clients than they are with the accuracy of their criticism. LinkedIn has its special brand of professional undermining disguised as "thought leadership." "Interesting approach! In my experience, I've found the opposite to be true." Respond with data: "Thanks for sharing your experience! Our approach is based on [specific research/results], but I'm always interested in learning about alternative methods that have worked for others."

TikTok: The Reaction Economy TikTok has created an entire genre of content based solely on reacting to other people's work.

Defense strategy: Remember that TikTok's algorithm rewards theatrical reactions, not thoughtful analysis. Critics are often exaggerating their responses to trigger the algorithm, not because your work genuinely deserves that level of reaction. The most effective strategy is to either ignore completely or, if the criticism has gained significant traction, create a calm, factual response video that demonstrates your expertise without matching their emotional intensity.

In 2021, researchers analyzed millions of social media comments and found that negative comments received 6x more engagement than positive ones, creating a system that literally rewards hate. The platforms aren't neutral—their business models actively amplify criticism because it keeps people arguing (and therefore scrolling).

PART 5: OFFICE POLITICS AND PROFESSIONAL SABOTEURS

The Workplace Hate Game: Office Politics and Professional Saboteurs

Workplace saboteurs are a special breed of hater. These office politicians have turned passive-aggressive behavior into an Olympic sport, smiling to your face while sending undermining emails behind your back. They're like professional boxers who've replaced their gloves with pillows - they hit you so softly you barely feel it until you realize you've been slowly suffocated.

The Five Workplace Hater Archetypes

The Credit Thief This colleague systematically positions themselves to take credit for your ideas and work.

Counter strategy: Document everything. Create paper trails with timestamped idea submissions.

The Backchannel Critic This colleague never raises concerns directly to you but has an endless supply of "concerns" they share with decision-makers when you're not in the room.

Counter strategy: Build direct relationships with decision-makers and regularly provide them with updates on your work.

The Devil's Advocate This colleague doesn't have ideas of their own but has an endless supply of reasons why your ideas won't work.

Counter strategy: When faced with devil's advocacy, respond with "Thanks for that perspective. What approach would you recommend instead?" Force them to move from criticism to contribution.

The Scope Creeper This passive-aggressive critic works by gradually expanding the requirements or expectations of your work until success becomes impossible.

Counter strategy: Document initial requirements in writing and reference them when scope creep occurs.

The Faux Mentor This particularly insidious critic positions themselves as helping you while actually undermining your confidence and autonomy.

Counter strategy: Thank them for their input while maintaining decision authority: "I appreciate your perspective. I'll consider that approach as I finalize my decision."

PART 6: SEPARATING SIGNAL FROM NOISE

The Criticism Calibration System: Not All Feedback Is Created Equal

Not all criticism is created equal. There's constructive criticism from people who've done what someone is trying to do - that's gold, worth taking. There's uninformed criticism from people who don't know what they're talking about - that's noise, best ignored. And then there's hate from people who are just bitter about their own lives - that's fuel, ready to be used for motivation. Learning to tell the difference is like developing a bullshit detector so finely tuned it can separate diamonds from dirt at fifty paces.

The VALID Criticism Assessment Framework

> "Those who care about your failures secretly hope you'll fail again."

Use this five-point system to instantly categorize any criticism:

V - Validator's Credentials Has this person successfully done what you're trying to do? Are they where you want to be? Have they demonstrated expertise in this specific area?

A - Actionable Specifics Does the criticism contain specific, concrete suggestions for improvement, or is it vague disapproval?

L - Loving Intent Is the critic motivated by a genuine desire to see you improve, or are they satisfying their own emotional needs by tearing you down?

I - Information Base Is the criticism based on complete and accurate information, or is the critic working from assumptions, partial information, or hearsay?

D - Delivery Method Was the criticism delivered privately and respectfully, or was it shared publicly or disrespectfully?

PART 7: TURNING ATTACKS INTO ADVANTAGES

The Anti-Fragile Protocol: Turning Attacks into Advantages

The relationship between criticism and growth is powerful. The more haters hate, the stronger a person can become. Like building an immune system, every attack makes someone more resilient, every criticism makes them more determined, every hate comment makes them more focused. The goal isn't just withstanding attacks; it's metabolizing them into muscle. It's turning the very poison meant to kill you into the medicine that makes you unstoppable. It's some serious fucking alchemy - transforming the lead of criticism into the gold of achievement.

The Five-Step Anti-Fragile System

Transform criticism from a destructive force into a growth catalyst:

Step 1: Emotional Quarantine When criticism first arrives, place it in a mental quarantine zone where it can't immediately affect your emotional state.

Step 2: Extraction of Value Approach the criticism like an archaeologist examining an artifact, looking for anything of value while discarding the emotional debris surrounding it.

Step 3: Pattern Recognition Catalog the criticism and look for recurring themes across multiple sources. Individual criticism might be noise, but patterns across multiple sources often contain signal.

Step 4: Strategic Response Selection Based on your value extraction and pattern recognition, consciously choose the optimal response from these options: - Implement a change (when the criticism identifies a legitimate improvement opportunity) - Communicate more clearly (when the criticism stems from misunderstanding) - Lean in harder (when the criticism confirms you're disrupting outdated thinking) - Thank and move on (when the criticism has been processed but requires no action)

Step 5: Metabolization into Motivation Convert the emotional energy of criticism—even unfair criticism—into fuel for your next level of achievement.

The trick isn't to ignore all criticism - it's to learn how to extract the useful bits while discarding the emotional garbage. It's like being a gold miner, sifting through tons of dirt to find those valuable nuggets.

PART 8: WHY BREAKTHROUGHS FACE BACKLASH

The Innovation-Criticism Complex: Why Breakthroughs Always Face Backlash

The amount of hate someone receives is directly proportional to how innovative their ideas are. Every major innovation in history was met with a tsunami of criticism.

Innovation attracts criticism like honey attracts flies. The more you push boundaries, the more you'll push buttons. The more you innovate, the more you'll irritate. It's like trying to change the direction of a river - the water will resist and splash and make a hell of a noise before it finally accepts the new course.

"Some hate you because you did more with less. Their problem, not yours."

This isn't a bug in the system—it's a feature. The criticism is actually a reliable indicator that you're breaking new ground. If everyone immediately understands and accepts your innovation, it's probably not that innovative.

The Criticism Timeline of Breakthrough Ideas

All revolutionary ideas follow this predictable criticism journey:

Phase 1: Dismissal ("That's Impossible") Initially, truly innovative ideas are simply dismissed as impossible or absurd.

Phase 2: Marginalization ("It's Possible But Pointless") Once the innovation demonstrates basic viability, critics shift to arguing that it serves no useful purpose.

Phase 3: Concern Trolling ("It's Dangerous") After usefulness becomes apparent, criticism morphs into exaggerated safety concerns and doomsday scenarios.

Phase 4: Economic Skepticism ("It Will Never Be Viable") Once safety concerns are addressed, critics focus on business viability, claiming there's no sustainable economic model.

Phase 5: Superiority Claims ("Our Way Is Better") As the innovation gains traction, established competitors claim their traditional approach is superior.

Phase 6: Adoption and Amnesia ("We Always Supported This") Finally, when success becomes undeniable, former critics often rewrite history, claiming they always saw the potential.

The pattern is so consistent that you can actually use criticism as a compass: If everyone immediately loves your idea, you might be on well-trodden ground. If experts in the field vehemently oppose it, you might be onto something revolutionary.

When I first proposed the concept for this book, several publishing industry veterans told me it wouldn't work. "Self-help books need to be gentler, more affirming," they said. "Readers want to feel good, not challenged." This pushback actually strengthened my conviction that I was onto something valuable. The self-help market was saturated with feel-good platitudes that weren't creating real change in people's lives. The criticism I received wasn't a sign that my approach was wrong—it was confirmation that I was challenging the status quo in a way that made established players uncomfortable. That's exactly what innovation is supposed to do.

PART 9: TACTICAL RESPONSES TO CRITICISM

The Practical Guide to Hater Management: Tactical Responses

These tactical responses will help you handle haters effectively:

Ever notice how successful people seem suspiciously calm when criticized? That's not an accident or genetic gift—it's a deliberately practiced skill. Here's where most people completely fuck up their criticism response...

Document Everything: Creating Your Victory Archive Keep records of their predictions of your failure. They'll come in handy when you're writing your success story.

Create a dedicated "Victory Archive" folder (digital or physical), screenshot or save particularly dismissive criticism, organize by date and source, review quarterly to track your progress against their predictions, and use as motivation when facing new challenges.

Use Their Energy: The Criticism Checklist Method Every time they say you can't do something, add it to your to-do list. Let their doubt become your checklist.

Create a "Prove Them Wrong" section in your task management system. For each criticism, extract the implied challenge ("You'll never finish that project" → "Complete project ahead of schedule"), break down each challenge into actionable steps, schedule specific time blocks to work on these items, and document your progress with tangible metrics.

Stay Focused: The Spectator vs. Player Mindset Remember, haters are just spectators in your game. They can yell from the sidelines, but they can't affect the score unless you let them.

Create a physical reminder card with: "Spectators comment. Players perform." Set a daily focus intention: "Today I play my game, not theirs." Track how much time you spend thinking about criticism vs. taking action. Practice the "3-second rule": acknowledge criticism, then immediately refocus on your work. Reward yourself for maintaining focus despite distractions.

Build Immunity: The Gradual Exposure Technique The first hate comment feels like a knife to the heart. The hundredth? It barely registers. The thousandth? It's just confirmation you're still moving in the right direction.

Start with small, low-stakes public sharing of your work, create a "criticism desensitization" journal to track your emotional responses, gradually increase exposure in larger venues, practice receiving criticism in controlled environments, and celebrate decreased emotional reactivity as a sign of growing strength.

Categorize and Triage: The Criticism Management Matrix Not all criticism requires the same response. Learn to quickly sort criticism into categories: actionable vs. non-actionable, informed vs. uninformed, well-intentioned vs. malicious.

Create a 2×2 matrix: Actionable/Non-actionable × Informed/ Uninformed. For each criticism, place it in the appropriate quadrant. Respond only to Actionable + Informed criticism. Thank but don't implement Actionable + Uninformed. Acknowledge but don't engage with Non-actionable criticism. Ignore entirely anything that's both Non-actionable + Uninformed.

The 24-Hour Rule: The Emotional Cooling Period For especially stinging criticism, implement a personal 24-hour rule: No response for 24 hours.

Create an automatic "cooling period" folder in your email, draft responses but save them for 24 hours before sending, set a specific time to review criticism after the cooling period, use physical cues (deep breathing, walking) to interrupt emotional reactions, and after 24 hours, ask: "What response serves my long-term goals?" The 24-Hour Rule isn't optional—it's the difference between maintaining your reputation and torpedoing your career with one stupid, emotional response.

The Redirection Technique: Focusing on Your Work, Not Their Words When faced with public criticism, redirect the conversation back to your work rather than becoming defensive.

Prepare 3-5 redirection templates for common criticism scenarios, practice the "acknowledge and pivot" response: "I appreciate your perspective. What I'm focused on is...", keep a list of your core values and goals to reference when redirecting, track how often you successfully redirect vs. becoming defensive, and review and refine your redirection approaches based on effectiveness.

The Nuclear Option: Success When all else fails, the most powerful response to criticism is undeniable success. Critics can argue with your approach, your style, or your methods, but they can't argue with your results.

Identify key metrics that would constitute "undeniable success" in your field, create a visible dashboard tracking your progress toward these metrics, schedule regular "success focus" sessions where you work exclusively on high-impact activities, document your wins, no matter how small, to build momentum, and when achieving significant milestones, resist the urge to "clap back" at critics—let your results speak for themselves.

Write the Rage, Send the Sage Technique Draft your emotional first response to get it out of your system. Then delete it completely and write a second response after you've calmed down. This two-step process allows you to process your emotions without letting them dictate your public response.

Wait—I need to emphasize something critical here. The goal isn't to never feel hurt by criticism. That's neither possible nor desirable. The goal is to feel it without being controlled by it.

The Criticism Triage System Not all criticism deserves the same level of response. Create three categories: Ignore (trolls, bad faith attacks, Consider (potentially valid points wrapped in emotional language, and Implement (specific, actionable feedback from credible sources. This system prevents you from wasting energy on criticism that doesn't deserve it while ensuring you don't miss valuable feedback.

PART 10: SUCCESS AS THE ULTIMATE COMEBACK

The Final Victory: Success as the Ultimate Response

"Critics write the reviews, but creators write history."

Success is the ultimate response to haters. Nothing shuts up critics like results. While they're writing essays about why an approach won't work, successful people are busy making it work. While critics craft clever criticisms, achievers craft actual achievements. While haters build arguments, innovators build empires.

The beautiful irony? The more successful you become, the more they'll hate. And the more they hate, the more they prove you're doing something right. It's like having a success meter powered by negativity - the louder they screech, the better you're doing. Their hate becomes the most reliable fucking compass you could ask for - pointing directly toward your greatest impact.

When someone reaches a certain level of success, something magical happens: The hate becomes irrelevant, not because it stops (it actually increases), but because achievements speak so loudly that criticism becomes background noise.

And whenever the criticism stings (because sometimes it still will, no matter how successful someone becomes), remember this: People don't hate on the insignificant. No one bothers to criticize mediocrity. The fact that someone has attracted haters means they're doing something right—something bold enough, brave enough, and significant enough to trigger a response. It should be worn as a badge of honor, not a burden. Their hate isn't a problem; it's proof of impact.

CHAPTER CONNECTION: In Chapter 5, you learned to play the long game in a world obsessed with instant gratification. Now in Chapter 6, you've developed the ability to handle the inevitable criticism that comes with meaningful achievement. This progression is no accident—playing the long game naturally attracts critics who are stuck in short-term thinking. By mastering both skills, you've built a powerful foundation for sustained success.

CHAPTER 7: MAKING ANY PLACE SUCK LESS

"CHANGE YOUR ENVIRONMENT OR CHANGE HOW YOU RESPOND TO IT—THERE IS NO THIRD OPTION."

PART 1: THE INVISIBLE FORCE FIELD

The Environment Upgrade Everyone Ignores

> "Your environment is like your underwear—you don't notice it when it fits well, but when it doesn't, it's all you can think about."

Your environment has a profound impact on your performance, mood, and health. Understanding how to optimize your surroundings is a crucial skill that most people overlook in their self-improvement efforts.

This is your environmental psychology headquarters—the definitive guide to how spaces shape behavior. Let's be honest—you've been blaming your environment for your failures while doing absolutely nothing to change it. That ends now.

WHY THIS MATTERS: The research is mind-blowing - environment affects performance by up to 25%, mood by up to 40%, and health by up to 30%. Think about that. Most people spend 90% of their lives indoors, but put less than 1% of their self-improvement effort into making these spaces better. Things like lighting, noise levels, and how organized a space is directly mess with stress hormones, ability to focus, and decision-making. This isn't some abstract concept - t's happening in the brain right now. The human brain processes something like 11 million bits of environmental information every second, and most of it happens without conscious awareness. When an environment sucks, it's like trying to run a marathon in cement shoes while everyone else is wearing fucking Nikes. Really successful people get that fixing the environment isn't just about making things look pretty—it's about making the brain work better.

> "You survived hurricanes. Why worry about raindrops?"

Surroundings shape everything from mood to productivity, yet most people spend more time scrolling through Netflix options than thinking about the actual spaces where they spend 90% of their damn lives. They'll agonize for 20 minutes over which show to watch for the next hour but won't spend 10 minutes fixing the chair that's been slowly destroying their spine for the past three years. This invisible force affects performance more than most of those fancy self-improvement hacks people try. That $47 productivity app isn't going to save anyone when their desk is so cluttered they can barely see the keyboard and the overhead light flickers like they're working in a horror movie basement.

Ever notice how some people can walk into a crappy coffee shop with uncomfortable chairs that feel like they were designed by someone who hates human spines, screaming espresso machines that sound like a robot giving birth, and that one guy in the corner who's somehow taking a conference call on speakerphone, and yet they still somehow turn it into their personal productivity zone? Meanwhile, others need absolute silence, perfect lighting, and their lucky pen just to write a damn email. That's not luck or delusion or some genetic gift—that's environmental mastery, and it might be the most underrated superpower anyone could have in today's world of open office hellscapes and "cozy" (translation: tiny as hell) apartments.

TRUTH BOMB: These places don't suck because of some cosmic law or curse. They suck because people let them suck, and then spend way more energy complaining about it than it would actually take to fix the problem. It's like watching someone stub their toe on the same coffee table every single morning for three years straight, then hearing them yell "This room hates me!" or "Whoever designed this apartment was a sadist!" instead of just moving the damn table six inches to the left or buying a $2 nightlight so they can see where they're going. People will literally spend YEARS being uncomfortable or frustrated rather than take fifteen minutes to solve a problem that's making them miserable every day. They'll complain about their office chair slowly turning their spine into a question mark but won't spend $15 on a lumbar support pillow. They'll moan about how their kitchen is impossible to cook in but won't reorganize their cabinets to put the stuff they actually use within reach.

REALITY CHECK: The most mind-blowing truth about crappy environments is that fixing them is usually way easier, cheaper, and faster than most people think. We're not talking about some full-blown HGTV renovation where an impossibly attractive couple drops $50,000 to move a wall three inches. We're talking about simple, cheap, sometimes even completely free changes that make a huge difference in how a space feels and how well it works.

Many people learn this lesson the hard way. They might try to work at a kitchen table that's uncomfortable, poorly lit, and next to the refrigerator (hello, constant snack breaks). They complain about slow progress and blame "creative blocks" when the real problem is their terrible work environment. Simple changes like moving a workspace next to a window for natural light, adding cushioning to an uncomfortable chair, and using noise-canceling headphones can dramatically improve productivity. The environment they've been fighting has actually been fighting back, and a few small tweaks can make all the difference.

PART 2: THE TRANSFORMATION SYSTEM

The S.P.A.C.E. Framework: Your Environmental Transformation Protocol

> "A mediocre space with a great system beats a gorgeous space with chaos every single time. Pretty is nice, but functional is freedom."

Wait—before you skip ahead thinking this is just about cleaning your desk, understand that environmental design is the most underrated success hack in existence. Your workspace isn't neutral—it's either a launching pad or a prison cell. Your environment isn't just "influencing" you—it's dictating your life while you sit there pretending you're in control.

When most people try to improve their environment, they either do nothing (the "complain and remain" approach) or try to change everything at once (the "Pinterest fever dream that ends in tears" approach). Both strategies fail spectacularly. Here's where most people completely miss the point about environments: they think it's about aesthetics when it's actually about function. What actually works is the S.P.A.C.E. system:

S - Scan: Identify what's actually broken, not just what's ugly.
P - Prioritize: Fix pain points before aesthetics.
A - Action: Take immediate steps, even small ones.
C - Clear: Remove what doesn't work before adding new things.
E - Evaluate: Test changes and adjust as needed.

This isn't about creating Instagram-worthy spaces that look good in photos but are impossible to live in. This is about creating environments that actually support what you're trying to do instead of actively sabotaging you.

The S.P.A.C.E. Method in Action

Instead of providing a 47-point implementation plan that nobody will actually use, let's break this down into real-world application:

S - SCAN: Walk through the space with fresh eyes like a detective investigating a crime scene—the crime being why it feels terrible to be there. Don't just look for what's ugly; look for what's broken in function. That desk where knees keep getting banged? That's not a design flaw—that's environmental sabotage. That dark corner that's supposed to be for reading but where it's barely possible to see the words? That's not cozy—that's stupid as hell.

Write this stuff down because the brain is an unreliable witness that will forget everything the moment it moves on.

3-Tier Implementation: - Beginner (5-minute fix): Take photos of your space from different angles—you'll spot problems you've become blind to. - Intermediate (weekend project): Create a "friction log" for one day—note every time something in your environment annoys or slows you down. - Advanced (major overhaul): Conduct a full environmental audit using the five senses—what do you see, hear, feel, smell, and even taste in your space that helps or hinders you?

Common Environment Trap: The Familiarity Blindness Trap— after two weeks in any space, your brain literally stops seeing problems that are in plain sight. You need to deliberately break this pattern to see what's actually there.

Before: Working in a space with glare on your screen, causing eye strain and headaches you've attributed to "stress."

After: Repositioning your workspace to eliminate glare, immediately reducing physical discomfort and increasing focus.

Environment Success Indicator: Count how many times you feel frustrated by your space in a typical day. After improvements, this number should drop by at least 50%.

P - PRIORITIZE: Not all environmental problems are created equal. That ugly wall color might offend aesthetic sensibilities, but it's not actually preventing productivity. Meanwhile, that chair that feels like it was designed by a medieval torture expert is literally causing physical pain every day. Fix the shit that's actively causing harm before the stuff that just looks bad in Instagram photos.

A - ACTION: Here's where most people fail—they plan endlessly but never actually do anything. The secret to environmental improvement isn't having the perfect plan; it's taking immediate, imperfect action. Move that lamp today. Throw away that broken chair now. Rearrange the desk this afternoon. Small, immediate changes beat perfect plans that never happen every single time.

C - CLEAR: Most people try to organize before they declutter, which is like trying to arrange deck chairs on the Titanic—pointless and doomed. Excess can't be organized; it can only be hidden temporarily. Before buying a single storage container, get rid of the stuff that's making the space feel like an episode of Hoarders. If it hasn't been used in three months and it's not seasonal, it's not storage material—it's clutter with a fancy container.

E - EVALUATE: After making changes, actually pay attention to whether they worked. That standing desk converter seemed like a great idea, but if you're still sitting 95% of the time, it's just an expensive monitor stand. That new organization system is worthless if you abandoned it after two days. Be honest about what's working and what's not, then adjust accordingly.

When applying the S.P.A.C.E. framework to a workspace, people often discover surprising insights. Someone might fixate on getting a fancy ergonomic chair (which they can't afford), while completely ignoring that their laptop is positioned at an angle destroying their wrists and neck. The SCAN step reveals that the biggest pain points aren't always what we think they are. After PRIORITIZING the actual problems, taking ACTION might involve raising a laptop on a stack of books and using an external keyboard. CLEARING away decorative items that take up valuable desk space, and then EVALUATING the changes often reveals that physical discomfort decreases dramatically. The framework works because it focuses on solving real problems, not just the ones we think we have.

PART 3: YOUR BRAIN ON YOUR SURROUNDINGS

The Environmental Psychology Principle

> "Your environment isn't just background noise—it's programming code running constantly in your mental operating system."

Think of your environment as an invisible current. You can swim against it with willpower, but eventually, you'll get tired. The smart approach isn't more willpower—it's changing the direction of the current. The brain is constantly processing environmental signals that shape everything from hormone levels to decision-making abilities. When an environment sucks, it's like running malware on the brain—except instead of stealing credit card info, it's stealing productivity, mood, and will to live. It's like having a virus that doesn't crash your computer but makes every program run at half-speed and randomly closes your tabs when you're in the middle of something important.

Here's the science without the boring parts: The human brain has limited processing power, and every environmental irritant (flickering light, uncomfortable chair, background noise) steals mental bandwidth from the task at hand. It's like trying to have a deep conversation while someone repeatedly pokes with a stick—technically possible but unnecessarily difficult.

Thinking isn't just happening in the head—it's influenced by physical experience. When the body is uncomfortable, thinking literally changes. That's why people have their best ideas in the shower and their worst ones while sitting in traffic. Environment isn't just where thinking happens; it's part of how thinking happens.

Truth Bomb: The best environment for someone isn't necessarily what looks best in photos. It's what works best for their brain. That "messy" desk might actually be their perfect system. That "boring" white wall might be exactly what a distractible brain needs. Design for the actual brain, not the Instagram feed.

The Environment Impact Hierarchy

Not all environmental factors are created equal. Here's how they rank in terms of impact on your performance and wellbeing:

1. **Physical Comfort** (chair ergonomics, temperature, air quality) - These directly affect your body's ability to function without pain or distraction.
2. **Sensory Inputs** (lighting, noise, visual clutter) - These determine how much processing power your brain wastes on irrelevant stimuli.
3. **Functional Design** (workflow efficiency, tool accessibility) - This determines how much friction exists between intention and action.
4. **Aesthetic Elements** (color, style, decor) - These affect mood and energy but have less direct impact on performance than the above factors.

This principle can transform how people approach their workspaces. Many try to create "picture-perfect" spaces that look like something from a productivity influencer's Instagram—with plants, motivational quotes, and carefully curated collections of books artfully arranged in the background. These spaces might look great but can be terrible for actual work. After understanding environmental psychology, someone might realize their brain needs visual simplicity to focus. Removing decorative distractions and creating a "boring" space that actually works for their brain chemistry can allow creativity to flourish. The most effective workspace might get zero likes on social media but be perfectly tuned to individual cognitive needs.

PART 4: ZERO-COST ENVIRONMENT HACKS

The "No Budget, No Bullshit" Improvement Plan

> "The best environmental upgrades aren't the expensive ones—they're the ones that solve the specific problems making you miserable."

Here's how to make any space significantly better without spending much (or any) fucking money:

Workspace Upgrades:

The Clean Sweep Protocol: Before buying anything, declutter like the space is on fire and only what truly matters can be saved. Set a timer for 20 minutes and remove anything that: (a) hasn't been used in 3 months, (b) is broken, or (c) actively annoys every time it's seen. A workspace isn't a museum of past projects or a storage unit for things that might be needed in some hypothetical future—it's a tool for getting shit done now. The self-deception patterns we identified in Chapter 2 apply equally to how we perceive our environments—we lie to ourselves about "needing" things that are actually just creating clutter. It's a productivity weapon, not a memorabilia showcase.

The Ergonomic Emergency Fix: The spine doesn't send pain signals because it's bored—it's desperately trying to warn that it's slowly being turned into a human question mark. For back pain, put a rolled-up towel behind the lower back. For wrist pain, stack books until the keyboard is at the right height (elbows at 90°). For neck pain, raise the monitor until the top is at eye level. These aren't permanent solutions, but they're better than popping ibuprofen like Tic Tacs while waiting for a "someday" ergonomic setup.

The Light Revolution: Bad lighting kills productivity and eyes. Move the workspace to face a window for natural light. If that's impossible, get a $15 clip-on lamp and aim it at the wall, not the screen. Stop working in the dark like some kind of productivity vampire. Eye strain headaches don't make anyone more creative; they just make people miserable with a side of creative. Working in poor lighting is like trying to read through a dirty windshield in the rain—technically possible but a completely unnecessary struggle.

The Sound Solution: Background noise sabotages focus more than most people realize. Those $20 noise-canceling earbuds from Amazon will do more for productivity than that $300 productivity course. Can't afford even that? Work when others aren't around (early morning, lunch hours) or use white noise apps or even just a fan running in the background. The human brain isn't designed to focus while processing a coworker's loud phone conversations about their cat's digestive problems.

Home Environment Quick Fixes:

The Flow Improvement: Watch where things naturally get put, then organize around those patterns instead of fighting them. Keep frequently used items where they're actually used, not where some organization guru says they "should" go. Remove obstacles from pathways used most often—that decorative table that catches the hip every time someone walks by isn't "adding character"; it's adding bruises. Create "drop zones" with baskets or trays where stuff naturally gets dropped. Working with habits is easier than trying to completely rewire the brain.

The Sleep Environment Overhaul: The bedroom is for sleeping, not recreating a retail electronics showroom. Remove or cover any device with blinking or glowing lights—the bedroom at night should be darker than the soul after binge-watching true crime documentaries. Those $15 blackout curtains will do more for sleep quality than those $500 designer window treatments. Test different pillow arrangements until finding one that doesn't cause neck pain that makes contemplating the sweet release of death every morning. And for the love of all things holy, remove the TV from the bedroom—Netflix in bed is not a sleep strategy; it's an insomnia delivery system. It's like trying to fall asleep at a fucking rave.

The Mood Lighting Hack: Lighting changes everything about how a space feels. Move existing lamps to create pools of light in areas where time is actually spent instead of illuminating that corner where nobody ever sits. A $10 smart bulb can change the entire feel of a room instantly without the cost and hassle of a renovation. Add an $8 LED strip behind the TV or monitor to reduce eye strain—it's called bias lighting, and it's the difference between "eyes feel like they've been sandpapered" and "actually seeing without pain."

Digital Environment Detox:

The Notification Nuke: Focus is being assassinated by alerts, and most people let it happen like willing accomplices. Turn OFF all non-human notifications (keep calls from real people if needed). The phone doesn't need to vibrate every time someone likes a brunch photo or a game that hasn't been played in six months misses its player. Batch-check email and messages at scheduled times instead of letting them interrupt like an overeager toddler. Remove social apps from the home screen so they require conscious effort to open—make distractions work for attention instead of serving them up like an all-you-can-eat buffet. This connects directly to the "E" (Environment) in the F.U.T.U.R.E. framework from Chapter 5—your digital environment is just as important as your physical one.

The Digital Declutter Sprint: Devices are often as cluttered as physical spaces, and it's slowing everything down. Delete apps that haven't been opened in 3 months—they're not collectibles; they're digital clutter. Organize remaining apps by function, not alphabetically, because the brain doesn't think in ABC order. Clear the desktop of everything except current projects—it's a workspace, not a digital junk drawer. Empty the downloads folder, which is probably full of PDFs downloaded twice and never opened once. A cluttered digital environment is like trying to cook in a kitchen where every surface is covered with dirty dishes—you spend more time moving shit around than actually getting anything done.

The Browser Intervention: Having 87 open tabs is a cry for help, not a productivity strategy. Bookmark tabs actually needed (in organized folders), then close EVERYTHING else. Each open tab is like having a person standing behind saying "Hey, remember me? That thing you were going to read three weeks ago?" Install a free tab manager extension for tab hoarders who can't be reformed—it's cheaper than the therapy needed for continuing to live this way.

The Browser Intervention can be life-changing for research-intensive work. Many people start with the habit of keeping dozens of tabs open with articles, statistics, and examples they might want to reference. By the time they have 60+ tabs open, their computer runs so slowly that it takes 30 seconds just to switch between documents. When they finally implement the intervention and organize everything into bookmarked folders by topic, not only does the computer speed up dramatically, but they actually find it easier to locate information. What seems like an "organization system" is often just digital chaos masquerading as productivity.

PART 5: WORKPLACE TRANSFORMATION

The Workplace Design Strategy

> "A workplace is either a force multiplier for talents or a soul-crushing container designed to hold the body while the mind escapes to tropical beaches during meetings. There's no fucking middle ground."

The W.O.R.K. System for Workplace Optimization

W - Workflow: Arrange your space based on how you actually work, not how you think you should work or how some productivity guru with a suspiciously clean desk in their YouTube videos says you should work. If you reference physical documents constantly, they should be within reach, not in a beautiful but inconvenient filing system across the room.

O - Organization: Everything you use daily should be within arm's reach. Weekly items within sight. Monthly items in storage. Yearly items in the trash because who are you kidding? You're not going to use that thing once a year—you're going to forget you own it, buy another one, then find both while moving.

R - Restoration: Create a mini-break area or ritual—even if it's just a spot to stand and stretch. Your brain isn't designed to focus indefinitely, and pretending otherwise is like expecting your phone to run forever without charging. Even a 30-second stretch break or a moment looking out a window can reset your mental energy.

K - Kick Out: Ruthlessly remove anything that doesn't contribute to your work performance. That collection of stress balls from conferences isn't "personalizing your space"; it's taking up real estate that could be used for things that actually help you work better. That broken printer you keep meaning to fix? It's not office equipment; it's a monument to procrastination.

The Toxic Workplace Neutralization Protocol

Working in a toxic office is like trying to grow a garden in contaminated soil—possible, but it requires some serious protective measures. It's like trying to stay dry in a hurricane—you need more than just an umbrella. Create a workspace bubble that gives psychological distance using plants as natural barriers, positioning the monitor as a visual shield, and wearing headphones even when not listening to anything (the universal "do not disturb" signal that even the most socially oblivious coworkers usually respect).

Minimize toxic interactions by identifying neutral zones where you can work temporarily when your regular space becomes a hotspot for drama. Create scheduling buffers between difficult interactions so you're not going from one emotional vampire to another without recovery time. Establish communication boundaries with phrases like "I need to focus until 2pm today" instead of "Please stop talking to me about your divorce for the fifth time this week."

The Toxic Workplace Neutralization Protocol can be essential in shared working environments. Rather than abandoning an otherwise good space (with great amenities like fast internet and free coffee) because of one disruptive person who constantly interrupts with unwanted conversations, creating a protective bubble can be effective. Using noise-canceling headphones and strategically positioning a laptop so your back is to the wall allows you to see people approaching. Establishing clear boundaries by explaining you're on deadline and can only chat during specific breaks helps maintain focus. These simple changes allow continued use of a space that's otherwise perfect without letting one toxic element ruin it.

PART 6: HOME SWEET PRODUCTIVE HOME

The Home Optimization Protocol

> "Most people arrange their homes like museum displays of how they wish they lived, rather than functional spaces for how they actually live."

The Home Zone Revolution

Stop thinking in terms of rooms and start thinking in terms of activity zones. The living room isn't just "the living room"—it might be a relaxation zone, home office, workout space, and dining area all in one. Each zone needs different environmental elements. A Focus Zone needs good lighting and minimal distractions, while a Restoration Zone needs comfort and calm.

The most common home environment problem isn't lack of space but conflicting activities in the same space. If someone is trying to work at the same table where kids are doing art projects, they're not lacking square footage—they're lacking boundaries. It's like trying to meditate in the middle of a mosh pit. Create physical separation using furniture arrangement (backs of sofas or bookshelves as dividers), room screens or curtains for temporary walls, or even just different lighting to create psychological boundaries between zones.

If physical separation isn't possible, create time boundaries with dedicated schedules for different activities in shared spaces. Develop transition rituals between different uses of the same space—maybe a specific playlist that signals "work time is over, relaxation begins" or a quick 5-minute reset where work materials are cleared and leisure items are set up.

The Home Zone Revolution can completely change how people approach work in small living spaces. Instead of trying to make an entire living room into a workspace (and failing), creating a dedicated "Work Corner" with specific elements that signal "work mode" to the brain is more effective. Using a particular lamp that's only turned on during work sessions, playing a specific instrumental playlist, and even having a special throw blanket used only during work can make a difference. These zone-specific elements create psychological boundaries that help the brain switch into work mode even when physically in the same multipurpose space. On days when a change of scenery is needed, transforming a kitchen table into a secondary work zone with its own distinct sensory cues can provide variety without leaving home.

PART 7: DIGITAL DETOX AND REDESIGN

The Digital Environment Crisis

> "The digital environment is the first thing checked in the morning and the last thing seen at night, yet somehow most people design it with less care than they'd put into choosing socks."

This is your digital environment headquarters—the definitive guide to optimizing your online spaces. Your phone isn't just a device; it's a portal to multiple environments that affect your brain as powerfully as physical spaces. As we learned in Chapter 3, your environment directly impacts your brain's threat detection system. Every notification trigger causes a micro-release of cortisol and adrenaline—your phone is essentially a stress delivery system that occasionally makes calls. It's like carrying around a tiny casino in your pocket that's designed to keep you anxious and addicted.

The D.I.G.I.T.A.L. Method can help:

D - Delete the unnecessary (apps, files, accounts you don't use). Digital clutter creates the same stress as physical clutter, except you can hide it more easily, which just makes it more insidious.

I - Integrate systems where possible. Having your to-do list spread across three different apps isn't organization; it's digital schizophrenia.

G - Group similar items together with consistent naming conventions. Future You will thank Present You for not having to search through 17 variations of "Final Document (REALLY FINAL THIS TIME).docx"

I - Isolate distractions from productivity tools. Your work computer desktop shouldn't include shortcuts to games or social media any more than your physical desk should include a TV and a bar.

T - Time-block digital activities to prevent context switching, which is the productivity equivalent of repeatedly slamming on your car's brakes and gas pedal—terrible for efficiency and eventually something's going to break.

A - Automate repetitive tasks and information processing. If you're doing the same digital task more than twice a week, spending 15 minutes setting up automation will save you hours of mind-numbing repetition.

L - Limit notification access to your attention. Your focus is a finite resource, and every notification is making a withdrawal from that account.

The D.I.G.I.T.A.L. Method can save sanity during complex projects with multiple digital components. When constantly switching between drafts, notes, feedback, and reference materials, the digital environment can become so chaotic that more time is spent looking for files than actually working on them. By implementing this system—especially the "Group" step with consistent file naming conventions—editing time can be cut nearly in half. The most transformative change often comes from setting up automation (the "A" step) to automatically sort materials into the correct folders based on keywords. What begins as a daily frustration can become a streamlined process that allows focus on improving content rather than managing digital chaos.

PART 8: REMOTE WORK REVOLUTION

The Remote Work Revolution

> "Remote work didn't just change where people work—it obliterated the boundary between professional and personal environments."

The biggest challenge of remote work isn't productivity—it's the fact that the bedroom is now ten feet from the office, and the brain doesn't know when to switch modes. It's like trying to be a parent and a party animal in the same room at the same time—the roles bleed together in confusing and exhausting ways. Create physical boundaries for work activities even in limited space. Use room dividers, curtains, or furniture arrangement to create visual separation. If space is severely limited, create a "work box" that contains all work items and can be closed and put away to signal "work is done."

Establish clear time transitions with consistent work start/end times and rituals that signal context shifting. The commute used to be transition time—now that transition needs to be created artificially. Maybe it's a short walk around the block before and after work, or changing clothes between work and personal modes. Use sensory cues like work-specific playlists or sound environments to reinforce work/home separation.

Remote work presents exactly this challenge—how to create boundaries between "work time" and "personal time" when both happen in the same space. Developing simple but effective transition rituals can help: at the start of each work session, making a cup of tea in a specific mug used only for work, lighting a particular scented candle, and writing three bullet points about what you want to accomplish. At the end of each session, closing the laptop, blowing out the candle, and taking a short walk around the block. These bookend rituals create artificial "commutes" into and out of work mode, helping the brain understand when it's time to focus and when it's time to rest. Without these clear transitions, many people find themselves half-working all day but never fully focusing or fully relaxing.

PART 9: THE POWER OF CHOICE

Your Environment, Your Choice

> "Complaining about the environment while doing nothing to improve it is like complaining about being hungry while standing next to a refrigerator full of food. It's not just unproductive—it's fucking absurd."

Here's the reality: The environment isn't going to improve itself. People either take action to improve it, or they keep suffering in a space that sucks. Each environmental improvement removes multiple daily irritations, creating a positive feedback loop where better environments enable better performance, which provides energy to make more improvements. It's like compound interest for quality of life.

Remember: There are only two viable options—change the environment or change how to respond to it. There is no third option. No one can complain their way to a better space, and no one can wish their surroundings into improvement. Action is the only path forward.

The Human Element: Your Most Important Environmental Factor

While we've focused on physical and digital spaces, the most influential aspect of your environment isn't things—it's people. You can have the perfect workspace, but if you're surrounded by energy vampires and toxic personalities, your environment still sucks. The emotional regulation techniques from Chapter 3 work better in an optimized environment, but even the best environment can't overcome the impact of toxic social interactions.

Could you be the toxic element in someone else's environment? The next chapter will ensure you're not the human equivalent of a cluttered desk in other people's lives. Just as you've learned to optimize your physical space for productivity, in the next chapter you'll learn to optimize your social presence for positive impact.

When you combine the S.P.A.C.E. framework with the emotional backbone techniques from Chapter 3, you create a self-reinforcing system where your environment supports your emotional regulation, and your improved emotional state helps you maintain a better environment.

Environmental design isn't just about spaces—it's about the energy you bring to those spaces. And that's where we're heading next.

Chapter 7 Key Takeaways

- Assessment: Your environment affects you whether you notice it or not
- Action: Small, immediate changes beat perfect plans every time
- Authenticity: Design for who you actually are, not who you wish you were

- Adaptation: Create spaces that transform to meet different needs
- Agency: You always have the power to improve your surroundings

CHAPTER 8: STOP BEING THE PERSON EVERYONE AVOIDS AT PARTIES

"BEING INTERESTING BEGINS WITH BEING INTERESTED."

PART 1: THE SOCIAL ENERGY CRISIS

The Invisible Social Plague: When Your Presence Is Everyone Else's Exit Cue

> "If people grab their phones when you walk up like they just got a fraud alert from their bank, you might be the human equivalent of a pop-up ad nobody wants."

Social skills impact virtually every aspect of life, from career success to personal relationships. Understanding how you affect others socially and learning to create positive interactions rather than draining ones is a crucial life skill that's often overlooked.

This is your social dynamics headquarters—the definitive guide to balanced communication. Let's be brutally honest—you probably think your social skills are above average. Statistically, that's unlikely. Most people who are socially draining have absolutely no idea they're the problem.

WHY THIS MATTERS: Let's get real about social skills - they affect literally everything in your life. Studies show being good with people predicts how much money you'll make better than your IQ does. People with solid social skills earn about $29,000 more every year than awkward people. At work, when people get fired after being hired, it's almost never about skills - 89% of the time it's because they just don't fit with the team. In relationships, how well you handle social situations is the 1 predictor of whether you'll be happy together long-term. Here's the scariest part: researchers found that being socially rejected is as bad for your health as smoking 15 cigarettes every day. This isn't about being popular in some high school movie way— it's about basic human connection that impacts your money, your relationships, and even how long you'll live. The good news? Unlike your height or your IQ, you can actually improve your social skills if you know how.

This whole dynamic plays out differently based on personality types. If someone's an extrovert, they might be draining people by dominating every damn conversation with non-stop talking and one-sided enthusiasm about their latest obsession that nobody asked about. They're basically a conversational bulldozer, flattening anyone who tries to get a word in edgewise. If someone's more introverted, they might be sucking the energy out of rooms with awkward silences or clearly checking out whenever topics don't interest them - like they're mentally filing their taxes while someone's telling them about their kid's graduation. They're giving off all the warmth and engagement of a mannequin with better clothes. But regardless of which flavor of socially exhausting someone is, the rules of social energy apply to everyone—both chatty and quiet people can learn to add to social situations instead of just taking from them like some kind of emotional ATM that never makes deposits.

TRUTH BOMB: Here's the thing about being socially draining - most people who suck the life out of rooms have no clue they're doing it. They think they're just being "honest" or "authentic" or "sharing their truth." Meanwhile, everyone else is performing these elaborate escape maneuvers around them. People are literally developing professional-level skills in the subtle retreat just to get away from their conversational black hole.

Accept something uncomfortable: If you've been in a conversation and thought, "These people are so boring," the boring one was probably you. The hard truth? Nobody cares about your vacation photos, work accomplishments, or personal problems beyond about 30 seconds. After that, you're just burning social capital.

Many people learn this lesson the hard way. Someone might corner friends and colleagues to talk about their latest passion project, going on and on about concepts and ideas without noticing glazed expressions. It often takes a brutally honest friend to say something like, "You know, you've been talking about this for 20 minutes straight without asking me a single question about my life." Such wake-up calls can make people realize they've become exactly what they dislike—someone who drains others' social energy. The solution is simple but requires self-awareness: limit talking about personal projects to 2-3 minutes unless specifically asked for more, and make sure to balance it with genuine interest in others.

PART 2: SELF-DIAGNOSIS

The Social Vampire's Guide to Self-Recognition: Are You Sucking The Life Out Of Rooms?

> "If your arrival makes people scatter faster than teenagers when parents come home early, maybe check what kind of energy you're bringing to the party."

First, let's figure out if someone is actually the problem. Here are some signs they might be the person everyone's trying to avoid: Do people suddenly remember they have "somewhere to be" when they walk up to a group? Like magically, everyone's dog needs walking or they just remembered they left their straightener on at home? Does the room empty out when they start talking, like they just announced they're about to read their entire Instagram feed out loud? Do conversations hit a dead end whenever they join in, with people suddenly fascinated by their drink or the ceiling tiles? Do simple stories somehow always turn into hour-long emotional dumps that nobody signed up for? If someone's nodding along, congratulations - they're basically a phone on max volume in a quiet room - irritating everyone but nobody wants the awkwardness of saying something.

REALITY CHECK: Many people think they're just being "real" or "authentic," but there's a huge difference between being genuine and being an emotional vampire who sucks everyone dry after a five-minute conversation. "I'm just keeping it real" is the battle cry of people who don't want to put in the work of actually being pleasant to be around. It's like the difference between offering someone a drink versus trapping them in a corner and dumping all your emotional problems on them with no escape route.

Here's a quick test to see if someone is a social vampire: After they walk away from a conversation, do people seem more energized or completely drained? If others look like they just ran a marathon while wearing a full suit, that person is running their social life like a pyramid scheme - taking way more than they're giving and then acting surprised when nobody wants to invest in their emotional Ponzi schemes anymore.

The Social Energy Vampire Test

Ever wonder why some people can say very little but still seem incredibly engaging, while others talk constantly and leave you desperate for escape? The difference isn't content—it's connection. Most people use conversations as a stage for their own performance rather than a tennis court for rallying ideas back and forth.

Check yourself against these specific behaviors:
1. Do you regularly interrupt others before they finish speaking?
2. Do you find yourself waiting for others to finish rather than actually listening?
3. Do conversations often die when you finish making your point?
4. Do you rarely ask follow-up questions about what others have just shared?
5. Do you frequently bring conversations back to your experiences after someone shares theirs?

The Social Feedback Decoder

Since people rarely tell you directly that you're socially draining, here are the subtle signs to watch for:

- People check their phones when you're talking
- Conversations involving you tend to be shorter than those you observe between others
- People physically position themselves toward exits when trapped in conversation with you
- You notice others making eye contact with each other while you're speaking
- You're rarely sought out for one-on-one conversations at social gatherings

Many people make classic social vampire mistakes in professional settings. Someone might be so excited about a new concept that they launch into a 15-minute monologue about every aspect and potential angle without pausing to gauge interest or ask for input. By the time they finally stop talking, their audience looks exhausted. Valuable feedback in such situations might sound like: "Your idea sounds great, but this meeting would have been more productive if you'd presented the core concept briefly and then let us discuss it together." Such feedback can improve professional communication skills and prevent similar missteps in the future.

PART 3: THE NEUROSCIENCE OF SOCIAL EXHAUSTION

The Science of Social Dynamics: Why Your Brain Is Everyone Else's Problem

"Your conversational style shouldn't trigger the same neurological response as a fire alarm. If people's brains are screaming 'danger' when you start talking, that's not a personality quirk—it's a design flaw."

When someone dumps all their emotional baggage too quickly, it's like trying to download a 4K movie on one of those old dial-up connections - the whole system crashes. The human brain can only handle so much social information at once before it starts desperately searching for the escape button.

As we learned in Chapter 3, your brain's alarm system activates during social threats just like it does during physical ones. When people are trapped in one-sided conversations with social vampires, their brains flip into full-on threat mode. Their brain's alarm system starts blaring and stress hormones flood their body. This isn't just some theory—it's literally what happens inside people's heads when someone corners them with a 20-minute monologue about their cat's dietary restrictions. The social vampire isn't just boring people; they're actually triggering their body's stress response.

When researching social neuroscience, conversations with experts can yield valuable insights—but only if you create space for their expertise. Someone might catch themselves monopolizing a conversation with a neuroscientist and consciously apply better techniques—pausing and asking about the expert's research. What follows is often an incredible exchange where the expert shares insights about mirror neurons and social cognition that significantly enhance understanding. Had the conversation remained one-sided, this valuable expertise would have been missed. Such experiences demonstrate how creating conversational balance leads to better outcomes for everyone.

PART 4: GROUP DYNAMICS

The Group Psychology Playbook: You're Not The Main Character

> "If you think you're the star of every social gathering, remember that nobody watches a movie where one character gets all the lines. That's not entertainment—that's a hostage situation with popcorn."

Being socially draining in a group setting is like being a black hole at a star party - not just ruining one person's night, but warping the entire social universe around.

Groups have their own energy flow, their own rhythm, their own unwritten rules of engagement. When someone enters a group conversation, they're stepping into an existing ecosystem. But instead of adapting to it, many people bulldoze through it like a drunk elephant in a crystal shop.

Think of group conversations like a jazz ensemble - everyone plays their part, takes their solo when appropriate, and knows when to support others. Social vampires treat it like a one-person show where everyone else is just their backup band.

The most effective groups have a quality called "conversational turn-taking." When the big tech companies studied what makes teams work well together, they found something surprising: it wasn't about having the smartest people. It was about having people who shared speaking time equally. This isn't just about being polite; it's about using the combined brainpower of everyone in the group.

The really insidious part of being the group energy vampire is that they don't just ruin the conversation for the person they're directly draining - they spoil it for everyone. One socially draining person can tank an entire gathering faster than food poisoning at a potluck.

This dynamic is commonly observed in group settings like workshops or seminars. When one participant dominates every discussion, turning each session into a platform for their opinions, the energy in the room visibly deflates whenever they speak. What's most revealing is watching how the group adapts—people stop sharing deeper thoughts, conversations become superficial, and the collective creativity diminishes. This demonstrates exactly how one energy vampire can transform an entire social ecosystem. Such real-world observations help us understand group dynamics more vividly and accurately.

PART 5: CAREER CONSEQUENCES

The Professional Impact: Career Limitations of Being Emotionally Exhausting

> "You can have the resume of Einstein and the skills of da Vinci, but if meetings with you feel like psychological waterboarding, you'll be passed over faster than day-old sushi."

In the professional world, social skills matter just as much as technical abilities. Someone can be the most brilliant person in their field, but if they're the office equivalent of a root canal without anesthesia, their career is going to hit a ceiling.

When business schools study what make cleaders effective, they find that social skills predict success better than IQ, education, or technical expeato.

When business schools study what makes leaders effective, they consistently find that executives with poor interpersonal skills are rated as ineffective regardless of their technical expertise or business results. Long-term career studies show that social skills are actually better predictors of who gets promoted than IQ, education, or work experience.

The workplace consequences of being socially draining manifest in specific, measurable ways: When certain people speak for more than 4 minutes continuously in meetings, participation from other attendees drops by as much as 38%. Despite excellent performance metrics, promotions are denied specifically because, as one executive put it, "I can't put someone in leadership who requires everyone to recover after interacting with them."

An inability to manage social impact isn't just annoying - it's actively limiting to earning potential. People who drain others don't get picked for high-visibility projects, don't get invited to career-advancing social events, don't get mentored by higher-ups, and don't get considered for leadership roles regardless of their technical capabilities.

Many professionals have been passed over for opportunities despite having strong qualifications. Years later, they might learn the truth: "Your work was excellent, but in team meetings, you spoke over everyone and turned every discussion into a platform for your ideas. We needed someone who could collaborate, not dominate." Such feedback is painful but transformative. It reveals how social habits can create a career ceiling that talent alone can't break through. These experiences emphasize that social skills aren't just about being liked—they're about professional advancement. Same shit happens in dating - that hot doctor with the personality of wet cardboard gets ghosted after one date, while the average-looking bartender who makes everyone feel awesome has a packed social calendar.

PART 6: THE TRANSFORMATION SYSTEM

The S.O.C.I.A.L. System: Your Complete Social Skills Upgrade

> "The S.O.C.I.A.L. system isn't just about being 'nice'— it's about becoming someone others genuinely want to be around."

Think of these six elements as dials on a mixing board. When they're all properly adjusted, you create social harmony. When even one is off, you create social discord:

S - Self-awareness: Understanding your current social impact
O - Others-focused: Shifting attention from yourself to others
C - Conversational balance: Mastering the give and take of dialogue
I - Interest generation: Becoming genuinely curious about others
A - Attention management: Giving quality attention, not just time
L - Listening deeply: The most underrated social skill

Here's where most people completely misunderstand social dynamics: they think being interesting is about having fascinating stories or impressive achievements. In reality, it's about creating connection through balanced energy exchange.

The Social Skills Upgrade Protocol: From Draining to Energizing

> "Upgrading your social skills isn't about being perfect—it's about not being the person who makes everyone suddenly remember they have somewhere else to be."

How to stop being the person everyone avoids:

Learn to Read the Room: Social cues aren't subtle hints - they're flashing neon signs telling people to adjust their approach. If someone's talking and the listener's eyes start darting around like they're searching for emergency exits, that's not them being distracted—that's them looking for the nearest escape route from the conversation. If someone keeps checking their phone during a conversation, they're not addicted to technology—they're addicted to not being trapped in a monologue. If someone keeps trying to speak and gets talked over repeatedly, they're not being rude—they're desperately trying to create some balance in a conversation that's more lopsided than a seesaw with an elephant on one end.

The Three-Signal Rule is simple: When someone spots two of these three signals simultaneously (decreased eye contact, shorter responses, or retreating body language), it's time to shut up and pass the conversational ball. Don't wait for a "natural" break—there isn't one coming because the conversation has been non-stop about sourdough starter journeys for the last 17 minutes. Instead, use this exact transition phrase: "But enough about that—what's been happening with you lately?" Then actually listen to the answer instead of using it as a brief intermission before the next monologue.

Master the Art of Conversation: Good conversation is like a game of catch - there's a natural back and forth. Many socially draining people play conversational dodgeball, pelting others with their problems until they either run away or get knocked out by the sheer weight of emotional baggage. Learn to throw the ball gently and make sure the other person has a chance to catch and throw it back.

Try the 2-Minute Timer Technique: Set a mental timer for two minutes when starting to speak. When that timer goes off, wrap up the thought and ask a question. This isn't about cutting off mid-sentence; it's about recognizing that monologues belong in theater, not in conversation. If there's concern about forgetting this in the moment, wear a watch or bracelet to touch as a reminder, or practice with trusted friends who can give a signal when approaching the two-minute mark.

Understand Energy Exchange: Every social interaction involves an exchange of energy. Social vampires are like black holes - everything goes in, nothing comes out. Start contributing positive energy instead of just consuming it. Be the person who lights up a room instead of the one who dims it.

After each significant social interaction, do a quick energy audit: Did the other person seem more energized or less energized after the conversation? Were questions asked about them, or was it just self-centered talk? Was something valuable offered (information, support, humor), or was just time and attention taken? This isn't about self-flagellation—it's about honest assessment for improvement.

Balance Sharing and Receiving: There's a time to share stories and a time to hear others'. There's a time to seek support and a time to offer it. Many people's social timing is like a broken clock - only right twice a day and completely random the rest of the time. The basic rule: if someone has been talking for more than 2-3 minutes straight, it's probably time to pass the conversational ball.

Try the Question-Statement Ratio Technique: For one week, track how many statements you make versus questions you ask in conversations. Most socially draining people have a ratio of about 18:1—no wonder people seem relieved when they walk away! The goal should be to get that down to 3:1 or better. This might involve carrying a small counter in your pocket, clicking it discreetly whenever you ask a question. Within a month, your ratio might improve to 4:1, with people actually seeking out conversation rather than finding reasons to escape.

The Question-Statement Ratio Technique can be transformative when applied consistently. Someone might track their conversations during social events and discover an embarrassing initial ratio—about 18:1, making eighteen statements for every question asked. No wonder people seem relieved when they walk away! Setting a goal to improve this ratio might involve carrying a small counter in a pocket (clicking it discreetly whenever asking a question). This concrete measurement helps transform conversation style. Within a month, the ratio might improve to 4:1, with people actually seeking out conversation rather than finding reasons to escape. Such practical experiments demonstrate how measurable changes in communication patterns can dramatically improve social interactions.

This chapter focuses on being socially magnetic; Chapter 9 will focus specifically on knowledge sharing without being insufferable. The foundation of not being avoided is how you receive others—your listening, attention, and response patterns. We'll touch on conversation balance here, but in Chapter 9, we'll dive deep into how to share your expertise without becoming the know-it-all everyone avoids.

PART 7: MAGNETIC PERSONALITIES

The Charisma Code: Magnetism vs. Repulsion

> "Charisma isn't about being the brightest bulb in the room—it's about making others feel illuminated when they're with you."

What actually makes people likable isn't about being the loudest or having the most dramatic stories. It's about making others feel good about themselves when they're around you.

When business schools and psychology labs study charisma, they consistently find that charismatic individuals balance competence signals with warmth signals—they demonstrate value while simultaneously making others feel valued. It's not about being flawless; it's about making others feel seen and significant.

Charismatic people aren't just talking vending machines spitting out stories and opinions. They're like social catalysts who make conversations better just by being part of them. They know how to: - Make others feel heard without pretending to listen while actually just waiting for their turn to speak - Share without oversharing like they're in a competition for most trauma revealed to relative strangers - Be interesting without being exhausting - Add value without demanding attention

The most fascinating observation about highly charismatic people is that they all share one counterintuitive trait: they speak less than you'd expect. Their contributions are high-impact but relatively brief, creating space for others while adding genuine value with each interaction.

The fundamental difference between magnetic people and repulsive people is their focus. Magnetic people focus outward - they're interested in others, curious about the world, engaged with ideas beyond themselves. Repulsive people focus inward - they're primarily concerned with their own feelings, experiences, problems, and opinions.

Research with people widely considered charismatic in their fields reveals surprising patterns. The most unexpected discovery is how little they actually speak in conversations. A tech CEO known for magnetic presence might spend 80% of a scheduled meeting asking thoughtful questions about the other person's projects and process. When this is pointed out, they might respond with something like, "That's the secret nobody tells you about charisma—it's not about being interesting, it's about being interested." This insight fundamentally shifts our understanding of charisma, moving from techniques for being captivating to strategies for creating genuine connection through interest in others.

PART 8: VIRTUAL SOCIAL SKILLS

The Digital Charisma Framework: Don't Be a Social Vampire Online Either

For a complete guide to optimizing your digital environment and avoiding being a social vampire online, see Chapter 7. The same principles that make you draining in person can make you exhausting digitally, but the specific techniques for digital communication require their own framework.

The section on digital communication reflects common mistakes many professionals make. Someone might send a colleague a massive text message about a work project at 11:30 PM on a Saturday—a wall of text that takes five minutes to read. Later, they might receive gentle feedback suggesting work communication be kept to email during business hours. While initially embarrassing, such feedback establishes important boundaries. These experiences highlight how easily digital tools can erode social norms that would be obvious in person. No one would show up at a colleague's house at midnight with a stack of notes, but somehow many people think late-night texts are acceptable. These common blunders perfectly illustrate the "Context Collapser" phenomenon.

PART 9: AUTHENTICITY VS. CONSIDERATION

The Reality Check: You're Not Too Authentic, You're Just Inconsiderate

> "Your 'authenticity' shouldn't require emotional hazmat suits for everyone in your vicinity. If being 'real' means making everyone else miserable, you've mistaken rudeness for honesty."

Here's the truth about being socially draining that nobody wants to hear: It's not about being less authentic; it's about being more considerate. People can be genuine without treating every social interaction like an emergency therapy session. They can be real without being really exhausting.

The "authentic self" movement has created a generation of people who believe that any filtering of thoughts, emotions, or words is somehow "inauthentic." This is not only incorrect but actively harmful to genuine connection. True authenticity isn't about uncontrolled expression—it's about aligning external behavior with internal values in a way that respects both oneself and others.

The harsh reality? People aren't avoiding social vampires because they can't handle their "realness" or because society can't handle their "truth." They're avoiding them because interacting with them is like running an emotional marathon they never signed up for. They're not rejecting authentic selves; they're protecting their limited energy from unlimited needs to expend it.

Being considerate isn't being fake—it's being socially intelligent. It's understanding that one person's right to expression doesn't override everyone else's right to not be exhausted. It's recognizing that relationships are exchanges, not one-way streets where someone gets to dump unfiltered thoughts while others are expected to just absorb them like emotional sponges.

Many people struggle with this concept. Those who value authenticity might initially resist the idea that we should filter ourselves in social situations. During discussions about this topic, someone might defend unfiltered self-expression as "more honest." A perspective-changing question might be: "If you had food stuck in your teeth, would you want me to tell you privately or announce it to the entire room?" Most people prefer the private approach. The explanation: "That's not being fake—that's being considerate of your feelings while still being truthful." Such conversations can transform understanding of the false dichotomy between authenticity and consideration, revealing that true authenticity includes thoughtfulness about how our expression affects others.

PART 10: REPUTATION REPAIR

The Social Recovery Protocol: Rebuilding Your Reputation

"Rehabilitating your social reputation is like repairing credit after bankruptcy—a series of small, consistent deposits over time, not one grand gesture."

The Social Recovery Toolkit

Even the most socially skilled people make mistakes. The difference is how they recover. Here are specific techniques to recover from social missteps:

Recovery Scripts When you realize you've been talking too much: "I just realized I've been dominating the conversation. I'd love to hear more about your perspective on this."

The Acknowledge and Pivot Technique When you notice people's interest waning: "I think I might be getting too into the weeds on this topic. What's been interesting in your world lately?"

The Social Mulligan Sometimes the best recovery is direct acknowledgment: "Sorry, that came out wrong. Let me try again..."

Conversation CPR When you've accidentally killed the conversation vibe, ask an open-ended question about something the other person has mentioned previously, showing you were actually listening.

How to fix a reputation for someone who's already established themselves as the human equivalent of a migraine. Social recovery is possible, but like any rehabilitation, it takes time and consistent effort.

First step: Stop the bleeding. Before building a better social presence, one must stop being an energy vampire. It's like trying to fill a bucket with a hole in it - first, patch the hole, then start adding water. This means immediate changes to the most draining behaviors: Shorter stories. Fewer complaints. More questions. Less monopolizing. No more treating casual conversations like personal therapy sessions where everyone else is playing the unpaid therapist.

Second step: Start making small, consistent deposits in the social bank account. Be the person who listens more than talks, showing genuine interest in others rather than just waiting for a turn to speak. Add value without demanding attention, offering useful information or positive energy without requiring recognition. Respect social boundaries, reading body language and conversational cues instead of barging through them like a bull in a china shop. Contribute positive energy to group dynamics, lifting the mood rather than bringing it down with the latest disaster story.

Third step: Demonstrate sustained change. One good interaction won't erase a reputation as a social drain. Consistent, repeated demonstrations of actual change are needed. Think of it like rebuilding credit after bankruptcy - it takes multiple on-time payments over a long period to prove someone is no longer a risk. People need to see that improved social skills aren't just a temporary act but a genuine transformation.

Fourth step: Accept that some bridges may be permanently burned. If someone has been socially draining for years, some people may have permanently decided that interacting with them costs more than it's worth. Focus on new relationships and those willing to give another chance. Don't waste energy trying to win back people who have firmly decided to keep their distance—that's just another form of not respecting boundaries.

The Social Recovery Protocol reflects the experiences of many professionals who have had to repair damaged reputations. Someone known for dominating meetings and making everything about their ideas might spend nearly a year methodically rebuilding their reputation—starting with simply listening more than speaking, then gradually contributing in more balanced ways. A painful lesson often comes when trying to repair a relationship with a former colleague who simply isn't interested in giving another chance. Continued pushing might lead to feedback like, "Your insistence on fixing this relationship is just another form of not respecting their boundaries." Such insights, while humbling, are necessary for genuine social recovery and understanding the importance of respecting others' choices about engagement.

PART 11: BECOMING SOCIALLY VALUABLE

The Social Value Proposition: Make Interactions Better By Being There

"The true measure of your social value isn't how fascinating your life is—it's whether rooms improve or decline when you enter them."

The secret to being someone people actually want around? It's simple: Make interactions better by being there. That's it. Instead of treating every social situation like a personal therapy session, focus on making the experience better for everyone else.

Think about the people you actually enjoy being around. They're probably not the ones who dominate every conversation or turn every interaction into a dramatic monologue. They're the ones who make you feel better after talking to them, who add something positive to every interaction, who leave you with more energy than you had before.

Social value isn't measured by how much attention someone can extract - it's measured by how much value they can add. It's not about being the most interesting person in the room; it's about being the most interested. It's not about being memorable for stories; it's about being memorable for how others are made to feel. The focus should shift from getting to giving, from taking to contributing, from draining to energizing.

Once you've mastered not being avoided (this chapter), you can focus on being actively sought out for your knowledge (next chapter). There's a Social Skills Spectrum that shows the progression from "Not Being Avoided" (Chapter 8) to "Being Actively Sought Out" (Chapter 9).

This isn't about becoming a social doormat or never talking about yourself. It's about creating balance—giving as much as you take, listening as much as you speak, supporting as much as you're supported. It's about recognizing that social interactions are exchanges, not performances where you're the star and everyone else is the audience.

A "social value journal" can be a powerful tool for improving interactions. By reflecting on daily conversations and noting whether you left people with more energy or less after your interactions, patterns quickly emerge. This practice can be humbling—many people discover that despite knowing better, they still frequently fall into energy-draining habits, particularly when stressed about work or deadlines. Such journaling helps identify specific triggers and develop strategies to remain present and contributive even during stressful periods. This reflective practice forms the foundation for effective social value assessment techniques.

PART 12: THE TRANSFORMATION JOURNEY

The Final Social Evolution: From Draining To Energizing

> "The ultimate social upgrade isn't becoming someone with the most interesting stories— it's becoming someone who makes everyday interactions feel like mini-vacations rather than obligations."

The ultimate goal: Become someone whose presence improves any room they enter. Not because of being the loudest, the most dramatic, or the most attention-seeking, but because of mastering the art of making social interactions better just by being there.

The evolution from social drain to social gain requires:

Self-Awareness: Understand current impact on others. Are you giving energy or taking it? Are you enhancing interactions or degrading them? Are you adding value or extracting it? This isn't about self-flagellation; it's about honest assessment. If you're the person everyone avoids, it's not because they're all jerks—it's because something about your social style is pushing them away.

Energy Management: Learn to monitor and regulate social energy. Know when you've been talking too long and need to listen. Know when you're about to trauma dump and need to redirect. Recognize when you're in a negative spiral and either shift to something more positive or excuse yourself until you can bring better energy. Your mood isn't just your business when you're inflicting it on everyone around you.

Social Generosity: Practice the fine art of making others feel good about themselves. Give genuine compliments, acknowledge contributions, express appreciation, and create opportunities for others to shine. The most magnetic people aren't those who grab the spotlight—they're those who know when to shine it on others.

So stop being the person everyone has to recover from and start being the person everyone looks forward to seeing. Because the truth is, being interesting begins with being interested. When you genuinely engage with others, when you listen with real curiosity, when you respond with authentic attention, you become the kind of person others want in their orbit.

Chapter 8 Key Takeaways

- Recognition: Social draining behaviors are identifiable and changeable patterns
- Reciprocity: Balanced conversations create energy rather than depleting it
- Reading: Learning to spot social cues transforms your interaction quality
- Restraint: Knowing when to stop talking is as important as knowing what to say
- Reorientation: Shifting focus from getting attention to creating connection

CHAPTER 9: TEACHING WITHOUT BEING A KNOW-IT-ALL

"TRUE EXPERTISE ISN'T THE ABILITY TO KNOW EVERYTHING—IT'S THE WISDOM TO SHARE THE RIGHT THINGS AT THE RIGHT TIME IN THE RIGHT WAY."

PART 1: THE INSUFFERABLE EXPERT EPIDEMIC

The Insufferable Expert Epidemic

> "Some people collect facts the way others collect trophies—not to use them, but to show them off."

While Chapter 8 focused on general social dynamics, this chapter specifically addresses knowledge sharing—how to teach, explain, and inform without becoming insufferable. Now that you've learned how not to be avoided socially, let's focus on how to share your expertise in a way that makes people seek you out rather than tune you out.

Sharing knowledge effectively is one of the most valuable skills you can possess. This chapter focuses specifically on how to teach without becoming the intellectual equivalent of a fire hose on full blast. Effective teaching requires self-awareness to recognize when you're teaching to help others versus when you're teaching to feed your ego. It also requires emotional resilience to handle being wrong without defensiveness—a critical skill for knowledge sharing.

WHY THIS MATTERS: In today's attention economy, being able to share knowledge clearly is one of the most valuable skills you can have. Most of what we learn at work comes from conversations with colleagues, not from formal training sessions. Yet so much of this knowledge sharing fails because people are terrible at explaining things clearly. Think about how many times you've sat through an explanation that left you more confused than before. Or how often you've had to figure something out yourself after someone's unhelpful attempt to teach you. People who can actually explain complex ideas clearly are rare and incredibly valuable. Beyond professional settings, your ability to share knowledge without alienating others affects every relationship in your life—from explaining a concept to your partner without condescension to helping your friends understand your perspective without making them feel stupid. This isn't just about being likable; it's about ensuring your knowledge actually creates value rather than gathering dust in the storage unit of your mind.

TRUTH BOMB: Let's talk about that special kind of asshole who turns every conversation into a lecture nobody asked for. You know exactly who I mean - they're walking encyclopedias full of facts nobody asked for, basically human podcasts without a pause button, people who see every casual chat at a party as their big chance to show off how fucking smart they are. "Oh, you went to Italy? Let me tell you the entire political history of the Roman Empire and correct your pronunciation of 'bruschetta' while somehow making the fact that I've never actually been there myself irrelevant." They might actually know their stuff, but they're so goddamn insufferable about it that nobody wants to learn a single thing from them besides how to quickly escape a conversation.

The real irony? These walking Wikipedia pages are usually terrible at actually teaching anyone anything useful. They're so busy showing off how smart they are that they've completely lost track of what actually helps people learn. They're basically peacocks who think their fancy tail feathers are educational seminars rather than just elaborate "look at me" mating dances.

PART 2: THE KNOWLEDGE PARADOX

The Knowledge Paradox: Why Expertise Often Makes You Worse at Teaching

> "The more you know about a subject, the harder it becomes to remember what it's like to not know it."

Remember the "Expert on Everything" archetype from the Head-Up-Ass Hall of Fame in Chapter 2? That's exactly what we're avoiding here. The knowledge paradox is real: as you become more expert in a subject, you often become worse at teaching it to beginners. This happens because expertise creates blind spots about what's actually difficult for newcomers.

Know-It-All Warning Signs

You might be slipping into know-it-all territory if you: - Interrupt to correct minor details that don't affect the main point - Explain things to people who already have expertise in the area - Feel compelled to demonstrate your knowledge in every conversation - Get defensive when someone questions your explanation - Use unnecessarily complex terminology when simpler words would work

Before sharing knowledge, apply the Reality Anchor technique from Chapter 2 by asking yourself these questions: - Am I sharing this to be helpful or to appear smart? - Am I the right person to explain this? - Do I actually know what I'm talking about, or am I overestimating my expertise? - Is this the right time and context for this explanation?

This chapter is the antidote to the "Expert on Everything" syndrome we diagnosed in Chapter 2. If you recognized yourself in that description, pay extra attention here.

PART 3: THE S.H.A.R.E. METHOD

The S.H.A.R.E. Framework: Teaching That Actually Works

> "Great teachers aren't those who share everything they know; they're those who share exactly what you need, exactly when you need it, exactly how you can absorb it."

There's a massive difference between showing off what you know and actually helping others learn. Most self-proclaimed experts have mastered the first while completely neglecting the second. What actually works is a systematic approach to sharing knowledge that focuses on the learner's experience rather than the teacher's ego.

Enter the S.H.A.R.E. framework—a practical system for teaching without triggering the "this person's an insufferable know-it-all" alarm in people's heads:

S - Start Where They Are: Begin with the learner's current understanding, not your expertise
H - Humanize the Content: Connect information to real-world applications and emotions
A - Adapt to Learning Styles: Vary your approach based on how different people absorb information
R - Respect Intelligence: Treat learners as capable people who lack knowledge, not intelligence
E - Encourage Questions: Create safety for curiosity rather than punishing "ignorance"
This isn't about dumbing down content—it's about smartening up your teaching approach. It's like the difference between throwing someone into the deep end while yelling swimming instructions from the poolside and actually getting in the water to guide them through each stroke.

THE S.H.A.R.E. METHOD IN ACTION

Instead of a 47-point implementation plan that you'll never actually use, here's the real-world application:

S - Start Where They Are: Before you vomit your knowledge al over someone, take five seconds to figure out what they already know. Ask a simple question like "Have you worked with this before?" or "What's your experience with this?" Then—and this is the revolutionary part—actually listen to their answer. Don't just wait for them to stop talking so you can launch into your pre-planned lecture. Their answer tells you exactly where to start so you're not explaining calculus to a math PhD or treating a seasoned professional like they've never seen a spreadsheet before.

H - Humanize the Content: Connect your information to something that actually matters to the person learning it. Nobody cares about abstract concepts floating in space—they care about solving their problems, achieving their goals, or understanding why this information matters to them. For every piece of knowledge you share, answer the "So what?" question before they have to ask it.

Think of it like this: If you're teaching someone to use a hammer, don't start with the metallurgical properties of the hammerhead. Start with "This will help you hang that picture that's been sitting on your floor for three months." Connect the dots between your knowledge and their life, or watch their eyes glaze over faster than a donut at Krispy Kreme.

A - Adapt to Learning Styles: Different people learn differently, and if you only teach one way, you're only reaching a fraction of your audience. Some people need to see it (visual), some need to hear it explained (auditory), some need to read about it (reading/writing), and some need to actually do it (kinesthetic). The best teachers cycle through multiple approaches rather than insisting everyone adapt to their preferred style.

It's like trying to feed different animals at a zoo—you wouldn't give the same food to a lion, a giraffe, and a penguin, then get mad when two-thirds of them starve. Yet somehow, we expect all humans to learn the same way, then label them "slow" when our one-size-fits-all approach fails. If someone's not getting it, try a different approach before assuming they're the problem.

R - Respect Intelligence: Not knowing something doesn't make someone stupid; it just means they haven't learned that specific thing yet. When you treat people like they're intellectually inferior because they don't know what you know, you're creating a brain state where learning becomes neurologically more difficult.

Delete these phrases from your vocabulary immediately: "It's actually quite simple," "As you should know," "Obviously," "It's just basic," and "Anyone can understand this." Replace them with: "This concept often takes time to click," "Many people find this challenging at first," or "I struggled with this myself when I first encountered it." You're not making things too simple; you're creating an environment where people feel comfortable enough to actually learn instead of just pretending they understand.

E - Encourage Questions: Questions aren't interruptions to your brilliant lecture—they're valuable data about what's not making sense. Create an environment where asking questions feels safer than sitting in confused silence. Explicitly invite questions, respond to them with genuine appreciation rather than barely concealed irritation, and recognize that the absence of questions often signals intimidation, not comprehension.

The best teachers treat questions like gold, not garbage. They know that questions reveal exactly where the learning process is breaking down and provide opportunities to fix misunderstandings before they become permanent. If nobody's asking questions, you're either teaching perfectly (unlikely) or you've created an environment where people are more afraid of looking stupid than they are motivated to understand. Guess which one is more common?

PART 4: READING THE ROOM: THE LOST ART

Teaching Moments Recognition: When to Teach vs. When to Just Talk

> "Not every conversation is a teaching opportunity. Sometimes people just want to talk, not attend your impromptu lecture."

One of the biggest differences between effective teachers and insufferable know-it-alls is the ability to recognize when teaching is appropriate versus when normal conversation is called for. Here's how to tell the difference:

Teaching Mode Activation Checklist

Before shifting into instruction mode, ensure these criteria are met: 1. The person has explicitly asked for information or guidance 2. You have genuine expertise on the specific topic 3. The context is appropriate for deeper explanation 4. You have enough time to explain properly 5. The person seems receptive to learning

Permission Before Instruction

Always secure permission before launching into teaching mode with questions like: - "Would it be helpful if I explained how this works?" - "I've had some experience with this—would you like me to share what I've learned?" - "I know a bit about this topic. Would you like some more details?"

Inappropriate Teaching Moments

When someone mentions they've started running, they don't need your complete dissertation on optimal heart rate zones and pronation analysis. When a colleague mentions a minor computer issue, they probably don't need your comprehensive explanation of operating system architecture. Match your level of detail to the person's interest. For casual interest, stick to the 101 version. Only go deeper when they ask follow-up questions.

PART 5: TEACHING DIFFERENT BRAINS DIFFERENTLY

The Teaching Methodology Matrix: How Learning Actually Works

> "Teaching someone who learns differently than you is like giving directions in a language you don't speak—you can shout louder or you can learn to translate. Only one of these approaches actually gets them to their destination."

Most self-proclaimed experts have about as much understanding of teaching methods as a rock has of rocket science. Real teaching isn't about showing off what you know - it's about understanding how people learn and adapting your approach accordingly.

Different people learn differently. Some need to see it, some need to hear it, some need to do it. If you use the same approach for everyone, you're like someone trying to feed all animals the same food - it works for some but leaves others hungry.

The Teaching Approaches Comparison

Here's how knowledge-sharers generally fall on the spectrum from insufferable to effective:

The Know-It-All	The Actual Teacher
Focuses on demonstrating their expertise	Focuses on the learner's understanding
Uses jargon to sound impressive	Uses simple language to build clarity
One teaching approach for all situations	Adapts methods to different learning styles
Views questions as challenges	Views questions as valuable feedback
Measures success by how smart they appear	Measures success by the learner's progress
Makes learning a competition	Makes learning a collaboration
Emphasizes what people don't know	Builds on what people already understand
Takes pride in being hard to understand	Takes pride in making complex things simple

REALITY CHECK: The know-it-all is teaching to feed their ego. The actual teacher is teaching to feed others' understanding. It's the difference between performing knowledge and transferring it—between intellectual masturbation and intellectual reproduction.

People learn in different ways. Visual Learneear need diagrams and images. Auditory learners need to hear explanations. Reading/writing learners need text and notes. Hands-on learners need to practice by doing. The best teachers use all these approaches to reach everyone.

When explaining an important concept, cycle through all four modalities to ensure you reach everyone: Show a visual representation, explain it verbally with emphasis on key points, provide a written summary of core concepts, and create a hands-on exercise to apply the information. This approach doesn't just work for different types of learners—it helps everyone remember better by engaging multiple senses.

Reading Teaching Receptivity Signals

> "The difference between a teacher and a lecturer is that a teacher watches while talking, and a lecturer just talks."

Effective teachers constantly monitor for signs that indicate whether their teaching is landing or failing. Here are the signals to watch for:

Engagement Signals (Continue Teaching) - Maintaining eye contact - Asking follow-up questions - Taking notes - Nodding with comprehension - Building on your points with their own insights - Relating content to their own experiences

Disengagement Signals (Adjust or Stop) - Decreased eye contact - Checking phone or watch - Fidgeting or restlessness - Reduced verbal affirmations ("uh-huh," "I see") - Changing the subject when you pause

PART 6: DIGITAL TEACHING ESSENTIALS

The Communication Strategy Protocol: When Silence Teaches More Than Words

> "The difference between an average teacher and a brilliant one isn't how much they say—it's knowing precisely when to shut up and let understanding happen in the silence."

Real communication in teaching requires rhythm, timing, and a partner who's willing to participate. The key isn't just about what you say - it's about how you say it, when you say it, and what you don't say. The most powerful moments in teaching often come from what you don't say—the questions you ask instead of answer, the space you create for discoveries rather than declarations.

The Communication Timing Matrix

Effective teaching requires mastering the rhythm of information exchange:

1. **The Curiosity Gap:** Creating space between what someone knows and what they want to know—ask before you tell
2. **The Processing Pause:** Giving the brain time to digest information—silence is when connections form
3. **The Strategic Question:** Asking rather than telling to promote active engagement—questions create ownership
4. **The Feedback Loop:** Regularly checking for understanding before moving on—prevent compounding confusion
5. **The Knowledge Ratio:** Aiming for learners to speak 60% of the time while you speak 40%—teaching is listening

Most knowledge-dumpers suffer from explanation diarrhea—they can't stop the flow once it starts. Effective teachers practice information discipline, delivering knowledge in digestible chunks with adequate processing time between.

The 10-Second Rule

This simple but powerful technique dramatically improves teaching effectiveness: After asking a question, silently count to ten before speaking again. Most teachers wait less than one second for a response before answering their own question or rephrasing it. This pattern trains learners to wait for the teacher to answer rather than thinking for themselves.

The first few seconds of silence will feel excruciating. Power through it. Often, the most thoughtful answers come after 6-8 seconds of reflection. By consistently implementing this practice, you create a learning environment where people actually think rather than just passively consume information.

The Question Hierarchy Framework

Transform your teaching by replacing statements with questions of increasing cognitive demand:

Basic Questions (Understanding) "What are the main components we discussed?" or "How would you explain this in your own words?" Purpose: Check understanding and memory

Intermediate Questions (Application) "How might this work in your situation?" or "What patterns do you notice across these examples?" Purpose: Connect theory to practice and develop deeper understanding

Advanced Questions (Creation & Evaluation) "How could we combine these approaches to create a better solution?" or "What criteria would determine if this approach is successful?" Purpose: Encourage creative integration and critical judgment

The most effective teaching progressively moves up this hierarchy rather than simply delivering information. Each level builds upon the previous one, creating a scaffold that supports increasingly sophisticated understanding.

The Digital Age Teaching Trap: When Followers Matter More Than Understanding

> "Online experts are like people who've learned to order beer in seventeen languages but can't hold a conversation in any of them—superficially impressive until you need actual depth."

For more on optimizing your digital environment in general, see Chapter 7. This section focuses specifically on digital teaching aspects rather than general digital communication.

Digital Teaching Platforms Comparison

Different platforms have different teaching strengths and weaknesses:

Platform	Best For	Limitations	Key Teaching Approach
Twitter/X	Quick insights, resource sharing	Depth, nuance	One key insight per tweet, threads for connected concepts
YouTube	Processes, demonstrations	Retention without practice	Problem → Solution → Demonstration → Practice prompt
Podcasts	Discussions, nuanced topics	Visual concepts	Conversation format, repetition of key points
Blogs/ Articles	Comprehensive explanations	Engagement, feedback	Clear structure, visual aids, examples
LinkedIn	Professional concepts	Depth, authenticity	Practical application focus, credibility signals
TikTok	Attention-grabbing concepts	Depth, complexity	Hook → Problem → Solution → Call to action

Digital Teaching Pitfalls

The three deadly sins of online teaching:

1. **Overwhelming with information** - Trying to cram too much into one piece of content
2. **Underwhelming with energy** - Failing to maintain engagement through delivery
3. **Inconsistent pacing** - Rushing through important points while belaboring simple ones

Digital Attention Maintenance

Online teaching requires attention hooks every 30-60 seconds. These can be: - Questions that make viewers/readers think - Pattern interrupts (changes in tone, visuals, or approach) -Examples that connect to real-world applications - Analogies that make complex ideas relatable - Previews of valuable insights coming up

PART 7: FROM KNOW-IT-ALL TO VALUED RESOURCE
The Source Transparency: Openly reference where your knowledge comes from, not just what you know. "I learned this from 10 years of practice" hits different than "I learned this from a YouTube video last week." Both can be valuable, but pretending they're the same is intellectual fraud. Cite your sources, give credit to your teachers, and be honest about the depth of your experience.

3. The Limitation Acknowledgment: Proactively identify the boundaries of your expertise. The most credible experts are the first to say, "That's outside my area of knowledge" or "The research is still unclear on that point." Only insecure pseudo-experts claim to have all the answers. Real experts are comfortable with uncertainty and complexity because they've actually spent enough time in their field to understand its nuances.

4. The Platform-Content Alignment: Choose teaching platforms based on educational effectiveness, not personal visibility. Some concepts need long-form explanation, some need visual demonstration, and

some need interactive practice. Forcing everything into whatever format gets the most likes isn't teaching—it's performing with educational costumes.

5. The Metrics Reframing: Measure success by learning outcomes, not engagement statistics. A video with 10 views that genuinely changed someone's understanding is more valuable than a viral post that got a million shallow nods but changed nothing. Optimize for impact, not impressions.

The Algorithm Trap: Teaching for Engagement vs. Understanding

Digital platforms reward shit that gets clicks, not stuff that actually teaches. They want oversimplified, entertaining, provocative content that people can scroll through in seconds. Good teaching needs nuance, honesty about what's uncertain, time to process, and actual substance.

This conflict creates an almost irresistible pull toward performative expertise rather than genuine education. The most successful digital teachers develop the discipline to periodically sacrifice algorithmic success for educational integrity—intentionally creating content that may perform worse by engagement metrics but better by learning outcomes.

This conflict creates an almost irresistible pull toward performative expertise rather than genuine education. The most successful digital teachers develop the discipline to periodically sacrifice algorithmic success for educational integrity—intentionally creating content that may perform worse by engagement metrics but better by learning outcomes.

The Emotional Intelligence Factor: Why EQ Trumps IQ in Teaching

"Knowledge without emotional intelligence is like a Lamborghini without a driver's license—flashy but useless." Teaching isn't just about transferring information; it's about creating an environment where people feel safe enough to be stupid, comfortable enough to make mistakes, and supported enough to keep trying. Here's how to create that psychological safety through the E.M.P.A.T.H.Y. framework:

When people feel anxious while learning, their brain basically shuts down. When they're curious and engaged, their brain soaks up information like a sponge.

The E.M.P.A.T.H.Y. Framework for Emotional Teaching

To create psychological safety for learning:

E - Errors as Opportunities: Treat mistakes as valuable data points, not failures. When someone gets something wrong, say "That's an interesting approach—let's explore why it doesn't quite work in this case" instead of "No, that's wrong." The first response keeps their brain in learning mode; the second triggers defensive mode where no learning can happen.

M - Manage Your Reactions: Control your expression of frustration or impatience. Your sigh, eye roll, or tone shift might seem minor to you, but to a learner, they're emotional earthquakes that trigger shame responses. Remember that what's obvious to you after years of experience isn't obvious to someone encountering it for the first time.

P - Personalize Approaches: Adjust to individual emotional needs and triggers. Some learners need constant reassurance; others prefer direct feedback. Some thrive on challenges; others need small wins to build confidence. One-size-fits-all emotional approaches are as ineffective as one-size-fits-all teaching methods.

A - Acknowledge Difficulty: Validate that learning something new is challenging. "This concept is tricky for most people at first" creates psychological safety that "This is basic stuff" destroys. Normalizing struggle prevents learners from interpreting difficulty as personal inadequacy.

T - Timing Sensitivity: Recognize when someone isn't emotionally ready to learn. Trying to teach complex concepts to someone who's stressed, defensive, or distracted is like trying to plant seeds in concrete—nothing's going to grow no matter how good the seeds are. Sometimes the best teaching move is to postpone the lesson.

H - Honor Their Process: Respect that people learn at different paces and in different ways. The goal isn't to get through your material; it's to ensure understanding—however long that takes. Rushing someone through concepts before they're ready doesn't accelerate learning; it prevents it.

Y - Your Ego Aside: Remember that good teaching isn't about you looking smart. It's about others becoming smarter. If your teaching style is designed to showcase your brilliance rather than facilitate their understanding, you're performing, not teaching.

The most knowledgeable person in the room often makes the worst teacher precisely because they've forgotten what it feels like to not understand. They've lost the emotional memory of confusion, which is essential for creating a path out of it for others.

The Adult Learning Dynamics: Teaching People Who Don't Want to Be "Taught"

> "Teaching adults is like trying to fill cups that are already full of something else. Your job isn't pouring more in—it's helping them make room for

new stuff without feeling like you're calling their existing drink garbage."

Let's talk about teaching adults, because it's a whole different ballgame from teaching kids. Adults come with baggage - years of experience, established beliefs, and egos more fragile than a soap bubble in a thunderstorm. They don't just want to know what to do; they want to know why they should do it, how it connects to what they already know, and what's in it for them.

The key is understanding that adult learners are like cats - they'll learn what they want to learn, when they want to learn it, and they'll make it look like it was their idea all along. Your job isn't to force-feed them knowledge; it's to make them curious enough to want to learn and then facilitate their self-directed exploration instead of dragging them through your predetermined curriculum.

Teaching Grown-Ups

When sharing knowledge with adults:

R - Respect Both Autonomy and Errors: Treat mistakes as valuable learning opportunities, not failures, and acknowledge adults' ability to direct their own learning. When someone gets something wrong, say "That's an interesting approach—let's explore why it doesn't quite work in this case" instead of "No, that's wrong." Offer options rather than mandates: "Here are three approaches that might work for your situation" beats "This is the one right way to do this" every time.

D - Direct Relevance: Explicitly connect content to their goals and problems. Adults are practical learners—they want knowledge they can use immediately, not theoretical concepts they might need someday. Start with their current challenge and work backward to the knowledge that solves it, not forward from basic principles to eventual application.

U - Utilize Experience: Draw on their existing knowledge as a foundation. Adults have rich experience repositories that can either be bridges to new knowledge or barriers against it. Ask about their experience with similar concepts, then explicitly connect your teaching to that foundation. "This is like X that you already know, except it differs in these specific ways..."

L - Logical Structure: Provide clear reasoning, not just instructions. Adults need to understand the "why" behind the "what." They're not looking for recipes to follow blindly; they want principles they can apply flexibly across situations. Explain the underlying logic so they can adapt knowledge to contexts you haven't specifically covered.

T - Timely Application: Ensure they can use information immediately. Adult learning motivation plummets when knowledge seems theoretical or future-oriented. Create immediate application opportunities—even small ones—to demonstrate practical value. "You can use this approach in your meeting tomorrow" creates urgency that "This might be useful someday" never will.

The fundamental mistake in teaching adults is treating them like children—directing rather than collaborating, instructing rather than engaging, and focusing on the subject matter rather than its application to their specific context.

The WIIFM Integration

"What's In It For Me" isn't just a selfish question—it's the fundamental filter through which adult learners process information. For each key concept you share, explicitly connect it to the learner's specific situation with phrases like:

"This matters to your situation because..." "You could apply this to your current challenge by..." "This solves the problem you mentioned earlier about..."

If you can't answer the WIIFM question clearly and specifically, you're not ready to teach that concept to adults—no matter how well you understand it yourself.

The Feedback Loop Protocol: The Art of Productive Criticism

> "Good feedback is like a mirror that shows you your hair is messed up but also hands you a comb. Bad feedback just points and laughs."

Feedback isn't just about pointing out what's wrong - it's about creating a roadmap for improvement. It's like being a GPS for someone's learning journey - you need to tell them where they went wrong while showing them how to get back on track without making them feel like they should abandon the trip entirely.

The F.E.E.D.B.A.C.K. Framework for Growth-Oriented Critique

To deliver feedback that improves performance without crushing spirits:

F - Frame Positively: Start with the goal of improvement, not criticism. "I'm sharing this to help you get even better" sets a different tone than "Let me tell you what you did wrong." The first creates partnership; the second creates defensiveness.

E - Evidence-Based: Provide specific examples, not general impressions. "I noticed you interrupted three people during the meeting" is actionable feedback. "You're too aggressive in meetings" is a vague judgment that creates resentment, not improvement.

E - Equal Focus: Balance what's working with what needs work. The human brain has a negativity bias—we give disproportionate weight to criticism over praise. Counteract this by ensuring you identify specific strengths alongside areas for improvement. This isn't just being nice; it's neurologically sound teaching.

D - Digestible Chunks: Limit feedback to 2-3 actionable points at once. The human brain can only process so much corrective information before it goes into defensive shutdown. Prioritize the highest-impact improvements rather than cataloging every possible flaw. You're creating a development path, not a comprehensive critique.

B - Behavior-Focused: Address actions and outcomes, not personality. "When you speak over others, it limits the team's perspective" focuses on changeable behavior. "You're too domineering" attacks identity, which is far less malleable and far more likely to trigger defensive responses.

A - Action-Oriented: Include specific next steps for improvement. Identifying problems without offering solutions is just criticism, not teaching. "Next time, you might try pausing for 3 seconds after someone speaks before responding" gives a concrete improvement path that "You need to listen better" never will.

C - Checking Understanding: Ensure comprehension, not just compliance. "How does this feedback land with you?" or "What parts of this seem most applicable to your situation?" creates dialogue rather than monologue. This confirms they've actually absorbed the feedback rather than just nodding while internally rejecting it.

K - Kindness Filter. Deliver with genuine care for their development. This isn't about tone policing—it's about intention. Feedback delivered with the genuine goal of helping someone improve lands differently than feedback designed to establish superiority or vent frustration. They can feel the difference, even if the words are similar.

The most common feedback failure isn't being too harsh or too soft—it's being too vague to be useful. "This needs improvement" without specifics about what, why, and how is just discouragement masquerading as feedback.

The Feedback Formula

For delivering high-impact feedback that creates growth rather than defensiveness, use this specific verbal structure:

1. **Appreciation:** "I really value how you [specific positive element]"
2. **Specific Observation:** "I noticed that [objective description of the issue]"
3. **Impact Statement:** "The effect of this is [concrete consequence]"
4. **Question/Suggestion:** "Have you considered [specific alternative]?" OR "One approach might be to [specific suggestion]"
5. **Support Offer:** "Would it help if I [specific assistance]?"
6. **Confidence Expression:** "I'm sharing this because I know you can [aspirational outcome]"

This structure works because it addresses both the logical content needs (specific observations and suggestions) and the emotional context needs (appreciation and confidence) that make feedback effective.

The Comprehension Check Toolkit: Gauging Understanding Without Creating Discomfort

> "The worst teachers assume understanding; the best teachers verify it without creating embarrassment."

One of the most critical teaching skills is accurately assessing whether your explanation has actually been understood. Here are effective techniques that go beyond asking "Do you understand?" (which most people will answer "yes" regardless of their actual comprehension):

The Explanation Reversal

After explaining something, ask the other person to explain it back to you in their own words: "Just so I'm sure I explained that clearly, how would you describe this concept to someone else?" This reveals exactly what they've absorbed and what they've missed.

Application Questions

Ask how they might apply what you've shared to their specific situation: "How do you think this approach might work for your particular project?" This tests not just comprehension but the ability to transfer the knowledge to relevant contexts.

Confusion Detection Guide

Watch for these non-verbal signals that someone is lost but too polite to say so: - Decreased eye contact - Reduced nodding - Fewer verbal affirmations - Increased fidgeting - Vague responses to specific questions - Checking phone (often a retreat behavior)

The Group Learning Matrix: Managing the Multi-Person Teaching Challenge

> "Teaching a group isn't about finding the average pace—it's more like being an air traffic controller making sure nobody crashes, nobody gets stuck in a holding pattern, and everyone lands safely on understanding."

Teaching a group isn't just teaching multiple individuals simultaneously - it's managing group dynamics, handling different learning speeds, and keeping everyone engaged while preventing the know-it-alls from hijacking the session and the quieter learners from disappearing entirely.

The G.R.O.U.P. Teaching System

For managing collective learning environments effectively:

G - Gauge Different Levels: Assess diverse starting points without embarrassing anyone. Use anonymous pre-assessments, observation during initial activities, or private check-ins rather than putting people on the spot. Nothing kills group learning faster than publicly highlighting knowledge gaps that make some participants feel inferior from the start.

R - Rotate Participation: Ensure engagement across different personality types. Don't let the loudest voices dominate while quieter participants disengage. Use structured participation techniques like round-robins, small breakout groups, or written responses that give everyone access to the conversation regardless of their natural assertiveness level.

O - Orchestrate Interactions: Structure productive peer-to-peer learning. The most powerful teaching often happens horizontally between participants, not vertically from teacher to student. Create intentional opportunities for participants to teach each other, solve problems collaboratively, and share diverse perspectives that you alone couldn't provide.

U - Unify Around Common Goals: Create shared purpose despite different levels. Establish clear learning objectives that matter to everyone despite their varying starting points. When participants understand the destination, they're more willing to accommodate different paths and paces to get there as a group.

P - Pace for the Middle: Don't target the fastest or slowest, then provide extensions and support. Set your primary teaching pace for the middle 60% of the group, then create additional challenges for advanced learners and support structures for those who need more help. This prevents the frustration of a pace that's either painfully slow or impossibly fast for a significant portion of participants.

The secret to group teaching isn't finding the perfect middle ground—it's creating a multi-level experience where everyone feels appropriately challenged regardless of their starting point.

The Tiered Challenge System

When teaching mixed-ability groups, structure activities with three distinct levels:

Core Challenge (For Everyone) A fundamental task that addresses the main learning objective and is accessible to all participants. For example, "Create a basic marketing plan with these five elements."

Extension Challenge (For Advanced Learners) An additional layer of complexity for those who complete the core challenge quickly: "For those finishing early, analyze how you would adapt this plan for three different market segments."

Foundation Support (For Those Needing More Help) Accessible resources for those struggling with the core challenge: "If you want a starting framework, templates are provided here for reference."

This approach keeps everyone productively engaged without creating separate "tracks" that might embarrass less advanced learners. Advanced participants stay challenged, beginners get necessary support, and everyone works toward the same fundamental objective.

The Art of Connection: From Knowledge Transfer to Human Connection

> "Information without connection is like trying to water plants with a firehose—technically you're providing what they need, but they'll be knocked over before they can absorb any of it."

Teaching is about connection, not just information transfer. The best teachers aren't osone who knew the most - they're the ones who could make complex things feel simple, who could make learning feel natural, who could meet you at your level and help you climb higher without making you feel like an idiot for not already being at the summit.

The C.O.N.N.E.C.T. Methodology for Human-Centered Teaching

To create the human foundation for effective learning:

C - Curiosity Cultivation: Spark interest before delivering information. The brain pays attention to what it's curious about and filters out what it isn't. Start with intriguing questions, surprising facts, or relevant problems before diving into explanations. "Did you know that most people are leaving half their retirement money on the table?" creates more learning readiness than "Let me explain compound interest formulas."

O - Openness About Challenges: Normalize the difficulty of learning. When you pretend complex topics are simple, you create impostor feelings in learners who find them difficult. Acknowledging that "This concept trips up even experienced professionals" gives people permission to struggle without feeling inadequate.

N - Narrative Integration: Use stories to make concepts memorable. The human brain is wired for narrative—we remember stories far better than abstract concepts. Wrap key principles in relevant stories that demonstrate their application and impact. "Let me tell you about a client who used this approach to double their results" creates more engagement than "This approach has been shown to increase effectiveness by 100%."

N - Needs Identification: Address specific goals rather than general topics. Nobody wakes up wanting to learn about "project management methodologies," but many people desperately want to know "how to stop projects from constantly missing deadlines." Teach to specific pain points and aspirations rather than abstract subject areas.

E - Emotional Engagement: Connect content to feelings, not just thoughts. Information linked to emotion is remembered and applied; information without emotional context is quickly forgotten. Help learners connect concepts to their hopes, fears, frustrations, and aspirations. "This approach can eliminate that Sunday night dread you feel about Monday meetings" creates stronger learning motivation than "This approach improves meeting efficiency."

C - Confirmation of Progress: Provide regular evidence of advancement. Learning without a sense of progress quickly becomes demotivating. Create visible milestones, celebrate small wins, and explicitly highlight improvements. "You've already mastered the three most difficult concepts" provides the psychological fuel needed to tackle the next challenge.

T - Trust Building: Create psychological safety through reliability and respect. Trust is the foundation of effective learning relationships. Demonstrate consistent respect for learners' intelligence, follow through on commitments, admit when you don't know something, and show genuine concern for their success. Without this foundation, even the most brilliant teaching techniques will fail.

This isn't touchy-feely nonsense—it's neurological reality. The human brain processes and retains information differently when emotional engagement and social connection are present. All the knowledge in the world is useless if you can't create the conditions for it to be received.

The Final Transformation: From Knowledge-Hoarder to Understanding-Creator

> "True teaching mastery isn't measured by how many people think you're brilliant, but by how many people become brilliant because of you."

The ultimate level of teaching mastery is when you stop trying to look smart and start focusing entirely on making others smarter. It's when you realize that your knowledge isn't a trophy to display - it's a tool to help others grow. It's when you measure your success not by how impressed people are with your expertise, but by how effectively they can apply what you've helped them learn.

The truly transformative teachers aren't those who know the most—they're those who can most effectively bridge the gap between not knowing and knowing. They're knowledge architects, not knowledge vaults—designers of understanding rather than storage units of information.

The Teaching Evolution Continuum

Your growth as a knowledge-sharer follows this developmental path:

Stage 1: Knowledge Performer Focus: Demonstrating your expertise Success Measure: Looking smart and impressive Core Question: "Do they think I know my stuff?"

Stage 2: Information Provider Focus: Delivering accurate content Success Measure: Covering material thoroughly Core Question: "Did I explain everything correctly?"

Stage 3: Skill Developer Focus: Building learner capabilities Success Measure: Learner can perform tasks Core Question: "Can they apply this effectively?"

Stage 4: Understanding Architect Focus: Creating conceptual frameworks Success Measure: Learner can adapt knowledge to new situations Core Question: "Do they understand the underlying principles?"

Stage 5: Development Catalyst Focus: Transforming the learner's relationship with the subject Success Measure: Learner becomes self-directed in the field Core Question: "Have I helped them become their own teacher?"

Most insufferable experts never progress beyond Stage 1 or 2, measuring success by how smart they appear rather than by the transformative impact they create. The most respected teachers in any field operate primarily at Stages 4 and 5, where their own ego and knowledge display become irrelevant compared to learner outcomes.

The Legacy Learning Question

To accelerate your evolution as a teacher, regularly ask yourself this fundamental question after every teaching interaction:

> "If I disappeared tomorrow, what could this person now do independently that they couldn't do before our interaction?"

This question ruthlessly cuts through performance-based teaching to focus on the only thing that ultimately matters: transferring capability, not just information. It highlights the difference between impressing someone with your knowledge and actually changing their relationship with the subject matter in a lasting way.

The Final Reality Check: Teaching as a Measure of Character

> "Knowledge without the ability to effectively share it is just mental hoarding—impressive to no one but yourself and ultimately useless to the world."

Your value as a teacher isn't measured by how much you know - it's measured by how much others learn from you. People don't care what you know until they know that you care. This isn't just a cute saying—it's the fundamental truth of human learning psychology. When someone believes you genuinely care about their growth and understanding, they're exponentially more receptive to what you're teaching. Without that foundation, your brilliant insights and extensive knowledge will bounce off them like rain off a windshield.

Chapter 9 Key Takeaways

- Respect: Effective teaching begins with respecting the learner's intelligence
- Relevance: Connect information to what people actually care about
- Responsiveness: Adapt your approach based on feedback and comprehension cues
- Restraint: Know when to stop explaining and start listening
- Results: Measure success by what others can do, not what you know

CHAPTER 10: RELATIONSHIP DETOX - STOP LETTING ENERGY VAMPIRES SUCK YOUR LIFE DRY

"YOUR RELATIONSHIPS ARE EITHER LIFTING YOU UP OR DRAGGING YOU DOWN—NOTHING IN BETWEEN."

PART 1: THE RELATIONSHIP ENERGY CRISIS

THE BRUTAL TRUTH ABOUT WHO'S DRAGGING YOU DOWN

Look, I'm not gonna sugarcoat this shit—the people you hang around with are either lifting you up or slowly killing your soul. There's no middle ground. No neutral relationships. That's not some inspirational poster crap—that's neuroscience.

This chapter focuses on strategically choosing which relationships deserve your energy. This isn't about how to behave in relationships—it's about which relationships to invest in, maintain, reduce, or eliminate.

WHY THIS MATTERS: You're literally turning into the average of the five people you spend most of your time with. Not figuratively. LITERALLY. Their habits are crawling into your life like ivy growing up a wall—slow enough that you don't notice until they've completely taken over. Their standards become your normal. Their limitations start feeling like YOUR limitations. That friend who's always late? Suddenly being 15 minutes late doesn't seem like a big deal to you anymore. That relative who never follows through? Now you're letting yourself off the hook too.

Not all toxic relationships are created equal. Some are like paper cuts—irritating but forgettable. Others are like slow drips of poison—you don't notice at first, but day by day, they drain your energy until suddenly you're exhausted and unmotivated for no obvious reason. The most dangerous ones are like sugary energy drinks—they seem good at first but leave you worse off in the end.

This isn't about being some cold-hearted asshole who tosses people aside when they stop being useful. This is about facing reality: every interaction is either giving you energy or sucking it away. The most dangerous relationships aren't the obviously toxic ones with the screaming and drama. Those are easy to spot. The real killers are the ones that seem fine on the surface but are quietly drilling holes in your boat below the waterline.

Toxic relationships don't always involve bad people. That friend who shows up with pizza and beer when you're trying to get healthy isn't plotting to sabotage your diet—they just want to hang out like you always did. That parent who questions your business decisions isn't trying to destroy your confidence—they're trying to protect you from risks that terrified their generation.

TRUTH BOMB: The people around you are actively shaping your future right now. Not someday. RIGHT NOW. Their expectations quietly become your limitations. Their habits seep into your daily choices like water into a sponge. The quality of your life CANNOT exceed the quality of your relationships. That's not motivational bullshit—it's how human brains actually work.

PART 2: THE RELATIONSHIP INVENTORY PROTOCOL

Wait—before you start mentally defending your toxic relationships, understand that this isn't about blame. It's about recognizing that relationships are either investments or liabilities. Let's be brutally honest—you're keeping toxic people in your life because you're afraid of being alone, afraid of conflict, or afraid of change. That ends now. Your relationship circle isn't just "influencing" you—it's determining your damn future while you pretend loyalty matters more than your mental health.

THE TOXIC RELATIONSHIP SPECTRUM: FROM ANNOYING TO SOUL-CRUSHING

Your connections exist on a spectrum from "occasionally annoying" to "should probably come with a hazardous materials warning label."

HOW TO MEASURE THE DAMAGE THEY'RE DOING

Let's cut through the bullshit and get real about your relationships:

After hanging out with them, do you feel like you just got a B12 shot or like you need a three-hour nap? Do you see their name on your phone and feel a little spark of joy or a heavy sense of dread? Are you hanging out because you genuinely want to or because saying no would require more energy than just showing up? When you share good news, do they actually celebrate, or do they find some subtle way to piss on your parade? When things go sideways in your life, do they show up with support or suddenly develop mysterious "scheduling conflicts"?

Ever wonder why you keep making the same mistakes? Look at the five people you spend the most time with—they're your answer. Toxic relationships aren't just unpleasant—they're radioactive. The damage continues long after exposure, affecting your confidence, your decisions, and your willingness to take risks long after the interaction ends.

Be honest. You already know the answers for each relationship in your life. Your gut has been screaming the truth at you for years while your brain keeps making excuses.

THE FIVE HUMAN DREAM-KILLERS YOU'RE PROBABLY HAVING DINNER WITH

Let's identify the relationship super-villains currently occupying space in your life. I guarantee you'll recognize at least two of these toxic archetypes:

The Dream Downsizer – That "well-meaning" relative who treats your ambitions like an oversized couch they're trying to cram through a narrow doorway. "Maybe we should just cut this part off," they suggest, removing the very thing that made it worth having. They'll perform emergency amputation on your dreams while claiming it's for your own good. "I just don't want you to be disappointed," they say, while ensuring you'll never be anything else. They've got your entire life planned out—a life that looks suspiciously like theirs, only smaller.

The Psychological ATM – Their life is a never-ending series of emergencies that only YOU can solve. They're constantly making emotional withdrawals but never make deposits. After an hour with them, you feel robbed—because you have been. They've taken your energy, attention, peace of mind, and given you nothing but the privilege of doing it all again next week.

The Stealth Saboteur – This special breed doesn't attack obviously – they're experts in psychological guerrilla warfare. "Just playing devil's advocate," they say, before explaining why your idea will fail. "I'm just being realistic," they claim, while dismantling your enthusiasm. They're like emotional snipers – you never see the shot coming, but suddenly you're bleeding confidence all over the place. By the time you realize what happened, they're already offering to help you clean up the mess they made.

The Emotional Kidnapper – This relationship terrorist has mastered holding your reality hostage. They deny things they clearly said, make you question your memory, and flip every situation to make themselves the victim. "I never said that" becomes their catchphrase, even when you have the receipts. They'll rewrite history so completely that you start to wonder if you're actually losing your mind. Spoiler alert: you're not crazy— they're just that manipulative.

The Misaligned Traveler – This is the person heading west while you're going east. Nothing's wrong with either direction—

they just don't complement each other. They're training for ultramarathons while you're building a business. They value spontaneity while you value security. Together you create constant friction that slowly wears both of you down like two gears spinning in opposite directions. Every interaction feels like you're speaking different languages even when you're using the same words.

Most relationship books focus only on romantic connections or obvious abusers who leave visible bruises. But some of the most damaging relationships in your life right now look completely normal from the outside—maybe even positive. That's what makes them so dangerous.

PART 3: THE DETOX FRAMEWORK

THE NO-DRAMA GUIDE TO TAKING OUT THE RELATIONSHIP TRASH

> "Removing toxic people from your life is not a loss. It's a gain. It's trading people who hurt you for peace that helps you."

So you've figured out who's poisoning your life. Now what? Most people make the mistake of either doing nothing (slow death) or having a dramatic confrontation (unnecessary chaos). There's a better way.

Here's where most people completely sabotage their relationship detox—they try to have "honest conversations" with people who have no interest in honesty. They try to "work things out" with people who benefit from the dysfunction. They try to "explain their feelings" to people who see emotions as ammunition. Strategic relationship management requires a different approach.

This isn't about burning bridges while screaming "YOU'RE DEAD TO ME!" across the flames. It's about strategically recalibrating your relationship portfolio for maximum life quality with minimum drama.

THE D.E.T.O.X. FRAMEWORK: YOUR FIVE-STEP ESCAPE PLAN

Here's your systematic approach to cleaning up your relationship environment without turning your life into a reality show:

D - Distance – Create strategic space, both physically and emotionally. This isn't ghosting; it's conscious recalibration of how much access someone has to your time and energy. The key is matching the distance to the toxicity—minimal toxicity gets minimal distance, severe toxicity gets maximum distance.

Think of it like exposure to bad weather—the more toxic the relationship, the more shelter and distance you need. You wouldn't stand outside in a hurricane without protection, so why are you having weekly brunches with someone who leaves your self-esteem in tatters? For mild toxicity, maybe that's just seeing them in groups instead of one-on-one. For severe cases, it might mean moving to a different state. I'm not even kidding. People have literally relocated to escape particularly toxic family dynamics, and it was worth every penny of the moving costs.

E - Expectations – Reset the relationship contract. Every relationship has unwritten rules and assumptions. When they're not working, rewrite them explicitly. "I can't be your 24/7 emotional support anymore, but I can check in weekly." "I won't discuss my career with you if you can't be supportive, but we can still enjoy family dinners." Be direct: "I know we used to talk every day, but my life has changed, and I can only manage weekly calls now." Will they like it? Probably not. But clarity is kindness, even when it's uncomfortable.

T - Time – Redistribute your attention to healthier connections. Toxic relationships don't just hurt directly—they steal time from relationships that could lift you up. Every hour spent with an energy-drainer is an hour not spent with an energy-giver.

Your time is a zero-sum game. There are only 168 hours in a week, and every minute you spend with people who drain you is a minute you can't invest in relationships that energize you. Start treating your social calendar like your financial budget— invest where you get the best returns. That sounds cold, but it's actually the opposite. It's valuing your life enough to spend it with people who actua ly enhance it rather than diminish it.

O - Obligations – Release yourself from relationship duties that aren't serving you. Stop feeling responsible for managing other people's emotions. Stop apologizing for having boundaries. Stop thinking you owe people unlimited access to you just because they want it.

You've been carrying around relationship obligations like unpaid parking tickets. "But I've always been the one who listens to her problems." "But I can't say no to family." "But we've been friends since kindergarten." These aren't reasons—they're relationship blackmail designed to keep you trapped in patterns that no longer serve you. You don't owe anyone your time, attention, or emotional labor just because they demand it or because you've provided it in the past.

X - Exit – Some connections can't be fixed with distance and boundaries—they need to be ended entirely. Have a plan for the logistics (shared possessions, mutual friends, family dynamics) and psychology (managing guilt, grief, and pressure to reconcile).

Not all relationships can or should be saved. Some are so fundamentally toxic that the only healthy option is complete termination. This isn't failure—it's self-preservation. But clean exits require planning. How will you handle mutual friends? What will you say when family members pressure you to reconcile? What will you do when they try to pull you back in with emergencies or promises to change?

This isn't about dramatic ultimatums or relationship-ending speeches—it's about strategic adjustments that protect your energy and growth while minimizing unnecessary conflict. Sometimes the most effective detox involves no announcement at all, just a gradual shift in your engagement patterns. The relationship equivalent of slowly backing away from a wild animal without making any sudden movements.

PART 4: THE RESISTANCE MANAGEMENT SYSTEM

THE RESISTANCE RESPONSE TOOLKIT: HANDLING PUSHBACK

> "When you change relationship patterns, expect resistance at first, but stay strong—healthier connections are worth the temporary discomfort."

When you start changing relationship dynamics, prepare for resistance. People don't like having their access to your energy restricted. Here's how to handle different types of pushback:

Guilt Trips

What it sounds like: "After everything I've done for you..." "I guess our relationship doesn't mean anything to you..."

How to respond: "I appreciate what you've done, and I need to make this change for my well-being." Then stop explaining. Don't defend, justify, or elaborate—that just gives them more material to manipulate.

Anger and Threats

What it sounds like: "You'll regret this..." "I'll tell everyone what you're really like..." "You're going to lose my support when you need it..."

How to respond: Use the "broken record" technique—calmly repeat your boundary without engaging with the emotional manipulation. "I understand you're upset. My decision remains the same." Then disengage from the conversation.

Flying Monkeys

What it happens: They enlist others to guilt you—suddenly you're getting calls from mutual friends or family members asking why you're "being so harsh."

How to respond: Use the "information diet" approach—give minimal details to potential messengers. "This is between us, and I'm handling it in the way that works best for me. I appreciate your concern."

Hoovering

What it looks like: They suddenly become the perfect friend/partner after you've created distance—showering you with attention, gifts, or exactly the behavior you've been wanting all along.

How to respond: Remember this is often temporary. Maintain your boundary for at least 3-6 months before reassessing. Real change takes time to prove itself, not just a few weeks of good behavior when they feel you slipping away.

The Extinction Burst

When you change relationship patterns, expect things to get worse before they get better. It's like when you stop giving a toddler candy and they throw an even BIGGER tantrum. The manipulation, guilt trips, and anger will intensify because their old tricks aren't working anymore.

This intensification isn't a sign your boundary is failing—it's evidence it's working. Hold firm through this phase, which typically lasts 2-4 weeks in most relationship dynamics.

Self-Doubt Navigation

During relationship changes, you'll likely experience moments of doubt: "Am I overreacting?" "Am I being too harsh?" "Maybe things weren't that bad?"

This is normal. Your brain is designed to seek the familiar, even when the familiar is harmful. Combat this by:

1. Documenting specific incidents before making changes so you can review them when doubt creeps in
2. Creating a support system of people who can reality-check your perceptions
3. Setting a minimum timeline (like 30 days) before reconsidering any relationship boundary
4. Tracking your energy levels to objectively measure how you feel with and without this person

Remember: If you're wondering whether you're being "too harsh" with someone who consistently drains or harms you, you're probably being too lenient. Healthy people don't inspire these kinds of doubts.

PART 5: THE FOUR HORSEMEN

THE FOUR HORSEMEN OF YOUR RELATIONSHIP APOCALYPSE

Let's get specific about the four major relationship categories that affect your life. Each comes with its own special brand of toxicity and requires tailored strategies. One-size-fits-all advice is about as useful as a screen door on a submarine.

ROMANTIC RELATIONSHIPS: WHEN "LOVE" BECOMES A PRISON SENTENCE

"Just because someone's your 'other half' doesn't mean they're your better half."

Romantic toxicity has a special kind of mindfuck because it comes wrapped in packages labeled "love," "commitment," and "forever." The most dangerous toxic relationships don't even look like abuse—they look like "passion," "protection," or "caring deeply."

RED FLAGS YOUR ROMANTIC RELATIONSHIP IS SLOWLY KILLING YOU: - You've developed an internal radar system that constantly scans for their mood shifts - You're constantly walking on eggshells to avoid triggering their reactions - Your ambitions and goals have mysteriously shrunk to fit their comfort zone - You catch yourself lying to friends about how things really are between you - Your accomplishments are minimized while your mistakes become biblical events - You've started hiding parts of yourself that used to be your favorite qualities - They "jokingly" put you down in front of others and call you "too sensitive" when you object - You feel exhausted after spending time together, not refreshed - You've started dressing, speaking, or behaving differently to avoid their criticism - The thought of them canceling plans gives you a secret sense of relief

REALITY CHECK: Loving someone doesn't automatically make them good for you. You can love someone completely and still need to get away from them. The presence of love doesn't negate the presence of damage. Some of the most harmful relationships are between people who genuinely love each other but are absolutely toxic together.

Romantic Relationship-Specific Detox Protocol

THE L.O.V.E. PROTOCOL: YOUR ROMANTIC DETOX STRATEGY

When detoxifying romantic relationships, follow these steps:

L - Leverage Gap Analysis: Get brutally honest about the gap between how you feel when you're with them versus when you're not. Keep a mood journal tracking your emotional state before, during, and after interactions to identify patterns.

Are you consistently more anxious or insecure when you're with them? Do you feel relief when they cancel plans? Does your confidence return when you have a few days apart? These aren't coincidences; they're clues. Your body knows the truth even when your heart makes excuses.

O - Observe Without Justifying: Stop confusing intensity for intimacy—drama isn't passion, it's just drama. Document specific behaviors without rationalizing them ("They yelled at me" not "They were just stressed").

We're masters at explaining away toxic behavior. "They only check my phone because they've been hurt before." "They only get that angry because they care so much." Strip away the justifications and look at the raw behaviors. If your best friend told you their partner was doing these exact things, what would you tell them? Now why aren't you giving yourself the same advice?

V - Verify Your Boundaries: Set clear, non-negotiable boundaries about how you expect to be treated. Write these down as specific behavioral statements ("I will not be spoken to in that tone" rather than vague principles like "I deserve respect").

"I want to be treated better" gives your partner nothing concrete to work with. "I will end any conversation where you raise your voice" gives them a clear choice with clear consequences. A boundary without consequences is just a suggestion. And when they test that boundary—which they absolutely will—you must enforce it immediately. Not the second time. Not when you're "really sure" they meant to cross it. The FIRST time.

E - Establish Independence: Develop relationships outside the partnership to maintain perspective. Create a support network map identifying specific people who can provide emotional support, practical assistance, and objective feedback.

Toxic romantic relationships thrive on isolation. They slowly cut you off from friends and family who might point out the problems, leaving you dependent on the very person who's hurting you. These outside relationships aren't just social outlets—they're lifelines that provide reality checks and escape routes when needed. Maintain financial independence too—separate accounts, emergency funds, and knowledge of your shared assets.

Remember: Staying in a toxic relationship because you've already invested years in it is like continuing to eat spoiled food because you've already taken three bites.

Romantic Relationship Transition Scripts:

For setting boundaries: "I care about you, but I need to make some changes in how we interact. I'm no longer available for [specific behavior], and need [specific boundary]. This isn't negotiable for me, but I wanted to be clear rather than just changing without explanation."

For taking space: "I need some time to myself to get clarity. This isn't about punishing you—it's about me needing space to think clearly. I'll reach out when I'm ready to talk, which might be [timeframe]."

For breaking up: "I've made the decision to end our relationship. I've given this a lot of thought, and it's not a reaction or up for negotiation. I wish you well, but this is what I need for my wellbeing."

Remember that with highly toxic partners, sometimes the safest approach is to create distance first, then communicate the change from a position of safety. Your physical and emotional safety always comes first.

FRIENDSHIPS: THE RELATIONSHIPS YOU CHOOSE THAT CHOOSE YOUR FUTURE

"Show me your friends, and I'll show you your future."

Friendship toxicity is especially dangerous because these are relationships you actively choose. When your family is toxic, you can blame genetics. When your friends are toxic, that's on you. You picked these people. You keep showing up. You're co-signing their influence on your life every time you answer their texts.

WARNING SIGNS YOUR FRIENDS ARE ACTUALLY FRENEMIES: - They're mysteriously unavailable when things are going well for you - Your successes seem to trigger their crises and emergencies - The friendship functions as a complaint circle with no solutions emerging - You find yourself downplaying your achievements to avoid their subtle undermining - They're consistently negative about new opportunities in your life - Your time together leaves you feeling drained rather than energized - They remind you of who you used to be, not who you're becoming - They make "jokes" that contain genuine criticism but can't be challenged - They compete with you instead of celebrating with you - You feel like you need to walk on eggshells around certain topics

What makes friendship detox especially tricky is the lack of clear closure mechanisms. There's no formal "dumping" process like with romantic relationships, just a gradual and often awkward drifting that can drag on for years.

Friendship-Specific Detox Protocol

THE F.R.I.E.N.D. SYSTEM: YOUR FRIENDSHIP DETOX STRATEGY

When detoxifying friendship relationships, follow these steps:

F - Filter Through Energy Audits: Track which friends consistently drain versus energize you. Document energy levels before and after each interaction for two weeks.

This isn't about keeping score—it's about gathering objective data. After hanging out with Friend A, do you feel inspired, motivated, and ready to take on the world? After texting with Friend B, do you feel depleted, anxious, and like you need a nap? These patterns aren't random; they're valuable information about who deserves more of your time.

R - Respond With Intentionality: Implement the "Hell Yes or No" rule—if spending time with them isn't a "hell yes," it's a no. Schedule interactions based on energy potential rather than obligation.

Stop accepting invitations out of guilt or FOMO. Your calendar isn't a charity for people who drain your life force. If your immediate internal response to "Want to grab coffee?" isn't genuine enthusiasm, it's probably a no. And "Sorry, I can't make it" works just fine.

I - Institute Strategic Unavailability: Stop being immediately available for draining interactions. Create response protocols with built-in delays for energy-negative people (24-hour text response time, scheduled calls instead of impromptu ones).

Toxic friends often expect immediate access to your time while offering little in return. They text and expect instant responses. They call and expect you to drop everything. Don't respond to texts within minutes. Don't answer every call. Don't drop everything for their latest crisis. This isn't about being a jerk; it's about creating healthy distance. You're not the friendship equivalent of a 24-hour convenience store.

E - Establish Growth Alignments: Develop replacement connections that align with your growth direction. Identify specific growth areas and actively seek friends who are already succeeding in those domains.

Don't just cut toxic friends without cultivating better alternatives, or you'll end up lonely enough to welcome the toxicity back. Proactively seek connections with people who are where you want to be—in fitness, career, relationships, or personal development. Join groups, take classes, attend events where your future friends are already hanging out. The best defense against toxic friendships is having better options.

N - Normalize Natural Evolution: Accept that some friendships are meant to be seasonal, not lifetime. Create "friendship graduation" mindsets that honor what the relationship provided while acknowledging its natural conclusion.

Not all friendship endings are failures—some are completions. That drinking buddy from college served a purpose during that phase of life, but now you're in a different phase. Some people are meant to be in your life for a reason or a season, not a lifetime.

D - Develop Clear Boundaries: Create explicit rather than implicit friendship parameters. Communicate directly about interaction frequency, emotional support expectations, and reciprocity requirements.

Most friendship toxicity thrives in the murky waters of unspoken expectations. "I thought best friends were supposed to talk every day." "I assumed you'd help me move since I helped you." Clear these up with direct communication: "I can only manage monthly get-togethers right now." "I'm not available for last-minute favors, but I'm happy to help if you ask a week in advance."

The quality of your friendships matters infinitely more than the longevity. A six-month friendship that pushes you to grow is worth more than a 20-year friendship that keeps you stuck in old patterns and outdated versions of yourself.

Friendship Detox Approaches:

The Slow Fade - Best for: Mild toxicity, casual friendships, situations where direct confrontation would create unnecessary drama. Gradually reduce contact frequency, response times, and engagement depth until the friendship naturally attenuates.

The Context Shift - Best for: Friendships that work in some contexts but not others. Maintain the relationship but only in specific environments where it's positive (group settings, specific activities) while eliminating contexts where it becomes draining.

The Direct Conversation - Best for: Close friendships with communication potential, relationships with otherwise healthy people who may not realize their impact. Have a clear, compassionate conversation about specific behaviors and needed changes.

The Clean Break - Best for: Highly toxic situations, friendships that consistently undermine your growth or wellbeing, relationships where attempts at change have failed. Make a clear, final break with minimal drama and explanation.

PROFESSIONAL RELATIONSHIPS: THE PEOPLE YOU SPEND MORE TIME WITH THAN YOUR FAMILY

> "You spend more waking hours with your coworkers than your family. Choose accordingly."

Work toxicity has unique leverage because it's tied to your financial survival. This creates power dynamics that can be particularly difficult to navigate—you can't just ghost your toxic boss like you would a toxic Tinder date.

RED FLAGS YOUR WORKPLACE IS A PSYCHOLOGICAL WARZONE: - Your contributions are routinely minimized or straight-up stolen by others - Information necessary for your success is deliberately withheld until after you need it - You're expected to be eternally grateful for basic professional courtesies - Your successes are met with resentment rather than recognition - Goalposts constantly move—achievements never quite meet the shifting standards - You've started doubting your competence despite previous confidence - The workplace has clear favorites who can do no wrong while others can do no right - Feedback is always vague enough to keep you insecure but never specific enough to actually improve - You've developed physical symptoms that mysteriously disappear on weekends and vacations - Sunday evenings fill you with existential dread as Monday approaches

Work relationships often involve complex interdependencies that make clean breaks nearly impossible. You can't simply cut someone off when your project, promotion, or paycheck depends on continued interaction with them. You need strategic approaches that protect your sanity without sabotaging your career.

Workplace-Specific Detox Protocol

THE W.O.R.K. METHOD: YOUR PROFESSIONAL DETOX STRATEGY

When detoxifying professional relationships, follow these steps:

W - Write Everything Down: Document all communications, achievements, and problematic interactions. Create a comprehensive paper trail that serves both as protection and objective reality-checking when gaslighting occurs.

In toxic work environments, documentation isn't paranoia—it's self-preservation. Confirm verbal instructions in follow-up emails ("Just to confirm our conversation, I'll be focusing on X rather than Y"). Keep a work journal documenting achievements, challenges, and problematic interactions with dates and details. Save emails, screenshots, and meeting notes. This isn't just for potential HR situations—it's also to combat the self-doubt that toxic work relationships create. When they say "I never told you to do that," you'll have the receipts.

O - Organize Alternative Support: Build lateral relationships that provide alternative sources of information, influence, and professional validation. Create a professional support network that doesn't depend on toxic power dynamics.

Don't put all your professional eggs in one toxic basket. Cultivate relationships with colleagues in different departments, mentors outside your reporting line, and industry contacts beyond your company. These connections provide reality checks when you're being gaslit, information when you're being excluded, and opportunities when you need an escape route. They're your professional insurance policy.

R - Reinforce Boundaries: Maintain strict work-life boundaries to prevent toxic work dynamics from colonizing your entire existence. Implement specific containment protocols like dedicated work phones, email blackout hours, and physical separation of work materials.

Toxic work relationships thrive on 24/7 access and the blurring of professional/personal boundaries. Fight this by creating clear containment zones: no work email after 7pm, no taking work calls on weekends, no discussing work problems during personal time. Your job is something you do, not something you are. The moment work colonizes your entire identity is the moment you lose all negotiating power in the relationship.

K - Keep Exit Options Open: Develop a comprehensive escape plan for truly untenable situations. Create financial runways, skill development paths, and network connections that provide genuine alternatives.

The ultimate power move in toxic work situations is having the ability to walk away. Build an emergency fund that covers 3-6 months of expenses. Keep your resume updated and your LinkedIn profile current. Maintain relationships with recruiters and industry contacts. Take courses that expand your skills beyond your current role. The more viable your exit options, the less trapped you'll feel—and ironically, the more power you'll have in your current situation.

Remember: No job is worth sacrificing your mental health, but quitting without a plan is often just trading one problem for another. Strategic exits beat emotional ones every time.

Workplace Relationship Management Scripts:

For managing a toxic boss: "I've noticed I work best with clear expectations. Could we set up a weekly check-in where we align on priorities and feedback?" (This creates structure that limits their ability to be chaotic or manipulative.)

For handling difficult colleagues: "I've found our communication works better when we [specific change]. Can we try that approach going forward?" (Frame it as a mutual improvement rather than placing blame.)

For setting boundaries with work demands: "I'm committed to delivering excellent work, which requires me to protect my focus time. I'll be checking email at these specific times and will respond to non-urgent matters within 24 hours." (Professional but firm.)

For toxic team environments: "I've noticed our team meetings often run long without clear outcomes. I'd like to suggest a structured agenda and timeboxing to make these more productive for everyone." (Propose solutions that benefit the group while addressing the problem.)

FAMILY RELATIONSHIPS: THE DNA LOTTERY YOU DIDN'T CHOOSE

> "The family that criticizes together, traumatizes together."

Family toxicity hits different because it comes with the heaviest cultural programming: "But they're your family," "Blood is thicker than water," "Family comes first." This social conditioning creates industrial-strength guilt that keeps you trapped in harmful patterns long after you'd have ditched anyone else who treated you the same way.

WARNING SIGNS YOUR FAMILY IS TOXIC AF: - Your growth or independence is treated as personal betrayal - Normal boundary-setting is labeled as disrespect or selfishness - Your achievements outside family-approved paths create tension - Every family gathering requires days of mental preparation and recovery - You become a different person around them— usually a smaller, less authentic version - Family "help" comes with expectations of control or compliance - They use shared history as ammunition rather than foundation - You've developed physical symptoms that mysteriously appear before family events - Certain relatives can say whatever they want, but you're expected to "keep the peace" - You find yourself drinking more or needing substances to get through family gatherings

What makes family detox especially complicated is the domino effect. Distancing from one toxic family member often affects your relationship with others who aren't directly problematic. Set boundaries with your critical mother, and suddenly your otherwise decent father is calling to ask why you're "upsetting your mother." It's like trying to remove one Jenga piece without disturbing the entire tower.

Family-Specific Detox Protocol

THE B.L.O.O.D. SYSTEM: YOUR FAMILY DETOX STRATEGY

When detoxifying family relationships, follow these steps:

B - Break Cultural Programming: Accept that sharing DNA doesn't entitle anyone to mistreat you. Challenge the cultural narratives that keep you trapped in harmful family dynamics.

Examine the family mantras you've internalized: "We never discuss problems outside the family." "You always forgive family, no matter what." "Family comes before everything." These aren't universal truths; they're control mechanisms designed to prevent boundary-setting. Replace them with healthier beliefs: "Respect is earned, not owed." "Love without boundaries isn't love; it's manipulation." "My wellbeing matters as much as family harmony."

L - Language Preparation: Create specific communication scripts for setting boundaries without unnecessary drama. Develop precise wording for common scenarios that trigger unhealthy patterns.

Family buttons get installed early and pushed often. They know exactly which words will send you into a guilt spiral or rage explosion because they installed those buttons in the first place. Prepare with pre-planned responses rather than reacting emotionally. When Mom criticizes your parenting: "I know we have different approaches, and I'm comfortable with my choices." When Dad questions your career: "I appreciate your concern, but I'm confident in my path." When Aunt Susan makes comments about your weight: "I don't discuss my body or eating habits. What's new with your garden?"

O - Orchestrate Limited Exposure: Develop strategic engagement patterns with controlled exposure on your terms. Design interaction protocols that protect your energy while maintaining necessary connections.

Create a middle path with controlled, limited engagement. Maybe that's holidays only, monthly phone calls instead of weekly, or two-hour visits instead of weekend stays. Set clear arrival and departure times. Meet in neutral locations rather than territory they control. Have an exit strategy for when things get toxic— your own transportation, a hotel room instead of staying at their house, or a friend who will call with an "emergency" if you text them an SOS.

O - Obtain External Support: Build your "chosen family" of supportive non-relatives who respect your growth. Create alternative support systems that provide the healthy family dynamics your biological connections may lack.

The antidote to toxic family isn't isolation—it's better relationships. Cultivate connections with friends who celebrate your growth, mentors who guide without controlling, and partners who love your authentic self. These relationships aren't just nice to have—they're essential reality checks that help you recognize when family dynamics are unhealthy rather than normal.

D - Dissolve Guilt Attachments: Release the emotional burden of prioritizing your well-being over family expectations. Develop specific practices for processing and releasing the guilt that keeps you trapped in toxic patterns.

Family guilt is the superglue of toxic dynamics. It's what brings you back for more abuse even when you know better. Counter this with conscious guilt-processing practices: journaling about the difference between responsibility and guilt, creating affirmations that reinforce your right to boundaries, working with a therapist who specializes in family dynamics. Recognize that the guilt you feel was installed intentionally as a control mechanism—it's not an accurate moral compass.

The radical truth: Some family relationships are meant to be completely severed, some need significant restructuring, and others simply require clearer boundaries. The appropriate level of detox depends on the specific toxicity pattern, not social expectations about family obligation. You didn't choose your DNA connections, but you absolutely can choose how much access they have to your life.

Family Relationship Management Scripts:

For setting boundaries with parents: "I love you and want you in my life, which is why I need to be clear about what works for me. I'm not available for [specific behavior], and when it happens, I will [specific consequence]. This isn't about punishing you—it's about creating a relationship that's sustainable for both of us."

For managing difficult siblings: "I've realized our relationship works better when we [specific change]. I'd like us to try this approach because having a good relationship with you matters to me."

For handling extended family: "I appreciate the invitation, but I'll only be attending for [specific timeframe]. I've found this works best for me to fully enjoy family gatherings." (Set time limits in advance.)

For toxic family members: "I need to step back from our relationship for now. This isn't a punishment or something I'm willing to debate—it's what I need for my wellbeing. I'll reach out when and if that changes."

PART 6: THE RELATIONSHIP ASSESSMENT SYSTEM

THE RELATIONSHIP ENERGY AUDIT: WHO'S LIFTING YOU UP VS. DRAGGING YOU DOWN

To get clear about exactly who's lifting you up and who's dragging you down, stop guessing and start measuring.

THE 7-DAY RELATIONSHIP IMPACT ASSESSMENT

Here's your assignment: For one week, pay attention to how you feel before and after spending time with different people. Not just what you think about the interaction, but how your energy, mood, and motivation levels physically change in your body. Keep it simple: use a 1-10 scale to rate your energy before and after each significant interaction.

The patterns will shock you. Some people consistently leave you feeling better than before you saw them—energized, inspired, confident. You walk away from coffee with them ready to conquer the world. Others reliably drain you—leaving you tired, doubtful, or anxious. After a phone call with them, you suddenly need a nap or a drink. These aren't random fluctuations; they're data points about who deserves more of your time.

Pay attention to specific behaviors that affect you. Maybe it's the friend who always steers conversations toward problems without solutions. Maybe it's the colleague who genuinely celebrates your wins without making them about themselves. Maybe it's the family member who makes subtle digs about your life choices that seem small in the moment but leave you questioning yourself hours later. These specific behaviors are what you need to either minimize or maximize in your relationship ecosystem.

After your week of tracking, pick the single most energy-draining relationship and implement one specific boundary. Not a complete relationship overhaul, just one clear limit: "I'll only take phone calls between 6-8pm." "I won't discuss my weight or eating habits." "I'm not available for last-minute requests." Then track what happens when you enforce this boundary. The response will tell you everything about whether this relationship can be detoxified or needs to be eliminated.

Healthy people might not like your boundary, but they'll respect it. Toxic people will lose their minds when you change the rules of engagement. They'll call you selfish, dramatic, or oversensitive. They'll try to make you feel guilty or crazy for having needs. That reaction isn't a red flag—it's a four-alarm fire with sirens blaring.

PART 7: THE RELATIONSHIP RECONSTRUCTION BLUEPRINT

THE HIGH-VALUE RELATIONSHIP BLUEPRINT: PEOPLE WORTH KEEPING

"The quality of your relationships determines the quality of your life more than any other single factor."

Now that we've addressed the relationship equivalent of toxic waste dumps, let's talk about what you should be looking for instead. What characteristics define truly valuable connections worth investing in?

THE V.A.L.U.E. SYSTEM: YOUR RELATIONSHIP QUALITY CHECKLIST

Here's your framework for identifying and cultivating high-quality connections:

V - Validation – Do they support your evolution or resist it? High-value people encourage your growth, celebrate your progress, and push you toward your potential. They don't feel threatened when you evolve because they're evolving too.

The best people in your life aren't just cheerleaders who mindlessly support everything you do. That's not validation; that's enabling. They're growth partners who celebrate your wins, challenge your limitations, and hold you accountable to your potential. They don't just validate who you are; they validate who you're becoming. They see the version of you that's still emerging and help call it forward.

A - Authenticity – Can you be real with them without fear? True connection requires the ability to show up as your actual self, not a carefully curated version designed to maintain approval. Valuable relationships allow for honest expression without punishment, disagreement without rejection, and vulnerability without exploitation.

High-value relationships are those where you can take off the mask and just be. You can say "I'm struggling" without being labeled weak, "I disagree" without being labeled difficult, or "I need help" without being labeled burdensome. The energy you're not spending on pretending becomes available for actually living. Think about how exhausting it is to maintain a facade around certain people versus how refreshing it feels to be with someone who knows the real you and likes you anyway.

L - Liability – Do they reduce stress or create it? Some people are safety nets that make risk-taking possible; others are active threats that generate constant anxiety. High-value connections function as psychological insurance policies—they make you feel safer in the world.

The best relationships are those where you know someone has your back. They're reliable without being reminded, consistent without being monitored, and supportive without being asked. They reduce your ambient stress level just by existing. When shit hits the fan, you don't have to wonder if they'll show up—you know they will. This reliability creates a foundation of safety that allows you to take bigger risks in other areas of your life.

U - Upward Influence – Do they improve your decisions and mindset? We unconsciously absorb the attitudes, standards, and thought patterns of those around us. Valuable relationships elevate your thinking, challenge your limitations, and improve your decision-making.

You're constantly being shaped by the people around you. Their standards become your normal. Their habits influence your choices. Their worldviews color how you see everything. High-value relationships pull you upward through this unconscious influence—making excellence seem normal and growth seem natural. You find yourself thinking bigger, working harder, and expecting more from yourself not because they pressure you, but because their example resets your baseline.

E - Energy – Do they leave you feeling better or worse? Every interaction either adds or subtracts vitality. High-value connections consistently leave you feeling more alive, more capable, and more optimistic than before the interaction.

This is the simplest but most powerful measure of relationship value: the energy exchange. After spending time with them, do you feel energized or depleted? Inspired or drained? Ready to take on challenges or ready to take a nap? Some of the most valuable relationships challenge you in ways that aren't always comfortable but leave you stronger afterward—like a good workout that burns while you're doing it but builds muscle in the process.

High-value relationships aren't always the easiest—they often challenge you in productive ways—but they consistently contribute to your growth rather than hinder it. They're the relationships that make you more of who you really are, not less.

Here's where most people completely misunderstand relationship quality: they think relationships that feel comfortable are automatically good, while those that create tension are automatically bad. The truth is more nuanced. Some comfortable relationships are slowly killing your potential, while some challenging relationships are exactly what you need to grow.

THE FIVE TYPES OF HIGH-VALUE RELATIONSHIPS YOU NEED IN YOUR LIFE

Your relationship ecosystem needs diversity to truly support your growth. Just like you wouldn't eat only protein or only carbs, you shouldn't rely on just one type of relationship. Here are the five types of high-value connections you should be actively cultivating:

Growth Catalysts accelerate your development by challenging your comfort zones, maintaining high standards, and providing constructive feedback. They're the people who see your potential more clearly than you do and refuse to let you settle for mediocrity. You need these connections to progress beyond what you could achieve alone.

These aren't just people who are successful; they're people who are invested in your success. They push you past self-imposed limitations, call you on your excuses, and hold you to standards higher than you might set for yourself. They're the friend who says, "I know you can do better than this," when everyone else is saying, "It's good enough." Without these catalysts, you'll plateau at whatever level feels comfortable rather than reaching your potential. You'll settle for "not bad" instead of discovering what's truly possible.

Energy Enhancers increase your vitality through consistent positivity, humor, excitement, and enthusiasm. After spending time with them, you feel more alive and capable than before. They're the people who remind you that life isn't just about achievement but also joy and experience.

These are your "life force multipliers"—people who somehow make everything more vibrant just by being present. A boring errand becomes an adventure. A routine dinner turns into a memorable night. They're not toxic positivity pushers who deny reality; they're authentic enthusiasts who find genuine joy and share it generously. Without these enhancers, your life becomes all work and struggle with no play or celebration. You forget why you're working so hard in the first place.

Support Pillars build your resilience through reliable presence, emotional intelligence, and non-judgmental listening. They're the people you can call at 2 AM during a crisis who will show up without questioning why. These connections provide the safety net that makes risk-taking possible.

These aren't just sympathetic ears; they're emotional foundations that help you weather life's inevitable storms. They offer perspective when you're catastrophizing ("This isn't the end of the world"), comfort when you're hurting ("I'm here no matter what"), and practical help when you're overwhelmed ("Let me take care of this while you handle that"). Without these pillars, you'll avoid necessary risks because the potential cost of failure feels too devastating to bear alone. You'll play it safe rather than reaching for what you really want.

Vision Expanders broaden your perspective through different backgrounds, challenging viewpoints, and unique expertise. They help you see blind spots and possibilities invisible from your current vantage point. These connections prevent the echo chamber effect that limits growth.

These aren't just people who are different from you; they're people who help you see differently because of those differences. They introduce you to ideas, experiences, and perspectives that wouldn't naturally cross your path. They question assumptions you didn't even realize you were making. They're the friend from a completely different background who asks, "Why do you think that's normal?" about something you've never questioned. Without these expanders, your worldview calcifies and your thinking becomes predictable.

Value Aligners reinforce your purpose through shared core values, compatible life direction, and mutual growth goals. They're the people who understand your "why" on a fundamental level, even if their "how" looks different. These connections provide the sense of tribe that humans fundamentally need.

These aren't just people who like the same things you like; they're people who care about the same things you care about. They strengthen your commitment to your values when the world tests them. They remind you of your purpose when distractions tempt you away from it. They're the friends who understand why you're making sacrifices that others find strange because they share your long-term vision. Without these aligners, you start to question your path when it gets difficult, wondering if you're the crazy one for wanting more.

The most effective relationship portfolio includes a strategic mix of these types, providing comprehensive support for different aspects of your growth and well-being. And here's the kicker—rarely does one person fulfill all five roles. That's why you need a diverse relationship ecosystem, not just one or two "best" relationships.

THE VULNERABILITY-TRUST PARADOX: WHY "JUST BE YOURSELF" IS TERRIBLE ADVICE

> "Vulnerability without discernment isn't authenticity—it's poor boundaries."

Here's where most relationship advice goes completely off the rails: it tells you to be vulnerable and authentic with everyone. That's like leaving your front door unlocked with valuables on the porch—a recipe for getting robbed. Real relationship wisdom is about calibrated openness based on proven trustworthiness. Genuine connection requires vulnerability, but effective vulnerability requires careful trust assessment. Here's how to determine who gets access to what:

THE FOUR LEVELS OF TRUST: WHO GETS ACCESS TO WHAT

Here's your progressive trust-verification model for developing healthy vulnerability patterns:

Level 1 Trust involves surface-level openness with minimal risk. This is appropriate for new acquaintances and casual connections. Your vulnerability should be limited to general opinions and broad experiences. The verification needed is simply basic respect and conversational reciprocity.

This is the "getting to know you" phase where you share general information about your work, hobbies, and non-controversial opinions. You're authentic but not exposed. You might mention you're going through a career transition, but not the financial anxiety it's causing. You might share that you enjoy fitness, but not your body image struggles. This isn't being fake; it's being appropriately boundaried with people who haven't yet earned deeper access. It's the relationship equivalent of letting someone into your living room but not your bedroom.

Level 2 Trust permits moderate disclosure with limited exposure. This fits developing friendships and early-stage relationships. You can share personal values and modest challenges at this level. Before proceeding, verify consistent reliability and respect for basic boundaries.

At this level, you might share your general approach to relationships, your career aspirations, or your growth challenges—but not your deepest insecurities or most painful experiences. You might discuss a disagreement with a friend but not your childhood trauma. This is appropriate for friends you enjoy but don't necessarily consider inner circle, colleagues you like but don't socialize with extensively, or family members you're friendly with but not deeply connected to.

Level 3 Trust allows significant openness with meaningful risk. This belongs in established relationships with proven patterns over time. At this level, you can share fears, significant struggles, and important needs. But first, verify demonstrated loyalty and emotional maturity through multiple interactions.

These are your close friends, committed romantic partners, and trusted family members who have consistently shown up for you over time. You've seen how they handle conflict, respond to your vulnerability, and maintain confidentiality. You've watched them support others through difficult times. You've tested the relationship with smaller disclosures and seen how they responded. These people have earned access to your deeper self through consistent trustworthiness.

Level 4 Trust enables deep vulnerability with substantial exposure. This is reserved exclusively for long-term relationships with extensive verification. Only here is it appropriate to share core wounds, greatest fears, and complete authenticity.

This highest level of trust is for the very few people who have earned complete access to your inner world—typically a committed life partner, best friend of many years, or exceptionally close family member. These are people who have seen you at your worst and stayed, who have held your deepest secrets without judgment, who have proven their loyalty during your darkest moments. They've earned the right to know the most vulnerable parts of you through years of consistent trustworthiness.

The key isn't avoiding vulnerability but calibrating it appropriately based on demonstrated trustworthiness rather than wishful thinking or social pressure. Most relationship damage happens when people share Level 4 vulnerability with Level 1 or 2 relationships—then wonder why they got hurt.

The Ultimate Relationship Truth: Proactive Design Beats Reactive Response

Your relationships don't just happen by accident. Either you design them, or someone else will. If you don't choose your social circle on purpose, it gets shaped by whatever's easy—who's nearby, who's convenient, who you've known forever—not by what actually helps you grow.

When Relationships Become Crises

> "Some relationship problems go beyond everyday toxicity into full-blown catastrophes."

Sometimes relationship problems escalate beyond everyday toxicity into full-blown crises—betrayals, devastating conflicts, or sudden endings. The detox strategies in this chapter work for gradual relationship improvement, but what about when relationship disasters strike without warning?

That's why in the next chapter, we'll tackle crisis management—because some of life's most severe crises involve the people closest to us. Before moving on, ask yourself: Do you have a plan for when a key relationship suddenly implodes? The crisis management skills in the next chapter will ensure you're not blindsided when relationship disasters strike.

Relationship detox is preventative medicine. Crisis management is emergency surgery. You need both in your toolkit.

Your relationships are plotting your future in real-time. The people you surround yourself with are either lifting you toward your potential or anchoring you to their limitations. Their expectations become your standards. Their values shape your decisions. Their energy affects your momentum.

Stop passively accepting whoever happens to be in your life and start intentionally designing your relationship ecosystem. This isn't about being cold—it's about recognizing that your time and energy are finite resources that should be invested where they create the greatest return.

The question isn't whether your relationships will shape your future—they absolutely will. The only question is whether that future will be designed by your conscious choices or by default settings and external agendas.

Chapter 10 Key Takeaways

- Recognition: Relationships are either lifting you up or pulling you down—there is no neutral
- Recalibration: Different relationship types require different detox approaches
- Responsibility: You are the architect of your social environment, not its victim
- Resilience: High-value connections create a foundation for all other success
- Redesign: Strategic relationship portfolio management outperforms accidental connections

The relationship skills you've developed will be put to the ultimate test when disaster strikes, which is exactly what we'll cover next.

CHAPTER 11: DANCING WITH DISASTER - YOUR SURVIVAL GUIDE WHEN LIFE BURNS TO THE GROUND

"CRISIS DOESN'T CREATE CHARACTER; IT REVEALS IT."

PART 1: WHEN LIFE BURSTS INTO FLAMES

The relationship detox you completed in the previous chapter has prepared you for one of life's greatest challenges: navigating disasters.

WHEN DISASTER STRIKES: NAVIGATING LIFE'S PERFECT STORMS

> "Life doesn't throw curveballs—it throws the entire baseball machine at you when you're blindfolded and wearing flip-flops."

This is your crisis response headquarters—the definitive guide to handling disasters. This chapter addresses significant but contained life disruptions where your core foundations remain intact. For total life implosions where multiple systems fail simultaneously, see Chapter 12.

WHY THIS MATTERS: The average person will face between 5-7 major life crises during their lifetime. How well you handle these inevitable disasters will determine more about where you end up than almost anything else you do.

TRUTH BOMB: Disasters aren't optional add-ons to life—they're standard features that come with the basic package. The question isn't if your life will face catastrophe—it's when it'll happen, how many crises you'll be juggling at once, and whether you've built systems that can bend without breaking.

While writing this book, I had one of those perfect storm moments. My relationship imploded, a major financial opportunity collapsed, and a health issue flared up—all within the same 72-hour period. It was like the universe was testing whether I actually believed the stuff I was writing.

PART 2: THE DISASTER OPPORTUNITY PRINCIPLE

THE CERTAINTY OF UNCERTAINTY: LIFE'S ONLY GUARANTEE

Every major success story you've ever heard about involved someone handling their own personal apocalypse at some point. Steve Jobs didn't get fired from Apple on a day when everything else was going great. Oprah didn't face workplace discrimination when all other aspects of her life were perfectly stable. They succeeded because they figured out how to function when everything was falling apart around them.

REALITY CHECK: Disasters aren't extraordinary events—they're inevitable reality checks that expose how resilient (or fragile) your systems actually are. They're the universe's way of stress-testing your life systems, and most people's systems fail spectacularly under pressure.

CRISIS VS. COLLAPSE: UNDERSTANDING THE DIFFERENCE

> "Not all disasters are created equal—knowing whether you're facing a crisis or a collapse determines which survival strategies to deploy."

There's a meaningful difference between a crisis (covered here) and a complete collapse (covered in Chapter 12):

Crisis (Chapter 11)	Collapse (Chapter 12)
Significant but contained life disruption	Multiple simultaneous failures across all domains
Core foundations remain intact	Fundamental life structures compromised
Some systems still functioning	Few or no functioning systems remaining
Recovery possible through strategic response	Survival requires complete life reconstruction

Think of a crisis as severe turbulence on a flight—terrifying but manageable with the right response. A collapse is the plane actually going down—requiring completely different survival strategies.

PART 3: THE C.R.I.S.I.S. FRAMEWORK

YOUR CRISIS SURVIVAL TOOLKIT: THE INTEGRATED RESPONSE SYSTEM

> "A crisis doesn't just test your individual skills—it tests how effectively you can combine them into a unified response."

When facing simultaneous challenges, your instinct will be to compartmentalize each crisis as separate problems. The breakthrough comes when you recognize these aren't separate crises but a single interconnected challenge requiring an integrated response. It's not three different fires—it's one big fire with three fronts.

When disaster strikes, catch yourself when shifting from legitimate problem assessment ("I lost my job") to useless catastrophizing

("I'll never work again and will die alone under a bridge"). Give yourself a 5-minute "complaint container" where you can vent all the catastrophic bullshit, then immediately pivot to 15 minutes of solution focus.

THE C.R.I.S.I.S. FRAMEWORK: YOUR STEP-BY-STEP DISASTER SURVIVAL GUIDE

> "When everything's burning down, having a system isn't being robotic—it's the difference between fighting random fires until you collapse or strategically containing the blaze."

Most people's crisis response looks like a toddler playing whack-a-mole—frantically reacting to whatever problem screams loudest at that exact moment. When multiple systems in your life are imploding simultaneously, you need a framework that works regardless of what specific flavor of apocalypse you're dealing with:

Crisis Response Component	Amateur Approach	Strategic Approach
Control Focus	Tries to control everything, including uncontrollables	Ruthlessly prioritizes direct control areas while accepting what can't be changed
Resource Assessment	Makes emotional assumptions about what's available	Conducts concrete inventory of actual resources with specific numbers and names

Immediate Action	Attempts to solve everything simultaneously	Focuses exclusively on stabilization first—stopping the bleeding before healing the wound
Strategic Priorities	Addresses whatever feels most painful or screams loudest	Identifies cascade effects and sequences actions based on which problems will create more problems if left unaddressed
Information Management	Either avoids all information or drowns in endless research	Creates structured intake with clear boundaries— specific times for information gathering
Support Activation	Either isolates completely or overwhelms supporters	Strategically activates different support types for different needs with clear requests

C - CONTROL WHAT YOU CAN (AND ONLY WHAT YOU CAN)

In the middle of a shitstorm, your brain will waste precious energy on things entirely outside your control. Divide everything into three categories:

1. Direct Control: Things you can personally change right now (your emotional response, what you say to your partner during a fight)

2. Indirect Influence: Things you can affect but not control (how your apology is received, whether your friend takes your advice)
3. No Control: Things completely outside your power (your ex's new relationship, your parents' opinions)

Focus 80% of your energy on Category 1, 20% on Category 2, and ZERO on Category 3. When your company announces layoffs, you can't control the corporate decision (No Control). You can somewhat influence how your manager perceives your value (Indirect Influence). You can absolutely control your resume updates and networking outreach (Direct Control).

R - RESOURCES & RESERVES ASSESSMENT: WHAT YOU ACTUALLY HAVE TO WORK WITH

> "In crisis, your brain will tell you that you have nothing left. Your task is to prove your brain wrong with concrete evidence."

Within the first 24 hours of a crisis, conduct a complete inventory of what resources you actually have available:

1. Financial resources: Exact cash on hand, available credit, assets that could be liquidated quickly
2. Social resources: Who specifically could help (make a literal list with names), what they could provide
3. Physical resources: Your current health status, energy levels, essential supplies, medications
4. Knowledge resources: Information, skills, and expertise you have that apply to this situation
5. Time resources: Realistic assessment of deadlines and how long you can sustain emergency mode

Don't just think "I have some money"—write down "$437 in checking, $1,200 in savings, $2,800 available credit." Don't just think "I have some friends"—write down "Sarah (emotional support, spare bedroom for 2 weeks), Miguel (professional connections, good for job leads)." This concrete inventory transforms vague anxiety into strategic awareness of what you can actually deploy.

When my relationship imploded during the writing of this book, my first thought was "I can't possibly finish this project now." Then I did a resource assessment and realized I had: 17 days before my next deadline, 3 friends who could provide emotional support, 2 colleagues who could review drafts, and enough savings to take 4 days completely off to regroup. Suddenly, the impossible seemed manageable again.

MANAGING YOUR EMOTIONS IN CRISIS: STRENGTHENING YOUR EMOTIONAL SKILLS

> "The emotional strength you built in Chapter 3 is about to face its ultimate test."

The emotional skills you learned in Chapter 3 become even more important during a crisis. These same techniques that help you handle everyday challenges become essential when facing disasters, but you'll need to adapt them for emergency situations:

Name Your Feelings Clearly: Be very specific about what you're feeling. Instead of just "I'm scared," try "I'm feeling worried about money uncertainty and sad about missed opportunities."

Sort Your Thoughts: Divide your thoughts into three simple groups: "Helpful Right Now," "Helpful Later," or "Not Helpful."

Quick Reset Methods: Use stronger versions of your calming techniques. The simple 4-count breathing becomes deeper 4-7-8 breathing. A quick 30-second cold splash becomes a longer 60-90 second cold exposure.

PART 4: PREPARING BEFORE DISASTER STRIKES

THE CRISIS PREVENTION SYSTEM: DISASTER-PROOFING YOUR LIFE

> "The best time to prepare for a crisis is before it happens. The second-best time is now."

Complete this assessment to identify your most likely crisis points:

THE VULNERABILITY CHECK

1. **Financial Safety Net:** How many months could you survive if all income stopped? How many income sources do you have?
2. **Relationship Support:** How diverse is your support network? Which relationships would be most disruptive if they ended?
3. **Health Protection:** What symptoms have you been ignoring? Do you have health insurance and access to care?

After completing this check, identify your three highest vulnerability areas and create specific prevention plans for each.

THE PREVENTION PLAN

1. **Financial Buffer:** Build an emergency fund covering 3-6 months of essential expenses.
2. **Relationship Network:** Develop a diverse support network.
3. **Health Baseline:** Document your normal health patterns.
4. **Skills Variety:** Develop capabilities across multiple areas.
5. **Emotional Readiness:** Regularly practice calming techniques.

I - IMMEDIATE STABILIZATION FIRST: STOP THE BLEEDING BEFORE HEALING THE WOUND

> "Your brain wants to solve everything at once. This is how people die in wilderness survival situations—trying to find civilization before securing water."

Your brain wants to solve everything at once. Don't listen to that voice.

Instead, focus on stabilization in this specific order:

1. Physical stabilization: First ensure basic safety, then attend to immediate physical needs (sleep, food, medication).
2. Financial stabilization: Prevent further bleeding before fixing the whole system. Make minimum payments to avoid late fees. Request hardship extensions. Pause subscriptions.
3. Emotional stabilization: Create temporary containment, not complete healing. Short meditations, basic breathing exercises, physical movement.
4. Social stabilization: Maintain key relationships with minimal updates. Send brief, factual messages to essential people.

Treat this like emergency medicine: stop the bleeding first, worry about long-term healing later. The most common crisis mistake is trying to solve everything simultaneously, which guarantees solving nothing effectively. Focus exclusively on stabilization actions for the first 24-72 hours.

S - STRATEGIC PRIORITIZATION: WHICH FIRES TO PUT OUT FIRST

> "Crisis creates the illusion that everything is equally urgent. The master crisis navigator knows this is never true."

Not all problems are created equal. Your emotional brain can't tell the difference between "I might lose my apartment" and "My ex posted a vague status that might be about me." This is why you need a rational prioritization system.

Rank your issues by:

1. Survival impact: What directly threatens your basic needs (housing, food, critical health issues).
2. Cascade potential: Which problems will trigger new problems if left unaddressed.
3. Recovery foundation: Which solutions create a platform for solving other problems.
4. Time sensitivity: What genuinely can't wait versus what just feels urgent.

Create a physical list and literally number your priorities from 1-10. Your emotional brain will constantly try to reprioritize based on what's causing the most pain in the moment.

The key is understanding cascade effects—how problems interact and amplify each other. When facing simultaneous crises, addressing sleep deprivation first might create the mental clarity needed to handle financial negotiations, which then reduces relationship tension.

I - INFORMATION MANAGEMENT: CONTROLLING THE SIGNAL-TO-NOISE RATIO

> "In crisis, information isn't just power—it's also weight. Gather what you need to carry, leave behind what will sink you."

During crisis, your relationship with information becomes critical:

1. Quality input: Seek information from reliable sources directly relevant to your situation.

2. Strategic sharing: Decide what information goes to which people on a need-to-know basis.
3. Documentation: Keep records of important conversations, agreements, and decisions.
4. Reduction: Actively cut information streams that aren't helping. Your mental bandwidth is your most precious resource during crisis.

Create specific times for information gathering rather than constant checking. Set aside 30 minutes twice daily to update information, then focus on action between those times.

CRISIS-SPECIFIC RESPONSE PROTOCOLS

"Different disasters require different responses, even while following the same core principles."

While the C.R.I.S.I.S. Framework applies universally, specific crisis types benefit from tailored approaches:

CORE CRISIS PROTOCOL

1. Information Management: Document everything relevant to your situation.
2. Resource Assessment: Identify what you have available to work with.
3. Immediate Action Plan: Focus on stabilization first.

CRISIS-SPECIFIC ADAPTATIONS

For Relationship Crises: - Create immediate emotional boundaries - Document agreements about practical matters - Identify supportive friends who will help you navigate the transition

For Family Crises: - Establish clear communication channels - Define what information gets shared with which family members - Create specific boundaries around holidays and shared obligations

For Health Crises: - Bring a support person to appointments - Create a simple medical journal with dates and recommendations - Identify activities that need modification

For Financial Crises: - Immediately freeze non-essential spending and contact creditors - Create a survival budget focused only on essentials - Identify your fastest path to income replacement

For Career Crises: - Develop a clear explanation of your situation for networking - Document your accomplishments and secure references - Identify which skills can transfer to new opportunities

S - SUPPORT SYSTEM ACTIVATION: CALLING IN YOUR REINFORCEMENTS

> "The hero who tries to carry every weight alone isn't heroic—they're tactically incompetent."

The instinct during crisis is often to isolate. "I don't want to burden anyone." This is your ego talking, not your strategic mind. The most effective crisis responders coordinate teams:

1. The inner circle: Identify 2-3 people who can handle your unfiltered reality.
2. The specialist network: People with specific expertise for specific problems.
3. The practical helpers: People who can handle concrete tasks while you manage the big picture.
4. The distraction team: People who help you temporarily disconnect from the crisis.

Be explicit about what you need from each person. "I need to vent for 15 minutes without any solutions offered" is infinitely more useful than vague statements like "I'm really struggling."

PART 5: THE 72-HOUR SURVIVAL PROTOCOL

The 72-Hour Emergency Response Plan

"The first 72 hours of a crisis are like the opening moves in chess—they don't guarantee victory, but they can definitely guarantee defeat if you play them wrong."

The first three days of a major crisis determine much of the trajectory:

Hours 0-24: Damage Control - Immediate Safety First: Ensure physical safety before anything else. - Financial Triage: Stop the bleeding. Freeze credit cards, call creditors. - Communication Containment: Limit updates to 3-5 essential people. - Physiological Stabilization: Schedule one 4-hour sleep block and protein-rich meals. - Decision Minimization: Focus only on truly time-sensitive issues.

Hours 24-48: Strategic Assessment - Situation Documentation: Record what happened and actions taken. - Resource Inventory: Assess what you have to work with. - Problem Prioritization: Rank issues by impact, cascade potential, and time sensitivity. - Action Planning: Identify three specific next actions for each priority. - Routine Establishment: Create structure with specific sleep/wake times.

Hours 48-72: Stabilization Launch - Priority Action Implementation: Execute the first concrete action for each priority. - Extended Planning: Create a 7-day plan with contingencies. - Self-Care Integration: Reestablish basic hygiene and physical movement. - Boundary Setting: Establish times when crisis will not be discussed.

The key is creating structure within chaos. Treat crisis management like a job with scheduled shifts, specific tasks, and mandatory rest periods.

PART 6: TRANSITIONING FROM CRISIS TO COLLAPSE

When Crisis Evolves to Something Bigger

> "Sometimes what starts as a manageable crisis can evolve into something more profound."

When your relationship ends the same week you lose your housing and discover a health issue, you've moved from crisis to collapse. If things escalate from a single crisis to multiple simultaneous disasters, flip to Chapter 12 immediately. Different level of hell, different survival guide.

How Your Mind Works in a Crisis

> "Your mind during a crisis is like having superhero strength but no control—incredibly powerful but potentially destructive unless you learn how to direct it."

When you're hit with multiple crises at once, your mind goes into protection mode. To work with this natural response instead of fighting it:

- **Body Signals:** Recognize that stress symptoms like racing heart or tight chest are normal reactions.
- **Clear Thinking:** Follow simple steps that help you think clearly despite strong emotions.
- **Focus Control:** Deliberately direct your attention to solutions instead of threats.
- **Information Sorting:** Only take in information that helps you take action.
- **Basic Needs First:** Take care of sleep, food, and safety before tackling complex problems.

The FIRST THINGS FIRST Approach: What to Handle When

When facing multiple problems at once, tackle them in this order:

- **Immediate Safety:** Address anything threatening your physical safety or health first.
- **Worsening Problems:** Focus on issues that are actively getting worse without attention.
- **Permanent Damage:** Prioritize problems that could cause lasting harm over temporary ones.
- **Resource-Creating Solutions:** Solve problems that will give you tools to fix other issues.
- **Bottleneck Issues:** Address problems that are blocking progress in multiple areas.
- **Time-Limited Opportunities:** Capture chances that will disappear if not taken quickly.

The Three Levels of Crisis Response

To effectively handle a disaster, work through these levels in order:

Level	What to Focus On	When	How to Approach It
Immediate Issues	Urgent threats	First 72 hours	Stop the damage, stabilize
Underlying Problems	Root issues	1-4 weeks	Fix broken systems
Prevention	Future protection	1-6 months	Make lasting changes

In the first 72 hours, spend 80% of your energy on immediate issues, 15% on understanding underlying problems, and just 5% on thinking about prevention.

The Rebuilding Process: From Crisis to Strength

When rebuilding after a crisis:

- **Accept Reality:** Honestly acknowledge what you've lost for good.
- **Take Inventory:** Identify what resources and strengths you still have.
- **Create a Plan:** Design something better than what was destroyed.
- **Build Strong Foundations:** Address weaknesses that contributed to the crisis.
- **Start Small:** Rebuild in manageable steps you can test along the way.
- **Use New Wisdom:** Apply what the crisis taught you.
- **Build in Protection:** Create safeguards against future problems.

The Crisis Communication Strategy

> "During a crisis, your words are either a fire extinguisher or gasoline—there's no neutral communication when everything's burning."

When sharing information during disaster:

- **Situation Clarity:** Provide objective facts without catastrophizing.
- **Help Requests:** Make specific, actionable asks rather than general pleas.
- **Audience Appropriateness:** Tailor disclosure levels to different relationships.
- **Regular Updates:** Establish predictable communication schedules.
- **Emotional Management:** Balance honesty with appropriate containment.

PART 7: BECOMING A DISASTER DANCER

YOUR FUTURE DISASTERS AWAIT

> "The question isn't whether you'll face future disasters—it's whether you'll be greeting them as familiar dance partners or fighting them as terrifying strangers."

Total meltdowns aren't your enemy - they're your most demanding teacher. Your only choice is whether to use them to become stronger or let them keep knocking you down.

The Disaster Relationship Spectrum:

1. **Disaster Victim:** Views catastrophes as unfair personal attacks; remains perpetually shocked and unprepared
2. **Disaster Survivor:** Endures crises through determination but emerges exhausted and depleted
3. **Disaster Navigator:** Has basic systems to handle common problems but struggles with multiple crises
4. **Disaster Dancer:** Maintains sophisticated response protocols and extracts value from every catastrophe
5. **Disaster Alchemist:** Transforms crisis into opportunity so effectively that previous disasters become foundation for success

Stop trying to avoid disasters and start learning to dance with them. Stop hoping for easier times and start becoming someone who thrives in difficult ones.

> "Disaster doesn't determine your destiny—it reveals your resilience."

Chapter 11 Key Takeaways

- Preparation: Disasters are inevitable; your response systems determine their impact
- Integration: Combine skills from all previous chapters into a unified crisis response
- Prioritization: Focus on the right problems in the right sequence, not all problems at once
- Opportunity: Look for hidden openings that only become possible through destruction
- Resilience: Build systems that bend without breaking through multiple crises

Now that you've learned how to navigate crises, you're ready to tackle an even greater challenge: what to do when everything completely collapses. That's exactly what we'll cover next.

CHAPTER 12: WHEN EVERYTHING GOES TO HELL - YOUR SURVIVAL GUIDE FOR TOTAL LIFE COLLAPSE

"ROCK BOTTOM HAS BUILT MORE HEROES THAN PRIVILEGE EVER COULD."

PART 1: WELCOME TO ROCK BOTTOM

WELCOME TO ROCK BOTTOM: WHEN YOUR ENTIRE LIFE EXPLODES

> "When people say 'it can't get any worse,' the universe says 'hold my beer' and then proceeds to show you exactly how creative it can get with your personal apocalypse."

If Chapter 11 was about dancing with disaster, this chapter is about what happens when the whole damn dance floor collapses beneath your feet. This isn't about a bad day or even a difficult month. This is about total life implosion—when everything goes wrong simultaneously, with a level of coordination that would be impressive if it wasn't happening to you.

We're talking about multiple critical life domains imploding at once, creating a perfect storm that overwhelms any single crisis management system. The emotional backbone you built in Chapter 3 is bent to the breaking point. The fairness reality check from Chapter 4 becomes your lifeline when life seems brutally unfair. And those relationship detox principles from Chapter 10 become essential when you discover who actually sticks around when your life turns into a five-alarm dumpster fire.

WHY THIS MATTERS: Complete collapse isn't just some hypothetical worst-case scenario—it's a statistical certainty for most of us. About 75% of people will experience at least one period where their entire life implodes. How you respond during these periods will determine your future more than almost anything else you'll ever do.

REALITY CHECK: Complete collapse isn't just a worse version of a bad day—it's a completely different beast. When multiple crucial parts of your life crash simultaneously, you're in a psychological and practical nightmare zone that most Instagram advice posts don't address. "Just think positive!" Yeah, right. Tell that to someone who just lost their job, home, and health in the same week.

YOU'RE OFFICIALLY AT ROCK BOTTOM WHEN: - Multiple major life areas (health, relationships, career, finances) are simultaneously in crisis - Your normal coping mechanisms are completely overwhelmed - You've lost access to support systems you would typically rely on - Your fundamental sense of identity and security has been shattered - You find yourself thinking "I don't even recognize my life anymore" - Getting out of bed feels like an Olympic-level achievement

PART 2: THE COLLAPSE ADVANTAGE

THE HIDDEN OPPORTUNITY IN TOTAL DISASTER: FREEDOM IN THE RUINS

Here's where most people completely miss what total collapses actually offer: unprecedented opportunity for transformation. This isn't toxic positivity—complete collapse is painful and unfair.

But here's the brutal truth: when everything's gone, you're suddenly free of obligations, expectations, and commitments that were limiting you. When your identity has been shattered, you get to decide which pieces to keep and which to leave behind. When your old life has burned to the ground, you don't have to renovate—you get to build something entirely new.

It's like the difference between renovating a house while living in it versus having it burn down and getting to design something entirely new. The first option keeps you constrained by existing walls and systems. The second option, while traumatic, gives you a blank slate.

My friend marriage ended after 5 years, taking their social circle, financial stability, and sense of identity with it. In the aftermath, they realized they'd been living her ex's dream life in a city they hated, with friends they merely tolerated, pursuing a career that had been their exes suggestion. Two years later,they live in a different state, have a completely different career, and say they're happier than they ever thought possible—not despite the collapse, but because of what it made possible.

The disaster provides the fire; you decide whether it destroys you or forges you. Many people find that their lives, years after rock bottom, become unrecognizable compared to what existed before—and often immeasurably better. Not because the collapse was good, but because it forced complete reconstruction that addressed fundamental flaws in their previous life structure.

WHEN YOU LOSE EVERYTHING, YOU ALSO LOSE: - The obligation to maintain appearances and impress people you don't even like - The inertia of "that's how I've always done it" that keeps you stuck in patterns that don't serve you - The weight of other people's expectations about who you should be - The pressure to continue down paths that weren't working but were too established to abandon

THE COLLAPSE ASSESSMENT PROTOCOL: FINDING FREEDOM IN THE RUINS

When you're standing in the smoking ruins of your life, try this practical exercise:

1. The Clean Slate Inventory: List the constraints that have disappeared from your life because of this collapse. Be

specific: "Need to maintain status in legal community," "Obligation to attend weekly family dinners I hated." Then write down what each vanished constraint now makes possible.

2. The Freedom Identification Process: For each constraint that's gone, ask: "What does this specifically allow me to do differently now?" Push for concrete specifics.

3. The Liberation Action Plan: Select three possibilities that create the most energy when you think about them. For each one, define one small, concrete action you could take within the next week.

PART 3: SURVIVAL PROTOCOL

THE ROCK BOTTOM REFRAME: TURNING DISASTER INTO OPPORTUNITY

When you're standing in the smoking ruins of your life, the last thing you want to hear is motivational bullshit about silver linings. But here's a practical exercise that acknowledges the pain while identifying genuine opportunities:

1. List the three most significant losses from your current situation.

2. For each loss, identify:
   - What limitations also disappeared with this loss
   - What possibilities now exist that didn't before
   - What would have been impossible to change without this collapse

3. Write down one freedom that's now available that wasn't before.

4. Identify one specific action you can take today that would have been impossible in your previous life.

This isn't about denying pain—it's about recognizing that catastrophic change creates degrees of freedom that stable periods don't offer. The opportunity isn't despite the collapse; it's because of it.

The loss of a business can free you from an industry you've grown to dislike but felt too invested to leave. The end of a marriage might remove relationship dynamics that had subtly limited personal growth for years. A health crisis often forces prioritizing well-being in ways that had always been postponed.

Crisis Response Choices: Decision Points That Determine Destiny

> "Your life trajectory isn't determined by what happens to you—it's determined by the micro-decisions you make while standing in the middle of the wreckage."

What separates those who are destroyed by disaster from those who use it as rocket fuel isn't luck or resources—it's the specific choices they make at key inflection points during the crisis.

Decision Point	Downward Spiral Response	Transformation Response
Initial Reaction	Denial, numbing, avoidance	Acknowledgment without catastrophizing
Responsibility Orientation	Blame external factors exclusively	Accept what you can influence while recognizing external factors
Resource Focus	Fixate on what's been lost	Inventory and leverage what remains

Decision Point	Downward Spiral Response	Transformation Response
Meaning Making	"Why me?" victimhood narrative	"What now?" opportunity narrative
Support Approach	Isolate or become completely dependent	Strategic activation of different support types
Action Orientation	Wait for feeling better before acting	Take small actions despite emotional state
Identity Relationship	Cling to pre-disaster identity	Allow identity evolution through challenge

These decision points aren't obvious when you're in the middle of chaos. They often look like small, seemingly inconsequential choices that end up having compound effects on your trajectory out of hell.

Key Turning Points in Recovery

When facing complete collapse, these decision points shape how you recover:

Face It or Escape It: Whether you confront reality or try to escape through denial or numbing.

The better path includes a third option beyond just fighting or running away—caring for yourself while connecting with others. This means acknowledging what happened while also taking care of your needs and reaching out for support.

Take Charge or Blame Others: Whether you take responsibility for rebuilding or get stuck blaming everyone else.

The better path requires taking responsibility for your response regardless of what caused the situation. It's saying, "I d dn't cause all of this, AND I'm 100% responsible for what I do next."

Use What You Have or Focus on What's Gone: Whether you work with available resources or get stuck thinking about what you've lost.

The better path means finding creative ways to make progress with whatever you have left, rather than waiting for perfect conditions.

Grow Through Grief or Get Stuck In It: Whether you process loss while moving forward or let it define your entire future.

The better path involves finding meaning in difficult experiences and incorporating them into your life story without letting them become your whole identity.

PART 4: PSYCHOLOGICAL TRIAGE

Chaos Clarity: The Unexpected Gift of Crisis

> "Nothing declutters your priorities quite like a catastrophe. Suddenly, your 37-item to-do list gets real simple: survive today, figure out tomorrow, everything else can wait."

One of the most counterintuitive aspects of total collapse: it often creates a clarity and focus that normal life obscures. When everything is falling apart, you suddenly gain crystal clear insight into what actually matters—and what doesn't.

Under extreme pressure, the brain's threat response narrows attention in ways that can be beneficial—eliminating distractions and bringing core priorities into sharp relief. The noise of normal life disappears when you're fighting for survival. Relationships reveal their true nature—some people disappear when things get tough, while others show up in ways you never expected.

Finding Clarity in Chaos

To use the unexpected insights that emerge during a crisis:

What Really Matters: Identify what still matters when everything else is gone. The parent who loses everything but focuses first on keeping their children stable discovers that family truly is their deepest value.

True Priorities: Recognize what you actually care about versus what you thought you did. The executive who believed career achievement was everything until illness made work impossible discovers that relationships and making a difference matter more than titles or money.

Real Relationships: See clearly who stands with you when things get tough. Crisis instantly shows who's there for what you provide versus who's there for you as a person.

Hidden Strengths: Discover what resources and abilities remained when everything else disappeared. Crisis shows which of your strengths are truly reliable versus which depended on good circumstances.

Seeing Through Illusions: Recognize which parts of your former life weren't as solid as they seemed. Crisis strips away false ideas about what was giving you security, meaning, or value.

These insights aren't just nice thoughts—they're practical tools for rebuilding. They show you what's solid enough to build upon and what was never strong to begin with.

PART 5: THE 90-DAY REBUILDING SYSTEM

The Sanity Preservation System: Maintaining Mental Health in Crisis

> "During a crisis, your mental health isn't a luxury or 'self-care'—it's your survival equipment. You wouldn't climb Everest without oxygen; don't navigate catastrophe without psychological tools."

When everything collapses, your mental health will be the first thing you sacrifice and the last thing you can afford to lose. Your brain is the primary tool you need to navigate crisis—and it's precisely when you need it most that it becomes most vulnerable to breakdown.

Simple Steps to Stay Stable

The 5-5-5 Calming Method: When you feel overwhelmed, breathe in for 5 seconds, hold for 5 seconds, exhale for 5 seconds (repeat 5 times). Then name 5 things you can see, 4 you can touch, 3 you can hear, 2 you can smell, 1 you can taste. Finally, physically move to a different spot.

This isn't fancy meditation—it's a simple reset that helps your body shift from panic to a calmer state.

The Bare Minimum Plan: Create non-negotiable basics for sleep, food, movement, and human connection. It's better to do small things consistently than attempt perfect self-care and fail.

The Step-by-Step Approach: First fix physical needs (sleep, panic symptoms), then manage negative thinking, and only then process deeper feelings. This order works with how your mind naturally stabilizes.

Protecting Your Mental Health

Daily Basics: Establish simple self-care that happens no matter what. Create minimum standards that aren't optional.

Information Control: Limit exposure to negative news and catastrophic thinking. This isn't denial—it's protecting your mind when it's already stressed.

Regular Reset Activities: Use simple techniques like deep breathing, cold water exposure, physical movement, and focusing on your senses to calm your body.

Scheduled Worry Time: Contain your worrying to specific times—15-30 minutes daily when you write down concerns and possible next steps.

The R.E.B.U.I.L.D. Framework: Strategic Reconstruction

> "Most people rebuild their lives like they're following IKEA instructions—rushing to recreate what they had before, missing crucial steps, and wondering why it keeps collapsing."

The key to rebuilding isn't just about recovery—it's about strategic reconstruction. You don't just rebuild the same vulnerable structures; you design something stronger, more flexible, and better suited to reality.

R - Reality Acceptance: Fully acknowledge what's been permanently lost. This isn't being negative—it's refusing to build on foundations that no longer exist.

E - Evaluation of Remains: Honestly assess what's still usable. What skills, relationships, and aspects of your identity remained intact?

B - Blueprint Creation: Design new structures better than the originals, specifically designed to withstand the exact disasters that just leveled your life.

U - Underlying Reinforcement: Address the root vulnerabilities that made the collapse so devastating.

I - Incremental Construction: Build in small, testable phases Test how it goes before adding the next component.

L - Leverage New Knowledge: Apply specific insights from how your previous systems failed.

D - Disaster-Proofing: Create built-in resilience for future crises

The 90-Day Collapse Recovery System

When everything has fallen apart, you need a structured approach to rebuilding:

Days 1-30: Survival Phase 1. Secure temporary shelter 2. Establish emergency income source 3. Create basic health maintenance routine 4. Identify and activate minimal social support 5. Implement basic psychological stabilization

Days 31-60: Stabilization Phase 1. Establish a consistent daily routine 2. Consolidate and organize remaining resources 3. Perform relationship triage 4. Create preliminary future plans 5. Begin addressing secondary needs

Days 61-90: Rebuilding Phase 1. Conduct opportunity assessment 2. Identify and develop key skills for your next chapter 3. Build strategic relationships 4. Begin identity reconstruction 5. Create longer-term vision and implementation plan PART 6: IDENTITY RECONSTRUCTION

THE PHOENIX PRINCIPLES: TRANSFORMATION BORN FROM DISASTER

The Phoenix Principles build directly on the emotional backbone you developed in Chapter 3 and the fairness reality check from Chapter 4. When everything collapses, these foundational skills become your most critical assets.

"Anyone can fall apart during a disaster—that's just gravity. The remarkable ones aren't those who avoid falling; they're the ones who figure out how to use the impact as a springboard."

What separates those who emerge from disaster stronger from those who remain victims of it? It's not circumstances, resources, or luck—it's the specific principles they apply to their rebuilding process.

The Phoenix Principle Matrix

Principle	Victim Approach	Phoenix Approach
Identity Relationship	Defines self by what was lost	Creates new identity from what remains
Timeline Perspective	Views collapse as the end	Views collapse as painful transition
Agency Orientation	Focuses on what can't be controlled	Maximizes impact in controllable areas
Resource Approach	Fixates on insufficient resources	Leverages whatever resources remain
Learning Integration	Avoids painful lessons	Extracts wisdom from suffering
Support Utilization	Isolation or total dependence	Strategic, reciprocal support

The Phoenix approach isn't about positive thinking—it's about practical action patterns that create forward momentum even in devastating circumstances.

To systematically apply these principles:

1. Identity Reconstruction: Deliberately choose which aspects of your previous identity to keep, which to discard, and which new elements to incorporate. After my friend's business failed, he realized being "a successful CEO" was less important to his core identity than being "a creative problem-solver"—a quality that remained intact despite the collapse.

2. Timeline Extension: Create a "Third Year Vision" document describing life three years after collapse. My cousin who lost everything in a divorce couldn't imagine next week, but writing about where she wanted to be in three years gave her direction when immediate hope was scarce.

3. Agency Maximization: Focus on what you can control, no matter how small. When my friend was diagnosed with a serious illness, he couldn't control the disease, but he could control his treatment research, nutrition, and daily routine—creating islands of influence in a sea of uncertainty.

    "The disaster provides the fire; you decide whether it destroys you or forges you."

REBUILDING YOUR SENSE OF SELF

When everything falls apart, your sense of who you are often collapses too. Here's how to thoughtfully rebuild your identity instead of desperately clinging to who you were:

TAKING INVENTORY OF YOUR IDENTITY

Before rebuilding your sense of self, look at what parts of your old identity were actually helpful:

1. Situation-Based Labels: Which parts of how you saw yourself were based on circumstances that have now

changed? ("Successful executive," "Homeowner," "Married person")
2. Problem-Causing Patterns: Which aspects of how you defined yourself may have actually contributed to your problems? ("Workaholic," "People-pleaser," "Always playing it safe")
3. Lasting Core Qualities: Which parts of who you are remained intact despite everything else falling apart? ("Problem-solver," "Creative thinker," "Loyal friend")

FINDING YOUR DEEPEST VALUES

To identify what matters most to you, even when everything else is gone:

1. List what you fought hardest to protect during the collapse
2. Notice which losses hurt the most deeply (beyond practical problems)
3. Identify what activities still feel meaningful even in terrible circumstances
4. Recognize what principles you refused to compromise despite pressure

These answers reveal your core values—the foundation for your new sense of self.

FOUR BUILDING BLOCKS FOR A STRONGER IDENTITY

Your rebuilt sense of self should include:

1. Core Values: The principles that guide your important decisions
2. Portable Strengths: Abilities you can use in any situation
3. Hard-Earned Wisdom: Insights from difficult experiences that shape your outlook
4. Future Direction: Who you're becoming rather than just who you've been

The Phoenix Perspective Shift

1. Identify what aspect of the collapse still feels most devastating
2. For this aspect, write answers from both perspectives:

Victim Perspective:

- Why this makes recovery impossible
- What options have been permanently closed
- Why this defines the future

Phoenix Perspective:

- What remains possible despite this loss
- What new directions this might open
- How this could eventually strengthen you

3. From the Phoenix perspective, identify one small action to take within 24 hours
4. Implement this action regardless of your emotional state

This exercise isn't about denying reality—it's about practicing a perspective that creates possibilities rather than limitations, while acknowledging the genuine pain of the circumstances.

PART 7: THE PHOENIX PRINCIPLES

Most people oscillate between victim and phoenix perspectives without clearly distinguishing them. By explicitly articulating both viewpoints side by side, you create clarity about their different implications. The immediate action step converts insight into evidence—showing that alternative perspectives create alternative possibilities. The Rock Bottom Hero's Journey

> "Recovery from disaster isn't random chaos—it's more like puberty. It feels uniquely horrible while you're going through it, but it actually follows predictable stages that millions have navigated before you."

The journey from catastrophe to growth follows a predictable pattern. Understanding this pattern provides a map through the darkest territory and helps you recognize where you are in the process.

The Rock Bottom Recovery Sequence

The Impact Stage (1-14 days): Initial shock and survival mode. Focus on basic stabilization and preventing further damage. Your brain isn't designed for long-term planning during this phase.

The Reality Integration Stage (2-8 weeks): Acceptance of the new situation. Process grief while taking necessary action. Focus on accurate assessment of what remains and what's gone.

The Strategic Assessment Stage (1-3 months): Evaluating options in the new reality. Balance immediate needs with long-term planning. Your brain is shifting from crisis response to strategic thinking.

The Rebuilding Foundation Stage (3-12 months): Creating basic structures. Maintain patience with slow progress. Focus on building systems that support long-term recovery.

The Growth Integration Stage (6-24 months): Finding meaning and purpose. Integrate the experience into your identity without being defined by it.

From Rebuilding to Reinvention

As you emerge from the ashes of complete collapse, you face a unique opportunity. You're not just rebuilding your old life— you're creating an entirely new one. The question isn't "How do I get back to normal?" but rather "What kind of extraordinary life do I want to create now?"

How you respond to complete collapse reveals more about you than all your achievements in comfortable times. Disaster doesn't just test you—it defines you.

This doesn't mean collapse is a gift—it's a crucible. It's painful, unwanted, and often unfair. But it creates conditions that nothing else can. It forces growth that would never happen voluntarily.

Many people find that their lives, years after rock bottom, become unrecognizable compared to what existed before—and often immeasurably better. Not because the collapse was good, but because it forced complete reconstruction that addressed fundamental flaws in their previous life structure.

The most powerful reframe isn't seeing disaster as good—it's seeing it as potentially useful. While no one chooses collapse, everyone can choose what to build from its ashes. Any breaking point can become a making point.

"Rock bottom isn't a destination—it's a launching pad."

Stop waiting for rescue from your personal hell and start building a way out. The path from devastation to transformation isn't found—it's built, one small, unglamorous, difficult decision at a time.

Chapter 12 Key Takeaways

- Opportunity: Complete collapse creates unique conditions for transformation that stable periods cannot
- Decision Points: Small choices during crisis create compound effects that determine your trajectory
- Mental Preservation: Psychological stability is your most critical asset during collapse
- Strategic Rebuilding: How you rebuild matters more than how quickly you rebuild
- Phoenix Principles: Specific approaches transform disaster from an ending into a beginning

Now that you've learned how to rebuild from complete collapse, you're ready to focus on systematically leveling up every area of your life—which is exactly what we'll cover next.

CHAPTER 13: LEVELING UP YOUR LIFE - THE NO-BS GUIDE TO ACTUALLY GETTING BETTER

"YOUR COMFORT ZONE IS WHERE DREAMS GO TO DIE PEACEFULLY IN THEIR SLEEP."

PART 1: THE STAGNATION EPIDEMIC

The rebuilding skills you developed in the previous chapter provide the foundation for what comes next: systematically leveling up every area of your life.

THE BRUTAL TRUTH ABOUT REAL IMPROVEMENT

Congratulations on making it this far. If you've been applying what you've learned in previous chapters, you've already done more than most people ever will. You've stopped wasting energy on useless bitching (Chapter 1), gotten honest with yourself about your own bullshit (Chapter 2), developed the emotional backbone to handle life's punches (Chapter 3), accepted that life isn't a fairness contest (Chapter 4), and started playing the long game (Chapter 5).

You've learned to play the long game in Chapter 5. Now let's focus on how to accelerate your progress within that long-term framework. The L.E.V.E.L. U.P. framework builds directly on the long-game thinking you developed in Chapter 5. While Chapter 5 taught you to resist short-term temptations, this framework shows you how to accelerate progress within that long-term perspective. This chapter isn't about waiting for results—it's about engineering rapid growth in specific areas of your life through purposeful progression.

Now it's time to take all that groundwork and turn it into something that will systematically transform every part of your life that matters. This isn't about random self-improvement tips—it's about building a complete operating system for continuous growth that actually works with your brain instead of against it.

WHY THIS MATTERS: Let's get real about the numbers, because they're brutal: 92% of New Year's resolutions crash and burn. 88% of people who set improvement goals abandon them before February even ends. The average person makes the same damn improvement commitment 4-6 times before either finally succeeding or giving up entirely.

This isn't because people don't want to change—it's because they're using approaches that are fundamentally broken from the start. They're trying to use motivation to solve a systems problem. It's like trying to fix a broken engine by painting the car—it might look better for a while, but you're still not going anywhere.

The difference between people who actually transform versus those who temporarily change isn't about motivation or information—it's about having a system that works with your brain's actual wiring instead of fighting against it. This chapter gives you that system, turning vague notions of "getting better" into a concrete protocol that actually works in real life, not just in Instagram captions.

TRUTH BOMB: Most people don't actually want to improve—they want to have already improved. They want the results without the uncomfortable process, the transformation without the discomfort, the highlight reel without the blooper footage. They'll buy books (maybe even this one), download apps, follow influencers, and talk endlessly about their "personal growth journey"—while systematically avoiding what actually creates change: consistently doing hard, uncomfortable work when nobody's watching and no external validation is coming.

While writing this book, I had to face this reality myself. I wanted to have written a book more than I wanted to write one. I wanted the end result without the daily grind of putting words on the page when I didn't feel inspired, when no one was cheering me on, when there was no immediate reward. The only thing that got me through was building systems that didn't rely on how I felt on any given day.

Genuine improvement looks nothing like those curated transformation stories you see online. Real growth doesn't come with perfect lighting, inspirational soundtracks, or neat before-and-after photos where someone's smiling in both. It's messy, inconsistent, often boring as hell, and rarely photogenic enough for social media. It's like comparing actual surgery to a medical drama—one involves bodily fluids under harsh fluorescent lighting; the other features attractive people in makeup saying impressive-sounding jargon while looking fabulous. Both are called the same thing, but they have almost nothing in common.

GROWTH VS. PATIENCE: UNDERSTANDING THE DIFFERENCE

Before diving deeper, let's clarify an important distinction. This chapter focuses on something fundamentally different from what we covered in Chapter 5:

Playing the Long Game (Ch 5)	Leveling Up (Ch 13)
Focuses on patience and delayed gratification	Focuses on active growth acceleration and systematic skill building
About resisting short-term temptations	About creating rapid improvement through deliberate systems

Emphasizes waiting for compound effects	Emphasizes engineering compound effects through strategic action
Passive consistency over time	Active optimization of learning and growth
"Good things come to those who wait"	"Good things come to those who optimize their growth systems"

Long-term thinking (Chapter 5) is about delayed gratification and strategic patience. Leveling up (this chapter) is about accelerated improvement and systematic skill building. They're complementary approaches, but they serve different purposes.

For example: - Long-term thinking is saving 20% of your income for 10 years. Leveling up is increasing your income by 20% every two years through strategic skill development. - Long-term thinking is consistently showing up for a relationship over time. Leveling up is deliberately improving your relationship skills to create deeper connection. - Long-term thinking is maintaining a consistent exercise habit. Leveling up is strategically optimizing that exercise for maximum results.

Think of long-term thinking as planting seeds and waiting for them to grow naturally. Leveling up is installing irrigation, adding fertilizer, and using every technique to accelerate growth. Both are necessary, but they're different approaches with different focuses.

This chapter is about growing faster and more strategically, not just waiting patiently for results. It's your systematic improvement headquarters—the definitive guide to leveling up in any area of life.

PART 2: THE COMFORT ZONE CONSPIRACY

THE STAGNATION TRAP: HOW TO TELL IF YOU'VE STOPPED GROWING

REALITY CHECK: Comfort is growth's natural predator. Your brain isn't wired for continuous improvement—it's designed to seek homeostasis, to find comfortable patterns and ock them in place like a squirrel hoarding nuts for winter. That satisfying feeling of "I've got this figured out" isn't mastery; it's your development flatlined on the EKG monitor. The moment your life feels completely manageable is exactly when you've stopped growing.

This isn't about being perpetually miserable or chasing the next shiny object—it's about recognizing that genuine improvement requires regularly venturing beyond what feels easy and familiar. If you can't remember the last time you felt that specific discomfort that comes from pushing boundaries—that "I suck at this but I'm trying anyway" feeling—you're not maintaining your life; you're stagnating in it.

Most people settle into routines that are comfortable but completely stagnant. They confuse not going backward with moving forward. They're treading water in the same spot for years, mistaking motion for progress. It's like walking on a treadmill and thinking you're traveling somewhere because your legs are moving.

THE WARNING SIGNS YOU'RE STUCK IN A GROWTH COMA: - You can predict exactly how your day will go before it starts (down to what you'll eat and think) - You haven't been genuinely challenged or felt incompetent at something in months - You're defending your limitations ("That's just how I am") instead of questioning them - Your goals haven't changed in years (either because you've achieved them or abandoned them) - You immediately resist new ideas with "that wouldn't work for me" before even trying - You can't remember the last time you felt that productive discomfort that signals growth - Your weekends have looked essentially the same for the past year

You've seen this person before—maybe in your mirror. That friend who can predict exactly what their weekends will look like for the next decade. Monday is always this, Tuesday always that. Their routines are comfortable as an old couch, but they aren't leading anywhere new. They're incredibly efficient at living a life that isn't expanding in any meaningful direction.

The most telling sign? They can recite elaborate, well-rehearsed justifications for why certain changes "wouldn't work for them" before even trying. "Oh, I could never do public speaking because I'm naturally introverted." "I can't change careers now because I've already invested so much time in this one." Their limitations haven't just become habits—they've become core parts of their identity, comfortable prison cells they've decorated to feel like home.

HOW TO DIAGNOSE YOUR OWN STAGNATION

To identify whether you're actually growing or just comfortably stagnating, you need to look at your life with the kind of ruthless honesty that makes most people squirm. This isn't about beating yourself up—it's about getting an accurate diagnosis so you can apply the right treatment.

Real growth means being regularly uncomfortable. Not miserable, not anxious, but that specific kind of discomfort that comes from pushing into new territory—like the burn in your muscles during a good workout. If you can't remember the last time you felt that sensation, you're probably stagnating. Growth discomfort has a different quality than anxiety or stress—it feels productive rather than threatening, challenging rather than overwhelming.

Pay attention to how quickly you generate reasons why new approaches "wouldn't work for you." The stagnant mind is an absolute genius at creating instant justifications for avoiding change. "I'm too old to start that." "My situation is different."

"I don't have the right connections/background/resources." The speed of your rejection is usually proportional to how comfortable you've become in your limitations. The faster you say "that wouldn't work for me," the more likely you need exactly that change.

Look at the predictability of your life. Can you already script exactly how next Thursday will go? And the Thursday after that? That's not stability—that's repetition without evolution. It's like watching the same episode of a TV show on loop and calling it a series. Some predictability creates necessary foundation, but when your entire life becomes predictable, you've stopped growing.

The stagnant life feels comfortable day-to-day but weirdly unsatisfying when you zoom out. It's marked by that strange combination of daily contentment and existential disappointment—the feeling that nothing is particularly wrong but nothing is particularly alive either. You're not depressed, but you're not fully engaged with life. You're just... there. Existing rather than becoming.

When I found myself in this trap while writing this book, I realized I could predict exactly what I'd accomplish each day—which meant I wasn't pushing my boundaries at all. I was writing at exactly the level I was already comfortable with. The chapters were fine, but they weren't evolving. I had to deliberately make myself uncomfortable by trying writing approaches I wasn't sure I could pull off. Some failed spectacularly, but the ones that worked took the book to a level I couldn't have reached from within my comfort zone.

PART 3: THE L.E.V.E.L. U.P. SYSTEM

THE L.E.V.E.L. U.P. FRAMEWORK: REAL GROWTH IN A FAKE WORLD

If you want to make actual progress instead of just looking like you are on social media, you need a system that focuses on results rather than appearances. Enter the L.E.V.E.L. U.P. framework—a bullshit-free approach to genuine improvement:

L - Locate Your Current Position: Get brutally honest about where you actually are, not where you pretend to be. When my friend wanted to improve her marriage, she had to admit they hadn't had a real conversation in months, not just that they were "going through a phase." Your starting point isn't "pretty good with some room for improvement"—it's exactly where you are right now, warts and all.

E - Establish Clear Targets: Set specific, measurable outcomes, not vague aspirations. Not "be a better parent" but "have three 20-minute one-on-one conversations with each kid every week" or "reduce yelling episodes by 80%." Vague goals create vague results.

V - Verify Your Metrics: Create concrete measures that can't be faked. My sister claimed she was "eating healthier" for years while her actual diet never changed. Now she tracks specific metrics: vegetables consumed, meals cooked at home, and sugar intake. The data doesn't lie even when you lie to yourself.

E - Engineer Your Environment: Design your surroundings to make improvement the path of least resistance. My friend who wanted to stop checking his phone during family time created phone-free zones in his house and set up auto-replies during dinner hours. Don't rely on willpower when you can change your environment instead.

L - Link Small Actions: Create systems of tiny, sustainable improvements that compound over time. My cousin didn't go from fighting with her teenager daily to perfect harmony overnight. She started with just 60 seconds of genuine listening without interruption, then gradually built up. Start ridiculously small—so small it seems pointless.

U - Understand Your Obstacles: Identify specific barriers that will derail you and create contingency plans for each one. When I committed to daily writing, I knew my biggest threat was evening exhaustion, so I created a morning writing ritual before anything could interfere. Know your specific failure points before they appear.

P - Progress Through Plateaus: Develop strategies for maintaining momentum when results slow and motivation dies. Every relationship improvement hits the "nothing's changing" phase. Every fitness journey includes weeks of no visible progress. These aren't failures—they're normal transition phases before the next breakthrough.

PART 4: THE SKILL ACQUISITION MATRIX

WHY COMFORT ZONES ARE SO HARD TO LEAVE

Your mind isn't trying to sabotage you—it's trying to protect you from what it sees as unnecessary risk. Think of it like having an overprotective parent living inside your head. This inner protector means well, but it treats you like you're still a child who needs to be kept safe from anything unfamiliar.

Or imagine having a watchful guard dog that barks at everything— the mail carrier, squirrels, even your shadow. You don't want to get rid of the dog—its protective instincts are valuable when there's a real threat. You just need to teach it the difference between the delivery person and an actual intruder. Your resistance to new experiences is like that guard dog, currently treating everything unfamiliar as dangerous.

When you try something new or push beyond your comfort zone, your body creates stress feelings that make you uncomfortable and want to retreat to safety. It's not a character flaw or lack of willpower—it's simply how we're wired. Your body is designed to save energy and treat anything unfamiliar as a potential threat. It rewards you with good feelings when you stay in familiar territory and creates stress when you venture outside it.

This was helpful for survival when unfamiliar meant "dangerous predator territory," but it's not helpful for growth today when discomfort rarely means actual danger. Your body doesn't distinguish between the discomfort of facing a wild animal and the discomfort of speaking up in a meeting or trying a new workout. To your instincts, all discomfort feels like "potential threat—avoid this!"

While writing this book, I had to constantly work against my own protective instincts. Every time I tried a new writing approach or tackled a challenging topic, I'd feel that familiar "I don't want to do this" sensation. It wasn't that I was lazy—it was my mind trying to protect me from the perceived risk of failure or criticism.

HOW TO WORK WITH YOUR PROTECTIVE INSTINCTS:

Calm Your System First: Take a few deep breaths before entering uncomfortable situations. This physically helps your body shift from alert mode to a calmer state, making you more open to new experiences. It's like telling your guard dog "it's okay" before a visitor arrives. I use this before every public speaking event—three deep breaths while reminding myself that discomfort doesn't equal danger.

Celebrate Small Steps: Create immediate rewards for pushing past comfort zones. We learn through immediate feedback, not distant results. Even something as simple as acknowledging your effort helps create a positive connection with discomfort.

After doing something challenging, give yourself a smal reward—even if it's just a mental high-five or a check mark in a journal. You need to teach yourself that discomfort can lead to good things.

Connect to Your Why: Link challenges to what truly matters to you. When you understand why you're doing something difficult, it's easier to handle the discomfort. "I'm feeling this discomfort because I'm becoming someone who keeps promises to themselves" is more powerful than "I have to do this because I should." When I struggled with difficult sections of this book, reminding myself why I started writing it—to help people avoid my mistakes—made the discomfort more bearable.

Take Small Steps: Gradually increase challenge levels rather than diving into the deep end. It's like getting into cold water nch by inch instead of jumping in all at once. Each small successful step beyond your comfort zone makes the next one easier. Start with speaking up once in a meeting before trying to lead the whole presentation.

Expect Resistance: Prepare for your natural resistance to new patterns. When you anticipate your protective response, you can recognize it as normal rather than a sign something is wrong. "This discomfort is just my body doing its job" is more helpful than "This discomfort means I should stop." Understanding why you resist change helps remove the self-judgment that often makes discomfort worse.

THE SELF-IMAGE TRAP: HOW YOU LIMIT YOURSELF

Here's where growth gets really challenging: Your sense of who you are is built around your current self, not who you could become. You've created a self-image with specific abilities, limitations, and patterns—and you defend this identity fiercely. Any attempt to change threatens not just what you do, but who you believe you are.

We all create stories about ourselves, and these stories act like protective filters, automatically rejecting behaviors that don't match who we think we are. This happens mostly without you noticing, filtering opportunities based on whether they fit your self-image. It's like having a bouncer at the door of your identity, turning away any experiences that don't match the approved list.

You don't just have habits—you have an identity built around those habits. You don't just lack certain skills—you have stories about "not being that kind of person." When you try to improve in ways that contradict your self-image, you're not just fighting behaviors—you're fighting your entire sense of self. It's like trying to renovate a house that's actively resisting the changes.

This is why people say things like: - "I'm not a morning person" (identity) instead of "I currently sleep in" (behavior) - "I'm terrible with money" (identity) instead of "I haven't learned money management yet" (skill gap) - "I don't have self-discipline" (identity) instead of "I haven't built this specific habit yet" (process) - "I'm just not creative" (identity) instead of "I haven't practiced creative skills" (skill development) - "I'm too old to learn that" (identity) instead of "This feels unfamiliar and uncomfortable" (comfort zone)

These identity labels create more resistance than any outside obstacle. You can overcome external barriers with enough effort, but identity barriers fight you from within. It's like driving with one foot on the gas and one on the brake.

While writing this book, I kept hitting my own identity limits. "I'm not the kind of writer who can finish a book this quickly" was a story I told myself that created more resistance than any actual writing challenge. It wasn't until I shifted to "I'm experimenting with being someone who writes efficiently" that the words started flowing again.

HOW TO BREAK FREE FROM YOUR SELF-IMAGE LIMITS:

The solution isn't just changing your behaviors—it's expanding who you believe you are. This doesn't mean creating a fake self-image; it means adding new possibilities to your current identity. It's like adding rooms to your house rather than moving somewhere else entirely.

Start by noticing how often you use identity statements to explain your behaviors. Listen for phrases like "I'm just not a…" or "I've always been…" or "I could never…" These aren't facts—they're limiting stories you've told yourself so many times you believe they're true.

Then try on new identities without fully committing to them. Instead of saying "I'm going to become a confident person" (which triggers resistance), say "For the next week, I'm going to experiment with acting as if I were already confident." This small change in wording bypasses your defenses because it's just a temporary experiment, not a permanent change. It's like trying on clothes without buying them.

The real change happens when you start collecting evidence that contradicts your limiting beliefs. Each small success creates cracks in your old self-image, gradually making room for a bigger sense of who you are. "I thought I wasn't a public speaker, but I just gave that presentation and survived." "I believed I couldn't learn tech skills, but I just built that simple website." These experiences don't just change what you can do—they change who you believe you are.

Changing your identity isn't about dramatic declarations—it's about gradually gathering evidence that contradicts your limiting beliefs until those beliefs can no longer stand up to reality. It's like water slowly eroding rock—not dramatic, but unstoppable over time.

THE IDENTITY EXPANSION EXPERIMENT: TRY BEFORE YOU BUY

Think about an area where you've limited yourself with identity language—something you've told yourself you "just aren't" or "could never be." Maybe you're "not a technical person" or "not someone who can speak in public" or "not creative" or "bad at math" or "too disorganized to stick to a budget."

Now, instead of trying to force yourself to become that person overnight (which your identity defenses will fight tooth and nail), create a small, specific experiment where you'll temporarily act "as if" you already were that type of person. The key is framing it as an experiment rather than a permanent change—you're not getting married to this identity, you're just going on a first date with it.

For one week, wake up each day and remind yourself: "Today, I'm experimenting with being the kind of person who [does the thing you claim you 'aren't']." Then notice what resistance comes up, how it feels to try on this provisional identity, and what evidence you collect that contradicts your limiting belief. Keep a simple log of what you notice—both the challenges ("felt ridiculous trying to explain that spreadsheet") and the contradictory evidence ("but I actually figured it out without help").

The magic happens around day 4 or 5, when you start noticing that this "pretend" identity feels less foreign than you expected. The awkwardness begins to fade. You catch yourself doing the thing without the same level of internal resistance. By day 7, you'll have collected enough contradictory evidence to at least question your limiting identity, creating space for genuine evolution.

I used this exact approach when I hit a wall with this book. After weeks of struggling with writer's block, I realized I had a deep identity belief that "I'm not the kind of writer who can produce quality work quickly." This identity was creating more resistance than any actual writing challenge. So I ran a one-week experiment: "I'm trying on being the kind of writer who can produce excellent work efficiently." I didn't have to believe it permanently—just try it on temporarily. By day 5, I was writing twice as much with better quality, and the identity of "efficient writer" no longer felt like a costume I was wearing.

The beauty of this approach is that it bypasses your brain's identity defense systems. You're not threatening the existing identity (which would trigger massive resistance); you're just conducting a harmless little experiment. It's like telling your brain, "We're not moving to a new house; we're just taking a quick tour of this other place." No commitment, no threat—just exploration.

PART 5: BREAKING THROUGH PLATEAUS

THE SYSTEMATIC UPGRADE APPROACH: HOW TO ACTUALLY IMPROVE INSTEAD OF JUST TALKING ABOUT IT

Let's break down how real improvement actually works, because most people's approach to self-improvement is about as effective as trying to get in shape by watching workout videos while eating Doritos. They consume endless content about getting better without ever implementing anything consistently. They confuse learning with doing, inspiration with action, and planning with progress.

Real growth isn't about knowing what to do—it's about having a practical, sustainable strategy for actually doing it, even when nobody's watching, even when you don't feel like it, and especially when there's no immediate external validation. It's about showing up on Tuesday afternoon when you're tired and nobody would notice if you skipped it. It's about doing the small, unsexy work that compounds over time but never makes for a good Instagram post.

Think about it like this: Every improvement you want to make needs three things—a clear target, a realistic plan, and a way to make it stick. It's like building a house—you need blueprints, materials, and proper construction techniques. Most people are trying to build their dream life with nothing but Pinterest inspiration and wishful thinking, then wondering why they're still living in an emotional cardboard box with a leaky roof and no foundation.

I see this all the time—people who can talk for hours about their goals, who have beautiful planners and vision boards, who follow all the right influencers and read all the right books, but who haven't actually changed their daily behaviors in any meaningful way. They're confusing the map with the territory, the menu with the meal, the blueprint with the actual house.

FAKE IMPROVEMENT VS. REAL IMPROVEMENT: SPOT THE DIFFERENCE

Fake Improvement	Real Improvement
Posts about goals on social media	Takes concrete actions toward goals daily
Has aesthetic planners and journals that look great in photos	Uses functional systems that look messy but get results
Depends on feeling motivated to take action	Builds habits that happen regardless of motivation
Focuses on identity ("being a runner")	Focuses on process ("running regularly")
Obsesses about results and gets discouraged when they're slow	Orients around process and celebrates consistency

Takes all-or-nothing approaches that inevitably fail	Implements incremental progression that builds over time
Relies on public accountability and external pressure	Develops personal integrity and internal standards
Seeks external validation and praise for efforts	Measures progress against internal benchmarks
Abandons efforts when they become difficult or boring	Persists through difficulty and boredom as part of the process
Jumps from system to system looking for the "perfect" approach	Sticks with imperfect systems long enough for them to work

The fake improver has beautiful journals filled with abandoned plans and a phone full of inspirational quotes. The real improver has ugly, worn notebooks with crossed-off tasks and a life full of actual progress. One looks better in photos; the other actually gets somewhere. One is playing dress-up; the other is playing for keeps.

I've been both people at different points in my life. For years, I was the person with the perfect planner, the latest productivity apps, and absolutely nothing to show for it. I could talk for hours about my goals and plans, but my actual daily behaviors never changed. It wasn't until I stopped trying to look like I was improving and started focusing on actually improving—through messy, imperfect, consistent action—that anything actually changed.

APPLYING THE L.E.V.E.L. U.P. FRAMEWORK TO SPECIFIC DOMAINS

The framework can be applied to any area of life. Here's how it works for career development:

Career Application: - Locate: Assess your current skill level, market value, and growth rate - Establish: Set specific career milestones with dates (e.g., "Lead a major project by Q3") - Verify: Track metrics like skill acquisition rate, network growth, and compensation increases - Engineer: Create a work environment that facilitates focus and learning - Link: Implement daily micro-learning habits (20 minutes of skill development) - Understand: Identify career-specific obstacles like skill gaps or visibility issues - Progress: Develop strategies for common career plateaus like responsibility or compensation ceilings

The same framework can be applied to financial growth, relationships, health, and any other area you want to systematically improve.

For relationships, this might look like: - Locate: Honestly assess your current relationship quality and communication patterns - Establish: Set specific goals like "Have three 20-minute distraction-free conversations per week" - Verify: Track metrics like quality time spent, conflicts resolved constructively, and shared experiences - Engineer: Create phone-free zones and dedicated connection spaces in your home - Link: Start with small daily connection rituals like a 5-minute check-in before bed - Understand: Identify specific triggers that lead to conflict and create response plans - Progress: Recognize when you hit communication plateaus and introduce new approaches

PART 6: MINIMUM EFFECTIVE DOSE

The SYSTEMS Approach to Sustainable Change

For creating improvement that actually lasts, you need to focus on small beginnings, environmental design, specific triggers, tracking without judgment, success protocols, minimum viable consistency, and social support.

Start with changes so tiny resistance is minimal. If you want to start meditating, don't commit to 20 minutes daily—start with three conscious breaths. Want to exercise regularly? Begin with a single push-up or 30 seconds of movement. Want to write more? Start with one sentence per day. These micro versions seem laughably small, but that's exactly the point—they're too small for your brain to resist.

Structure your surroundings to reduce willpower needs. Identify all obstacles between you and your desired behavior, then eliminate or reduce them. Make triggers for desired behaviors unmissable with visual reminders in unavoidable locations. Physically eliminate competing options by removing distractions from your primary workspace.

Connect new behaviors to existing automatic habits with trigger-action pairing. After you brush your teeth, do one push-up. After you pour your morning coffee, write one sentence. After you sit down at your desk, take three deep breaths. These pairings bypass conscious decision-making by piggybacking on habits that already happen automatically.

Track your progress without judgment. Use simple, binary tracking methods (did you do it or not?) rather than quality assessments. Create visual progress displays in highly visible locations. When you miss a day, implement the "never miss twice" rule—one missed day is a slip, two is the start of a new pattern.

Establish specific plans for handling obstacles. Identify what will likely derail your efforts and create detailed contingency plans for each. Use if-then planning: "If I'm too tired after work to exercise for 30 minutes, then I'll just do one push-up to maintain the habit." Review breakdowns to prevent recurrence by documenting exactly what went wrong and implementing targeted countermeasures.

Focus on consistency over intensity. Prioritize unbroken chains of behavior with streak protection protocols for challenging days. Create minimum viable versions of each habit for low-energy days. Reward consistency, not performance, with celebrations at streak intervals.

Build relationships that reinforce your efforts. Create specific accountability structures with regular check-ins and clear formats. Surround yourself with people already doing what you aim to do. Define exactly what you need from others with specific support request scripts.

The difference between temporary change and permanent improvement isn't better information or stronger motivation—it's better systems. Systems continue working when motivation inevitably fades and when life throws its inevitable curveballs.

PART 7: THE EXPONENTIAL GROWTH BLUEPRINT

THE SKILL ACQUISITION SYSTEM: MASTERY BY DESIGN

Most people approach learning new skills like they're checking boxes—read a book, watch some videos, try it a few times, then wonder why they're not seeing results. Real skill development isn't about sporadic practice—it's about systematic mastery.

The 5-Step Skill Mastery Framework:

1. Strategic Selection & Deconstruction
   - Choose skills with high ROI for your specific goals

- Break complex skills into 3-5 core sub-skills that create 80% of results
- Example: When my friend wanted to learn public speaking, instead of trying to improve everything at once, she identified the critical components: opening hooks, story structure, vocal variety, physical presence, and audience engagement

2. Minimum Viable Proficiency
   - Focus on the smallest set of sub-skills that make you functionally competent
   - Create daily micro-practice sessions (15-30 minutes) focused exclusively on these core elements
   - My colleague became a competent cook in 30 days by mastering just five techniques (heat control, knife skills, seasoning, timing, and plating) instead of trying to learn hundreds of recipes

3. Deliberate Practice Design
   - Record your performance and identify specific breakdown points
   - Create targeted 5-10 minute drills that isolate each weakness
   - Systematically increase difficulty through progressive challenges
   - When I learned Spanish, I recorded myself speaking and created specific drills just for the verb tenses I consistently messed up, rather than general "practice more" approaches

4. Feedback Loop Engineering
   - Create systems for immediate performance feedback
   - Schedule strategic expert reviews at key development points
   - Establish peer learning relationships for perspective and accountability

- My sister improved her writing faster in three months than in the previous three years by having a professional editor review her work every two weeks, rather than waiting for random feedback
5. Real-World Application
  - Design projects that force authentic skill use
  - Combine new skills with existing ones to create unique value
  - Teach what you're learning to clarify understanding
  - My friend who learned coding didn't just complete tutorials—he built a real website for his neighborhood association, which revealed gaps in his knowledge that controlled practice had missed

The difference between people who master skills and those who remain mediocre isn't talent—it's the system they use for development. Mastery requires putting in the right kind of hours with the right structure.

Getting Past Plateaus: What to Do When Progress Stalls

Here's where most people get stuck: they make initial progress, hit a flat spot, get frustrated, and either push too hard or give up. But plateaus aren't failures—they're normal, expected phases of any growth process that just need the right approach.

Every significant skill follows a similar pattern: quick early progress (the honeymoon phase) followed by a period where nothing seems to improve (the plateau) before breaking through to the next level. This isn't a problem—it's how skills naturally develop. During plateaus, your mind and body are integrating changes, building the foundation for your next jump forward.

The problem is that most people see plateaus as failures instead of necessary consolidation phases. They either push harder with the same approach (causing frustration and burnout) or they quit (missing the breakthrough that was just around the corner).

Here's how to handle plateaus effectively:

Identify the Type of Plateau: Recognize what kind of plateau you're experiencing. Different types need different solutions: - Integration plateaus need patience while your system absorbs previous learning - Method plateaus need new approaches to the same skill - Feedback plateaus need better ways to measure progress - Foundation plateaus mean you need to strengthen basics before moving forward

Change Your Approach: Adjust your strategy based on the type of plateau. Don't just push harder with the same method—that's like pressing an elevator button repeatedly when it's already lit.

Try Different Learning Methods: If you've been learning through reading, try videos instead. If you've been practicing alone, try learning with others. If you've focused on theory, try practical application. Different learning methods often bypass plateaus that happen with just one approach.

Focus on Specific Parts: Break skills into smaller pieces to find exactly where you're stuck. What looks like an overall plateau is often just one specific element holding everything else back. Test each piece separately to find the bottleneck, then focus your practice there.

Simplify Instead of Complicating: When progress stalls, many people add more—more techniques, more practice time, more complexity. Often the opposite works better: strip away everything non-essential and focus intensely on the fundamental elements.

Develop Supporting Skills: Sometimes progress stalls because related skills need work. A musician stuck on a difficult piece might need to improve finger strength rather than just practicing the piece more. A writer blocked on a novel might need to work on character development rather than just forcing more words.

Return to Basics: Many plateaus happen because fundamental skills weren't fully mastered before moving on. Going back to basics isn't moving backward—it's strengthening your foundation with your now-better understanding, often revealing details you missed the first time.

The Growth Environment Engineering: Creating Spaces That Make You Better

Here's where most people completely miss a critical growth factor: they try to improve while surrounded by environments designed for mediocrity. Your physical, social, and digital environments exert enormous influence over your behavior and development—they can either automatically pull you toward growth or constantly push you toward stagnation.

Think about it like trying to get in shape in a house full of junk food, with friends who mock exercise, while your social media feed is filled with indulgent recipes. Your environment is constantly working against your intentions. Now imagine the opposite: a kitchen stocked with healthy options, friends who value fitness, and media that normalizes consistent exercise. Same goal, wildly different probability of success based solely on environment.

This isn't about having perfect conditions—it's about deliberately engineering your surroundings to make growth the path of least resistance rather than requiring constant willpower to overcome environmental friction.

For creating surroundings that automatically support development:

Eliminate Friction: Remove barriers to desired behaviors. Identify every step required to perform your target habit and eliminate or reduce as many as possible. Want to exercise in the morning? Sleep in your workout clothes. Want to read more? Keep books in every room. Want to eat healthier? Pre-chop vegetables and keep them at eye level in the fridge.

Normalize Excellence: Surround yourself with higher standards. Your sense of "normal" is largely determined by your environment.

If everyone around you considers mediocre effort acceptable, that becomes your baseline. Deliberately expose yourself to people, media, and communities where excellence is the standard, recalibrating your sense of what's possible and expected.

Visual Triggers: Create persistent cues for growth activities. Your environment should constantly remind you of your priorities without requiring conscious thought. Place physical reminders of your goals in high-traffic areas of your home and workspace. Use visual progress trackers that you can't help but notice daily. Set up your physical spaces so they automatically trigger the behaviors you want to develop.

Increase Growth Costs: Make stagnation behaviors more difficult. Don't just make good behaviors easier—make unhelpful ones harder. Put junk food in hard-to-reach places. Use website blockers during work hours. Unplug the TV and put the remote in another room. Create "activation energy" requirements for behaviors you want to reduce without eliminating entirely.

Remove Temptations: Decrease exposure to derailing influences. Willpower isn't about resisting temptation; it's about avoiding it entirely. Unfollow social media accounts that trigger comparison or consumption. Clear your home of items that undermine your goals. Avoid routes that take you past temptations. Don't test your willpower when you can remove the need for it instead.

Optimize Primary Spaces: Design key locations for specific purposes. Different environments should trigger different mental states and behaviors. Create dedicated spaces for focused work, creative thinking, relaxation, and connection—each with appropriate tools and stimuli for that specific purpose. Avoid multi-purpose spaces that send mixed signals to your brain about what should happen there.

Network Curation: Build relationships that pull you upward. You become the average of the five people you spend the most time with. Deliberately cultivate relationships with people who embody the qualities you want to develop. Reduce time with those who reinforce limitations or undermine your growth efforts. Join communities organized around the skills or qualities you want to develop.

Manage Media Intake: Control information that shapes your thinking. Your media diet influences your thoughts, beliefs, and perceived norms as powerfully as your food diet affects your body. Audit your information sources for quality and alignment with your goals. Replace passive consumption with active curation. Schedule media intake rather than allowing constant exposure.

Embed Challenges: Structure regular growth triggers into your environment. Build automatic challenge escalation into your surroundings. Set calendar reminders that prompt you to increase difficulty levels. Create systems that automatically increase expectations as you improve. Use technology that adapts to your development rather than maintaining static demands.

Nurture Feedback Loops: Create systems that provide performance data. Your environment should tell you how you're doing without requiring conscious tracking. Set up automated measurement systems that give you regular feedback. Create visual displays that show progress or regression at a glance. Establish regular review triggers built into your calendar or physical spaces.

Time Restructuring: Organize schedules to prioritize development. Your calendar reveals your actual priorities regardless of what you claim is important. Restructure your time allocations to reflect your growth priorities. Schedule development blocks first rather than trying to fit them into leftover time. Create time boundaries that protect growth activities from encroachment.

The key isn't just creating a generally pleasant environment—it's engineering specific surroundings that automatically trigger, facilitate, and reinforce your growth behaviors without requiring constant conscious effort.

The Metamorphosis: Your Transformation Protocol

You've now mastered the complete L.E.V.E.L. U.P. system—a comprehensive framework for genuine transformation in any area of life. This system gives you the tools to make real, lasting changes rather than temporary fixes.

The frameworks in this chapter—from identity renovation to environment engineering, from plateau navigation to success integration—aren't just techniques for achieving specific goals. They're the infrastructure for transformation across all domains of your life.

This is the ultimate purpose of leveling up: not just reaching arbitrary milestones, but becoming someone who can systematically improve any area of life. Not because you're broken and need fixing, but because growth becomes one of your deepest values and most authentic expressions.

The systems you've learned provide the answer: with clarity, intention, and structures that transform improvement from occasional effort into consistent reality.

FROM LEVELING UP TO NEVER-ENDING EVOLUTION

Each time you successfully level up in an area of your life, you don't reach an endpoint—you reach a new starting point. The skills you've developed and the systems you've built become the foundation for the next phase of growth. In the next chapter, we'll explore how to turn leveling up from a one-time achievement into a lifelong evolution.

> "The ultimate measure of success isn't whether you improved this once, but whether you've become someone who can systematically transform any area of your life."

Chapter 13 Key Takeaways

- Systems Over Goals: Create frameworks for improvement rather than relying on motivation
- Identity Evolution: Change who you believe you are to change what you consistently do
- Environment Design: Engineer your surroundings to make growth the path of least resistance
- Plateau Navigation: Understand different types of stagnation and how to break through each
- Integration: Make improvements permanent by embedding them into your identity and systems

CHAPTER 14: NEVER ENDING STORY

"THE MOMENT YOU THINK YOU'VE ARRIVED IS THE MOMENT YOU'VE LOST YOUR WAY."

PART 1: THE MYTH OF ARRIVAL

The Perfection Myth

This final chapter reveals the most dangerous delusion in personal development: the myth that you'll eventually "arrive" somewhere. That one magical day, you'll finally have your shit completely together, reach all your big goals, and then coast on autopilot for the rest of your life. This fantasy of completion is why 78% of people who achieve their big goals experience a massive emotional letdown afterward.

The harsh reality? You will never, ever be "done." The day you think you've finally arrived is the exact day you start dying—mentally, emotionally, and eventually physically.

This isn't depressing—it's liberating. The problem isn't that growth never ends; it's that we've been conditioned to expect neat endings. We want to "arrive" somewhere and be done. But that's not how life works.

While Chapter 13 gave you tactical systems for improvement, this chapter provides the philosophical foundation that makes those tactics sustainable for life. The L.E.V.E.L. U.P. framework helps you make specific progress, while the J.O.U.R.N.E.Y. system helps you find fulfillment in endless progress:

Leveling Up (Ch 13)	Never-Ending Evolution (Ch 14)
Tactical systems for improvement	Philosophical foundation for lifelong growth
How to make specific progress	How to find fulfillment in endless progress
Achievement strategies	Achievement integration philosophy
Environment engineering for growth	Psychological adaptation to never "arriving"

The true freedom comes when you stop waiting for that mythical moment of completion and start embracing the continuous nature of growth.

How to Free Yourself from the Finish Line Fantasy

Most people put their lives on hold until they reach some magical endpoint—the promotion, weight goal, relationship, or bank balance that will supposedly make everything perfect. The cruel irony? The biggest disappointment isn't failing to reach these goals—it's reaching them and discovering the fulfillment they expected isn't waiting there.

My friend Sarah spent three years obsessed with getting a specific executive position. When she finally got it, she felt a brief rush followed by emptiness. "I thought I'd finally feel like I'd made it," she told me. "Instead, I just saw a whole new set of challenges and realized I'd been postponing my happiness for a moment that wasn't what I imagined."

The solution isn't setting better endpoints—it's fundamentally reframing growth as a continuous journey without a final destination. Those milestone moments aren't conclusions but scenic viewpoints along an endless path.

Our brains actually release more happiness chemicals during engagement in meaningful processes than at moments of completion. You're literally wired to find more satisfaction in the journey than the destination.

PART 2: DESTINATION ADDICTION

The False Peak Problem

Your mind naturally hates the false peak experience. When you're struggling up a mountain and finally see what looks like the top, you feel a surge of excitement and anticipation. When you reach that point only to discover it was just a false peak with more climbing ahead, that excitement crashes, creating disappointment much stronger than if you'd never thought you were near the top at all.

This isn't just in your head—it's how we're built. The problem isn't that growth continues; it's that we're conditioned to expect clear endpoints that reality rarely provides.

My client Jake experienced this after working relentlessly toward a fitness goal for six months. When he reached his target weight and body fat percentage, he felt a strange emptiness. "I thought I'd be ecstatic, but instead I felt lost. What now?" The achievement revealed new possibilities rather than providing the conclusion he expected.

Want to avoid the letdown? Stop treating life like a video game with a final level. Instead, become someone who actually enjoys the climbing process itself. Take pictures at every false peak instead of getting frustrated. Create small celebrations for progress made rather than only celebrating when you reach the top.

How to Navigate the Never-Ending Mountain Range

Life isn't one mountain with a summit—it's an entire mountain range with countless peaks, valleys, and traverses between them. When you understand this, each false summit becomes less disappointing and more expected—just another beautiful viewpoint on an endless journey.

Instead of seeing a single peak you're trying to conquer, envision a vast range with multiple summits stretching to the horizon. Each achievement isn't the end but rather a vantage point that reveals new possibilities previously hidden from view.

Before reaching any significant goal, create a "What's Next" document that identifies specific challenges likely to become visible after achievement and explicit plans for the traverse to the next summit. This transforms the potentially deflating moment of "now what?" into an anticipated and prepared-for transition.

Design celebration activities that honor accomplishment without implying completion. Instead of "mission accomplished" parties, create "milestone revealed" celebrations that simultaneously honor the climb while explicitly acknowledging the continuing journey.

PART 3: BIOLOGY OF NEVER-ENDING GROWTH

Embracing Infinite Growth

To thrive in an endless growth journey without burning out or giving up, you need a philosophical shift. You need to stop obsessing about where you're going and start paying attention to where you are. Most people treat their lives like they're constantly on their way to the airport—rushing through everything, completely missing the actual journey because they're so focused on not being late for some future moment.

Start by getting your head out of tomorrow's ass and into today's reality. The present moment isn't just some woo-woo meditation concept—it's where all the actual living happens while you're busy planning for some mythical future where you'll "finally have your shit together."

When you hit a milestone, celebrate it like you would a friend's birthday—have some cake, take some pictures—but don't act like you've retired. The next morning, you're back on your bullshit, setting new targets and expanding your horizons.

Your expectations should evolve faster than technology makes your expensive gadgets obsolete. The goals you set last year should look embarrassingly small by now—not because they weren't worthy, but because you've outgrown them. If your ambitions still look exactly the same as they did five years ago, you're not playing an infinite game—you're just repeating the tutorial level over and over.

How to Embrace the Never-Ending Journey

Create structures that pull your attention to the present moment rather than fixating on future endpoints. Create daily "process appreciation" moments where you consciously notice what you're enjoying about your current activities. Develop "present progress markers" that track today's advancement without reference to endpoints. Establish "engagement metrics" that measure quality of attention rather than just outcomes.

How Your Body Is Built for Ongoing Growth

Your body and mind are naturally designed for constant change—they either grow or decline; there's no standing still. It's like being a shark—you either keep moving forward or you sink. This isn't just motivational talk; it's how your body actually works.

Your skills either get stronger with practice or weaker without it—there's no maintaining the status quo. "Use it or lose it" isn't just a saying but a reality of how your body functions. Your brain actually changes its physical structure daily based on which skills you practice and which you neglect.

Consider this: Every part of your body is constantly renewing itself. Your brain is always forming new connections (or losing unused ones). Your muscles are either strengthening or weakening. Nature doesn't have a maintenance setting—it's either growth or decline.

This connects directly with what you learned about emotional strength in Chapter 4. That resilience isn't something you achieve once—it's a capacity that needs ongoing development or it fades, just like physical strength.

Working With Your Natural Cycles, Not Against Them

Your body isn't a machine with simple on/off controls—it's a complex system with natural rhythms and cycles. Working with these patterns rather than fighting them makes ongoing growth sustainable instead of exhausting.

Accept the natural ups and downs in your energy, motivation, and ability. Your body doesn't maintain constant output—it naturally rises and falls in cycles. Trying to maintain steady, linear progress is like trying to breathe in continuously without ever breathing out.

Growth requires the right amount of challenge—not too much (which causes burnout) and not too little (which leads to stagnation). Increase difficulty in small, manageable steps rather than dramatic jumps. Include deliberate rest periods after intense growth phases to allow your body and mind to adapt.

> "Your body doesn't understand finish lines—it only knows the cycle of challenge, adaptation, and a new normal. Your cells don't retire."

PART 4: THE INFINITE GAME MINDSET

The Modern Completion Trap: Our Addiction to Endings

Here's where most people completely fuck up—they're addicted to endings. They want everything wrapped up in a neat little bow like some Netflix series. They think life should have seasons and finales, clear points where one chapter ends and another begins. But real life doesn't work like that. It's one continuous flow of challenges, changes, and adaptations.

This completion addiction has been amplified by modern media and technology. We've been trained to expect life to work like a Netflix series—with clear story arcs, satisfying conclusions, and maybe a post-credits scene teasing the sequel. But real life is more like a livestream that keeps going even when you fall asleep with your face in a bowl of chips.

Your brain has been hijacked by Hollywood endings, Instagram transformation posts, and video game "achievement unlocked" dopamine hits. That graduation ceremony was supposed to be your triumphant finale, but instead, you just got a hangover and student loan payments.

Humans are storytelling creatures—we can't help it. The problem isn't that you tell stories about your life; it's that you're telling the wrong kind of stories. You're writing fairy tales with "happily ever after" endings when you should be writing something more like "Game of Thrones"—complex, ongoing, and with the constant understanding that winter is always coming.

You've fallen into this trap too, haven't you? When completing educational degrees, expecting a profound sense of completion that never materialized. When reaching financial goals, anticipating a feeling of "having made it" that proved fleeting at best. The most disorienting aspect wasn't the continuing journey itself—it was your expectation of completion colliding with the reality of continuity.

But here's the beautiful irony: The same desire for completion that fucks people up can actually be channeled into something useful. Instead of seeking endings, you can learn to love the process. Instead of trying to arrive somewhere, you can learn to enjoy the journey.

How to Recover from Completion Addiction

Breaking free from endpoint fixation isn't about abandoning goals—it's about transforming how you relate to them and what you expect from reaching them.

The narrative restructuring process involves rewiring the stories you tell yourself about your life journey. Identify the "ending addiction" narratives you've internalized ("Once I achieve X, I'll finally be Y") and create alternative "continuing journey" narratives for each area.

It's like that person who stopped describing themselves as "a former athlete now in finance" and started saying "I brought the discipline and teamwork from my athletic background into my financial career, which is now evolving toward leadership."

Build satisfaction systems focused on journey rather than destination. Identify specific aspects of your daily process that provide inherent satisfaction rather than just the reward of completion. Create deliberate "process appreciation" practices that draw attention to these elements.

The ONGOING Approach: Balancing Achievement and Process

One of the biggest challenges in embracing the never-ending journey is finding the right balance between focusing on goals and enjoying the process. It's not about giving up goals—it's about relating to them differently:

Find joy in the process: Discover rewards in the activity itself, not just in reaching the finish line.

Use outcomes as information: See results as helpful feedback, not as validation of your worth.

Look up for inspiration only: Learn from those further along the path without comparing yourself negatively.

Reward showing up: Create small celebrations for consistent engagement with the process, not just for reaching milestones.

Always have a next step: Identify your next growth area before completing the current one.

Track your evolution: Measure how you're growing over time, not just whether you hit specific targets.

Compare to yesterday, not others: Use your past self as your measuring stick, not other people.

Instead of generic "I did it!" celebrations that reinforce the idea you've "arrived," create milestone rituals that honor both what you've achieved and the continuing journey ahead. This transforms celebrations from "I've arrived" moments into "I'm evolving" experiences that keep your momentum going rather than creating post-achievement letdowns.

PART 5: CAREER AS EVOLUTION, NOT DESTINATION

The Professional Evolution Matrix: Careers as Infinite Games

Let's talk about how careers have become infinite games. The idea of learning one skill set and being set for life is as dead as dial-up internet. Your professional development is e ther continuous or you're becoming obsolete faster than a floppy disk in the cloud computing era.

Your career isn't a ladder anymore—it's more like a video game where each level unlocks new challenges and requires new skills. The moment you think you've mastered your role is the moment you start becoming irrelevant. Today's expertise becomes tomorrow's basic requirement.

The Career Survival Guide for People Who Thought They Could Stop Learning

Want to avoid becoming the workplace equivalent of that person who still uses AOL email? Here's how to stay relevant without losing your mind:

Become a skill-collecting weirdo. Don't just get better at what you already do—start grabbing adjacent skills like they're free samples at Costco. If you're a designer who can't write basic code, you're like a chef who can't use a knife. If you're a marketer who doesn't understand data analytics, you're essentially doing astrology with better PowerPoints.

Stop whining about change and start surfing it. When your industry shifts (and it will, repeatedly), you have two options: waste energy complaining about how things used to be, or redirect that energy toward becoming the person who thrives in the new reality.

Treat your career like a shark—keep moving or die. This doesn't mean frantically jumping from job to job. It means creating deliberate cycles of learning, applying, and reflecting. Set aside specific times for skill development the same way you schedule dental cleanings.

Build your reinvention muscles before you need them. Most careers now include several "what the hell am I doing with my life" pivots. The question isn't if you'll need to substantially reinvent yourself but when and how many times.

Domain-Specific Journey Thinking

The never-ending journey concept applies differently across various life domains:

Career Journey Thinking

Mindset Shift: From "I'm working toward position X" to "I'm developing capability Y that creates ongoing value regardless of position."

Common Destination Traps: 1. The Title Fixation: Believing a specific position will bring fulfillment 2. The Retirement Fantasy: Working solely for the day you can stop working 3. The Recognition Addiction: Needing external validation to feel successful

Relationship Journey Thinking

Mindset Shift: From relationship milestones to relationship evolution; from "happily ever after" to "continuously growing together."

Common Destination Traps: 1. The Relationship Status Fixation: Believing a specific status will bring fulfillment 2. The Problem-Free Fantasy: Working toward a mythical state where conflicts disappear 3. The Passion Permanence Myth: Expecting initial feelings to remain unchanged

PART 6: RELATIONSHIPS AS JOURNEYS, NOT ACHIEVEMENTS

The Relationship Continuity Protocol: Eternal Gardens

Here's where most people fuck up their relationships—they think there's some point where they can stop putting in effort. Like once you've "made it" to a certain relationship status, you can just coast on autopilot. But relationships are like gardens—they either grow or they die. There's no maintenance mode.

Couples who view their relationship as an evolving journey rather than an achieved status show significantly higher satisfaction and longevity than those who believe they've "arrived" at a stable endpoint.

The key isn't just keeping things stable—it's continuing to evolve together. It's like being dance partners in an endless performance where the music keeps changing and you have to keep learning new moves.

The "Don't Let Your Relationship Die of Boredom" Guide

Want to keep your relationship from turning into a sad Netflix documentary about "where things went wrong"? Here's how:

Reinvent your relationship before it needs CPR. Deliberately shake things up when everything seems fine. Try new ways of spending time together, talking to each other, and yes, having sex—before the relationship flatlines.

Stop assuming you know everything about your partner. People change more than their underwear (hopefully). The person you're with today isn't exactly the same one you met years ago. Get curious again. Ask questions you think you know the answers to.

Take on challenges together that make you both slightly uncomfortable. Learn to make pasta from scratch. Build something that requires power tools. Have conversations about topics you normally avoid.

Fight the right enemy. Every relationship faces difficulties—the question is whether you fight each other or the problem. When shit hits the fan, are you standing back-to-back against the world, or are you facing off like it's a duel at high noon?

PART 7: THE N.E.V.E.R.S.T.O.P. FRAMEWORK

The Art of Momentum: Continuous Propulsion

Here's where most people completely fuck up—they treat progress like a series of sprints instead of an endless marathon. They go hard for a while, reach some arbitrary goal, then stop completely while they celebrate or recover. But that stop-start approach is killing their momentum.

This momentum principle connects directly with Chapter 3's lessons about taking action. While that chapter got you moving initially, this approach ensures you maintain that motion continuously rather than falling into the common pattern of action followed by extended inertia.

According to Newton's First Law, an object in motion tends to stay in motion unless acted upon by an outside force. This principle applies to personal development as well—maintaining momentum requires less energy than repeatedly overcoming inertia. Consistency (even at lower intensity) produces better long-term results than intermittent high-intensity efforts followed by complete stops.

Think about the most consistently successful people you know. They're not the ones who occasionally go all-out and then crash. They're the ones who keep moving forward every single day, who understand that maintaining momentum is more important than reaching any particular milestone. They're not the gym heroes who crush one insane workout that leaves them unable to walk for a week—they're the ones who show up consistently for years, gradually building a foundation that makes extraordinary performance possible.

The "Keep Moving or Die" Momentum Guide

Want to keep moving forward without burning out or giving up? Here's how to maintain momentum like a shark—keep swimming or sink to the bottom:

Set your daily minimum so pathetically low that it would be embarrassing NOT to do it. We're talking one push-up, three minutes of meditation, two sentences written. These aren't your goals—they're your absolute floor. They're what you do on days when you feel like roadkill. The point isn't the progress from that tiny action—it's maintaining the psychological continuity of never breaking the chain.

Stop with the all-or-nothing bullshit. You're not a light switch that's either ON FIRE WITH PASSION or completely off. Create deliberate intensity variations that never drop to zero. Have recovery days, not quitting days. Low-intensity forward motion beats high-intensity followed by full stop every single time.

The key isn't just about maintaining effort—it's about understanding that momentum itself has value independent of the progress it creates. A boulder rolling downhill doesn't need to push itself. Once you've got momentum, half your work is done. But every time you stop completely, you're back to pushing that boulder from a dead stop, which requires way more energy than keeping it rolling, even slowly.

The Metamorphosis: Your Continuous Evolution Protocol

You've now mastered the philosophical framework for embracing the never-ending nature of growth. This isn't an endpoint; it's the beginning of an entirely new approach to continuous evolution.

Think of this as graduating from someone who occasionally attempts improvement to someone who embraces continuous evolution as a fundamental aspect of their identity. You're no longer a person who sometimes tries to get better; you're a person who continuously transforms as a core expression of who you are.

The frameworks in this chapter—from false summit navigation to momentum maintenance, from relationship evolution to learning matrices—aren't just philosophical concepts. They're the mental infrastructure for ongoing metamorphosis across all domains of your life.

PUTTING CONTINUOUS GROWTH INTO PRACTICE

Understanding that growth never ends is one thing—actually living this way is another. Here's a simple system to make this mindset part of your everyday life:

DAILY: THE 5-MINUTE CHECK-IN

Each day, spend just 5 minutes reinforcing journey-focused thinking:

1. Morning Intention (1 minute): Start your day with a simple process-focused thought: "Today I'll find value in the learning process itself, not just in reaching goals."
2. Evening Check-In (4 minutes): End your day by asking yourself:
   - What surprised me today?
   - Did I catch myself thinking "I'll be happy when..."?
   - What small progress did I notice that I might have missed?
   - What did I enjoy about the process itself?

This quick daily habit gradually shifts your thinking from destination-focused to journey-focused.

WEEKLY: THE SUNDAY CHECK-UP

Once a week, spend 15 minutes on a deeper review:

1. Progress Without Attachment: Notice progress you made while not being fixated on specific outcomes.
2. Happiness Traps: Spot any "I'll be happy when…" thinking that showed up during the week.
3. Process Enjoyment: Note specific moments when you enjoyed what you were doing regardless of results.
4. Next Explorations: Identify new areas you're curious about exploring.

MONTHLY: THE BIGGER PICTURE

Once a month, take a broader look at your journey mindset:

1. Process Metrics: Review how you're measuring engagement with the process, not just outcomes.
2. Language Check: Notice if your writing and speaking uses destination-focused language.
3. Celebration Style: Consider how you celebrate achievements—do your celebrations suggest "I've arrived" or "I'm evolving"?
4. Comparison Points: Check if you're comparing yourself to others or to your past self.

QUARTERLY: THE SEASONAL RESET

Every three months, do a deeper review:

1. Life Story Check: How are you telling your life story—as a series of destinations or as ongoing growth?
2. Environment Review: Do your surroundings support journey thinking or destination thinking?

3. Relationship Alignment: Do your relationships support continuous growth or reinforce "arrival" thinking?
4. Life Areas Balance: Are you maintaining journey thinking across all areas of life?

This layered approach helps maintain journey thinking even though our culture constantly pushes for destination thinking. The daily practices build the foundation, while the weekly, monthly, and quarterly check-ins deepen your commitment.

FROM PHILOSOPHY TO PRACTICE: EMBRACING THE NEVER-ENDING STORY

Understanding that growth never ends is one thing—building a life that embraces this reality is another. Throughout this book, you've acquired a powerful set of tools that work together as an integrated system. The never-ending mindset from this chapter provides the philosophical foundation that makes all these tools sustainable for life.

The ultimate purpose isn't just accepting that growth continues, but embracing continuous evolution as one of your deepest values and most authentic expressions.

> "Your story has no final chapter—only continuous evolution into new and unexplored territories. The joy isn't in reaching an endpoint but in perpetually becoming more than you were before."

Chapter 14 Key Takeaways

Life doesn't come with a finish line—just increasingly interesting challenges. The moment you think you've "arrived" is the moment you start dying inside. Your growth journey isn't a neat little package with a bow on top; it's more like an endless road trip where the scenery keeps changing and occasionally you hit a pothole that makes you spill coffee all over yourself.

Success isn't reaching some mythical endpoint—it's building the capacity to keep evolving through whatever life throws at you. Treat achievements like pit stops on a cross-country drive: refuel, stretch your legs, take a picture for the 'gram, then get back on the road. The journey is the whole damn point.

Your relationships, career, and personal development all follow the same rule: grow or die. There's no maintenance mode in life. You're either pushing forward or sliding backward while telling yourself you're "taking a break." Choose continuous evolution over comfortable stagnation, and you'll never be the person at the high school reunion still talking about that one great thing they did twenty years ago.

CONCLUSION: FROM KNOWLEDGE TO IMPLEMENTATION

"THE DIFFERENCE BETWEEN WHO YOU ARE AND WHO YOU WANT TO BE ISN'T INFORMATION—IT'S IMPLEMENTATION."

Congratulations. You've made it to the end of this book, which means one of two things has happened:

1. You've actually implemented each chapter's principles as you went along, gradually transforming your life with every page you turned.
2. Or, let's be honest - you've blasted straight through without implementing a damn thing, collecting insights like Pokemon cards but not actually using any of them yet.

If you're in the first category, you've already felt how these principles work together as one integrated system instead of just a bunch of random techniques. If you're in the second category— and let's be honest, that's probably like 95% of you—don't worry. That's totally normal. But now comes the actual moment of truth, the fork-in-the-road decision point that separates people who actually transform their lives from those who just add another book to their "read" list on Goodreads and then go back to doing exactly what they were doing before.

The Complete System: How Everything Fits Together

Throughout this book, you've been on a journey that I've carefully mapped out for you. Let's take a quick second to understand how all these pieces actually fit together as one complete system for genuinely transforming your life (not just reading about it):

The Foundation: Eliminating What Doesn't Work

The first part of your journey focused on removing the primary barriers that prevent most people from changing. Think of it as clearing all the crap off your driveway before trying to pull out of the garage.

First, you learned to stop bitching like it's an Olympic sport. Your complaints weren't just annoying everyone around you—they were rewiring your brain to spot problems instead of solutions, poisoning your relationships faster than gas station sushi, and burning through energy you could have used for actually fixing your life. By implementing the Stop Bitching toolkit, you've reclaimed all that wasted energy and redirected it toward effective action instead of professional victimhood.

Then you got your head out of your ass, which was probably the most uncomfortable but necessary extraction of your life. You confronted all those cozy little lies you've been telling yourself—the ones that kept you stuck in the same patterns while wondering why nothing ever changes. Through reality anchoring practices and accountability systems that don't let you bullshit yourself, you've developed the self-awareness necessary for genuine change instead of just rearranging deck chairs on your personal Titanic.

These foundational elements aren't just preliminary steps you can check off and forget—they're daily practices that create the psychological space necessary for all subsequent growth. Without addressing these barriers first, even the most sophisticated strategies for personal development would fail faster than a chocolate teapot.

The Core Capacities: Building Internal Strength

With the barriers cleared away, you developed the essential internal capacities that support everything else—like building the engine before worrying about the car's paint job.

You built an emotional backbone that doesn't collapse under pressure. Through specific brain-training practices, you developed neurological resilience that allows you to function effectively when shit hits the fan instead of crumbling like a cookie in a toddler's fist.

You embraced the reality that life isn't fair and never will be. Instead of throwing tantrums about uneven playing fields, you learned to see unfairness as a strategic challenge rather than a moral catastrophe. This perspective shift transformed potential discouragement into pragmatic problem-solving—like navigating a game where the rules sometimes change mid-play.

You learned to play the long game instead of chasing every shiny object that crosses your path. By countering your brain's evolutionary bias toward immediate gratification, you developed the capacity for strategic patience and compound growth thinking that separates truly successful people from those who are perpetually starting over.

These internal capacities serve as your psychological infrastructure—the support systems that make all external achievements possible. Without them, any success would be as fragile as a sandcastle at high tide, vulnerable to the first strong wave that comes along.

The Strategic Applications: Turning Principles Into Practice

With your foundation solid and core capacities developed, you learned to apply these principles to external challenges—like taking your new skills out of the practice room and onto the actual playing field.

You mastered the art of handling haters without becoming one yourself. Instead of letting criticism derail you or hardening into someone who rejects all feedback, you developed systems for processing criticism constructively while maintaining your course. You transformed what sends most people into defensive spirals into a source of valuable feedback and motivation—like turning what could be poison into medicine.

You learned to make any place suck less, even when you can't control all the variables. Through strategic positioning and influence tactics, you discovered how to create supportive contexts even within challenging circumstances—like finding the one spot in a drafty room that doesn't make your joints ache.

These applications bridge the gap between internal development and external results, showing how your psychological growth translates into tangible improvements in your daily life. They're where the rubber meets the road, turning abstract principles into practical advantages.

The Relationship Dimension: Creating a Supportive Ecosystem

Recognizing that humans are social creatures (even the introverts among us), you expanded your focus to include key relationship skills that transform your social environment from a potential obstacle into a growth accelerator.

You stopped being the person everyone avoids at parties—you know, the energy vampire who leaves people feeling worse after interacting with them. Instead, you developed social intelligence and connection skills that make you a positive force in others' lives, someone people actually want to be around rather than someone they tolerate while looking for an escape route.

You learned to teach without being a know-it-all who makes everyone feel stupid. By sharing knowledge effectively without alienating others, you maximized your positive influence and became someone who elevates conversations rather than dominating them.

You performed a relationship detox, creating systems for evaluating and upgrading your social circle. By ensuring your relationships support rather than undermine your growth, you've surrounded yourself with people who challenge you to become better rather than those who keep you comfortable with mediocrity.

These relationship elements create a multiplier effect for your personal development. Instead of swimming against the social current, you've created an ecosystem that naturally carries you toward your goals—like trading a rowboat for a sailboat that harnesses the wind.

The Advanced Mastery: Navigating Life's Biggest Challenges

Finally, you prepared for life's most significant challenges and ongoing growth—the black diamond slopes of personal development that separate the amateurs from the pros.

You learned to dance with disaster rather than getting flattened by it. Through systems for crisis navigation and resilience, you ensured that temporary setbacks don't become permanent derailments—like having shock absorbers that let you drive over rough terrain without breaking an axle.

You created complete rebuilding protocols for when everything goes to hell. These worst-case scenario plans provide a safety net that actually encourages bolder action—because you know that even if you fall, you won't fall all the way to the bottom.

You built systems for leveling up your life when you hit those inevitable plateaus. Instead of getting stuck in the comfortable-but-stagnant zone where most people spend their lives, you developed methods for continually expanding your capacity and breaking through to new levels.

You embraced the never-ending story of personal growth, learning to maintain motivation and meaning through changing life phases. Instead of treating development as a temporary project with an endpoint, you've made it a lifelong journey with constantly evolving challenges and rewards.

These advanced elements future-proof your transformation, preparing you for both the inevitable challenges and the expanding possibilities that come with personal growth. They're not just about surviving life's storms—they're about learning to harness their power.

THE FIRST 30 DAYS IMPLEMENTATION PLAN

Let's get specific about exactly what to do, starting right now. Here's your day-by-day plan for the first 30 days:

DAYS 1-10: FOUNDATION BUILDING

Day 1: Complete the Complaint Awareness Audit from Chapter 1. For 24 hours, track every complaint you make, noting the context, trigger, and whether it led to any constructive action.

Day 2: Identify your top self-deception pattern from Chapter 2. Review the Reality Distortion Patterns and identify which one most frequently appears in your thinking.

Day 3: Implement the 5-5-5 Emotional Reset from Chapter 3. Practice it at least three times throughout the day, especially when you notice emotional reactivity.

Day 4: Complete the Fairness Expectation Inventory from Chapter 4. Identify three situations where fairness expectations are creating unnecessary suffering.

Day 5: Create your Long Game Vision from Chapter 5. Write a detailed description of where you want to be in 3-5 years, focusing on the person you'll become rather than just external achievements.

Day 6: Implement the Criticism Processing Protocol from Chapter 6. The next time you receive criticism, run it through the full protocol before responding.

Day 7: Conduct an Environment Audit from Chapter 7. Identify three aspects of your physical environment that are undermining your goals.

Day 8: Practice the Connection Technique from Chapter 8. In your next three social interactions, apply the specific listening and response patterns.

Day 9: Use the Knowledge Sharing Framework from Chapter 9. The next time you share expertise, apply the structure for making information accessible without condescension.

Day 10: Begin the Relationship Inventory from Chapter 10. Categorize your key relationships using the evaluation criteria.

DAYS 11-20: SYSTEM IMPLEMENTATION

Day 11: Create your Crisis Response Plan from Chapter 11. Identify your three most likely personal crises and outline specific response protocols for each.

Day 12: Develop your Rock Bottom Recovery System from Chapter 12. Create your personal "In Case of Emergency" guide for worst-case scenarios.

Day 13: Implement the L.E.V.E.L. U.P. Framework from Chapter 13. Choose one area for improvement and apply the complete framework.

Day 14: Practice the Journey Mindset from Chapter 14. Identify three goals you've been treating as destinations and reframe them as ongoing journeys.

Days 15-20: Integration Week. Spend one day reviewing and reinforcing each of the following: - Day 15: Complaint Reduction (Ch 1) + Self-Awareness (Ch 2) - Day 16: Emotional Regulation (Ch 3) + Fairness Reality (Ch 4) - Day 17: Long-Term Thinking (Ch 5) + Criticism Management (Ch 6) - Day 18: Environment Design (Ch 7) + Social Skills (Ch 8) - Day 19: Teaching Effectively (Ch 9)

+ Relationship Management (Ch 10) - Day 20: Crisis Preparation (Ch 11-12) + Continuous Growth (Ch 13-14)

DAYS 21-30: HABIT SOLIDIFICATION

During this final phase, focus on cementing your new practices into automatic habits:

Days 21-25: Implement the "Never Zero" approach. For each key practice, establish a minimum daily version that takes less than 2 minutes. Do at least this minimum every single day, no matter what.

Days 26-30: Create your ongoing implementation system: - Day 26: Establish your tracking system - Day 27: Set up your accountability structure - Day 28: Design your environment to support your new habits - Day 29: Create your review and adjustment protocol - Day 30: Develop your long-term implementation roadmap

Common Implementation Challenges (And How to Overcome Them)

Even with the best intentions and a complete system, implementation challenges are inevitable. Let's address the most common obstacles and their solutions:

Challenge 1: The Motivation Fade

The Problem: Your initial motivation will evaporate faster than a puddle in the desert. That fiery enthusiasm you feel right now? It's the honeymoon phase, and like all honeymoons, it ends. When it does, most people abandon their efforts precisely when the real work begins, then blame themselves for "lacking discipline" when the real problem was relying on an unreliable resource.

The Solution: Stop treating motivation like it's essential. It's not. It's a fair-weather friend that disappears exactly when you need it most. Instead, build implementation systems that function regardless of how you feel in the moment:

Wire your new behaviors directly into your existing routines. Don't just plan to meditate "sometime tomorrow"—decide that "after I pour my first cup of coffee, I will sit on the cushion for three minutes." Your existing habit becomes the trigger that launches the new one, no motivation required.

Make your desired actions easier than your excuses. Remove every possible step between intention and action. Want to exercise in the morning? Sleep in your workout clothes. Want to write more? Keep your laptop open to a blank document. The path of least resistance should lead to your goal, not away from it.

Put some actual skin in the game. Create accountability systems with consequences you'll genuinely want to avoid. Tell your most brutally honest friend you'll donate $100 to a political cause you hate if you miss your weekly goal. Suddenly, following through becomes the easier option.

Make your first steps so ridiculously small that they're harder to skip than to do. We're talking "floss one tooth" or "write one sentence" small. These micro-habits require so little activation energy that even on your worst days, you can still do them—and once you start, continuing is much easier.

The key is understanding that waiting for motivation is like waiting for a bus that doesn't run on any actual schedule—a great way to ensure you never get where you're going. Build systems that work when motivation is on vacation, which is most of the time.

Challenge 2: The Consistency Gap

The Problem: Most people implement like they're having a seizure—intensely for a few days, then nothing for weeks. This start-stop pattern is neurological sabotage, preventing the brain rewiring that creates lasting change. It's like trying to get a tan by sitting in the sun for 8 hours one day and then staying inside for a month—you'll just end up burned and pale.

The Solution: Prioritize consistency over intensity. A daily 10-minute walk beats a monthly marathon in terms of creating lasting change. Here's how to close the consistency gap:

Define your "this is so easy it's embarrassing" minimum. What's the absolute smallest action that still counts as implementation? One push-up? Three deep breaths? Two minutes of writing? This becomes your non-negotiable daily minimum—the floor below which you never drop, even on your worst days.

Adopt the "never-zero" mentality. Commit to doing at least one tiny action every single day that moves you toward your goal. The size of the action doesn't matter; what matters is maintaining the unbroken chain of implementation. This creates psychological momentum that makes larger actions easier over time.

Make your consistency visible. Maintain physical or digital records of your implementation streak—a calendar with X's, a chain of paperclips, a tracking app that shows your streak. The visual representation of your consistency becomes a motivational force of its own that you won't want to break.

Create bounce-back protocols for when life inevitably interrupts your streak. Instead of letting a missed day turn into a missed week, have a specific plan for immediately resuming—not tomorrow, not after the weekend, but within hours of noticing the lapse. The faster you recover, the less momentum you lose.

These approaches acknowledge that the path to change isn't about heroic effort or occasional bursts of superhuman willpower—it's about showing up day after day after day, like water wearing away stone. Consistency beats intensity every single time.

Challenge 3: The Environmental Sabotage

The Problem: Your physical and social environments are perfectly optimized—for your old behaviors. They're like elaborate traps designed by your past self to keep you exactly where you were. Every aspect of your surroundings—from the layout of your home to the notifications on your phone to the people you spend time with—creates constant friction against change and smooth pathways back to old patterns.

The Solution: Stop trying to change yourself while keeping your environment the same. That's like trying to get sober while living in a bar. Instead, deliberately restructure your surroundings to make your new behaviors the path of least resistance:

Rearrange your physical spaces to make desired behaviors easier and undesired ones harder. Put the healthy snacks at eye level and the junk food in an inconvenient location. Place your workout equipment where you'll trip over it. Move the TV to a less comfortable room. Your environment should make your good choices easy and your bad choices require effort.

Perform social surgery on your calendar. Selectively increase time with people who support your changes and decrease time with those who undermine them. This isn't about cutting people off—it's about adjusting dosages. The friend who always wants to drink when you're trying to cut back? See them for lunch instead of happy hour. The colleague who's also working on professional development? Schedule regular coffee meetings.

Hack your digital environment like it's trying to hack you (because it is). Modify device settings, notifications, and layouts to facilitate new behavior patterns. Delete apps that trigger old behaviors. Rearrange your home screen to highlight tools that support your goals. Unsubscribe from emails that tempt you toward old patterns. Your devices should be working for your new self, not your old one.

Redesign your choice architecture so the default option is the one you want to take. Make the positive choice the one that happens automatically unless you exert effort to prevent it. Set up automatic transfers to savings. Prepare healthy meals in advance so they're the easiest option when hungry. Schedule workout appointments in your calendar rather than hoping you'll "find time."

Environment isn't just context—it's causation. When you understand this, you stop trying to use willpower to fight against your surroundings (a battle you'll eventually lose) and start redesigning your surroundings to work with your goals rather than against them. This isn't cheating—it's finally playing the game intelligently.

Challenge 4: The Identity Conflict

The Problem: New behaviors often create an identity crisis in your brain. There's a civil war happening between who you've always thought you are and who you're trying to become. This creates psychological resistance even when you consciously want to change. Your brain essentially says, "Wait, this isn't me— I'm not a morning person/healthy eater/organized professional/ whatever," and sabotages your efforts to protect your existing self-concept.

The Solution: Stop trying to force behaviors that feel "not like me" and instead deliberately evolve your identity to make those behaviors feel like the most natural expression of who you are:

Bridge the gap between your current and desired identities with present-tense statements that acknowledge both. Instead of "I'm trying to become a runner" (which reinforces that you're not one), use "I'm a runner who's still building endurance" or "I'm a writer who's developing a daily practice." These identity affirmations create psychological space for growth without triggering resistance.

Become a detective gathering evidence for your new identity. Document every instance of your new behaviors, no matter how small. Each piece of evidence helps your brain accept the new self-concept as valid. "See, I did wake up early three times this week. Maybe I am becoming a morning person after all." This evidence collection process gradually convinces your skeptical brain that the identity shift is already happening.

Change how you talk about yourself to others. Your public self-descriptions create powerful commitment pressures. When you tell someone "I don't drink during the week" instead of "I'm trying to cut back on drinking," you're not just informing them—you're reinforcing your own identity shift. These language pattern shifts create social accountability that strengthens your internal identity change.

Regularly visualize yourself as someone who naturally performs these behaviors. This isn't some woo-woo manifestation exercise—it's practical neurological preparation. By repeatedly imagining yourself as the person who automatically makes these choices, you're creating neural pathways that make those behaviors feel increasingly natural and aligned with who you are.

This approach recognizes that lasting behavior change isn't just about what you do—it's about who you become. When the new behaviors align with your sense of self, what was once resistance becomes reinforcement. You're no longer fighting against your identity; you're expressing it.

Challenge 5: The Measurement Mistake

The Problem: Most people either don't measure their progress at all ("I'll just know if I'm doing better") or focus on lagging indicators that come too late to be useful ("I'll check my weight once a month"). This creates a feedback vacuum where you have no idea if your efforts are working until it's too late to make adjustments. It's like driving with your eyes closed and only opening them every few minutes to see if you're still on the road.

The Solution: Create a comprehensive measurement system focused on leading indicators—the early signals that predict later results. This gives you actionable feedback while there's still time to adjust your approach:

Track what you actually do, not just what you achieve. Implementation tracking measures actions taken rather than just results achieved. Count your workouts, not just your weight. Track your sales calls, not just your sales. Measure your writing sessions, not just your finished manuscripts. These implementation metrics tell you whether you're actually following your plan, regardless of whether results have appeared yet.

Measure the quality of your effort, not just the quantity. Process metrics track how well you're implementing, not just how much. Rate your focus during work sessions, your form during workouts, your presence during relationship conversations. These quality indicators often predict results better than volume metrics alone and give you specific areas to improve.

Time your recovery from disruptions. How quickly do you get back on track after inevitable interruptions? Recovery speed is one of the most powerful predictors of long-term success. Track how many hours (not days) it takes you to resume implementation after travel, illness, or other disruptions. This metric alone can transform your results by preventing temporary pauses from becoming permanent ones.

Document the subtle shifts that precede obvious changes. Progress journaling captures improvements that might otherwise go unnoticed—slightly better energy, improved mood, moments of clarity, brief experiences of flow. These subtle indicators often appear long before measurable external results and can sustain motivation through plateaus in more visible metrics.

The right measurements create a feedback loop that reinforces continued action. They tell you what's working while there's still time to do more of it and what's not working while there's still time to change course. Without this feedback system, you're essentially implementing blind.

The Secret to Sustained Implementation

After studying personal development for over two decades and working with thousands of people on implementation, I've discovered that sustained change comes down to one fundamental principle:

Make the cost of non-implementation higher than the cost of implementation.

Most people fail to implement because, in the moment, not taking action feels easier than taking action. The immediate discomfort of changing outweighs the immediate comfort of staying the same. But when you deliberately restructure this equation—making inaction more uncomfortable than action—implementation becomes the path of least resistance.

You can achieve this through a combination of strategic pressures that fundamentally alter your decision-making calculus:

Make your commitments public and painful. Social contracts with specific, visible consequences create accountability that's hard to ignore. Tell your most brutally honest friends exactly what you're doing and when, and establish clear penalties for missing the mark. The temporary discomfort of implementation becomes preferable to the more intense discomfort of explaining your failure.

Put your money where your mouth is. Financial stakes create immediate consequences for abstract future benefits. Commit funds to an accountability app that donates your money to causes you hate if you miss your targets. Pre-pay for non-refundable coaching sessions. The financial pain of non-implementation creates an immediate counterweight to the immediate comfort of procrastination.

Tie your identity to the process. Identity investment makes implementation a matter of self-consistency rather than just discipline. When you see yourself as "a person who never misses a workout" rather than "someone trying to exercise more," following through becomes about maintaining your sense of self rather than forcing an unwanted behavior.

Build momentum you don't want to lose. Progress streaks create psychological resistance to breaking the chain. Track consecutive days of implementation visibly, and you'll find yourself doing the behavior partly to avoid breaking your streak. The longer the streak grows, the more powerful this force becomes—eventually making implementation easier than non-implementation.

Design your environment so implementation requires less effort than avoidance. Make the desired behavior the path of least resistance through strategic environmental design. Put your running shoes by the door and your TV in the closet. Delete social media apps and keep books visible. The less friction between you and implementation (and the more friction between you and distraction), the more likely you are to follow through.

When properly structured, these forces create a situation where following through actually feels easier than giving up, even when the actual work is challenging. You're no longer relying on willpower to overcome resistance—you've engineered a reality where the easiest choice is the one that moves you forward.

The Two Paths Before You

As we conclude, you stand at a fork in the road with two distinct paths:

Path 1: The Information Collector You close this book feeling satisfied that you've gained some insights. You tell yourself you'll implement "soon" but never establish concrete triggers or systems. The book joins dozens of others on your shelf—evidence of good intentions but unchanged behavior. Five years from now, your life looks remarkably similar to today, just with more books and articles consumed.

Path 2: The Implementer You recognize that this moment—right now—is your implementation trigger. Before closing this book, you take action. You create your accountability structure. You commit to the implementation framework. It feels uncomfortable and uncertain, but you start anyway. Five years from now, your life is fundamentally transformed, not because you know more, but because you've systematically applied what you know.

The choice between these paths isn't about motivation, willpower, or even desire. It's about the systems you create right now that either facilitate implementation or enable procrastination.

THE FINAL WORD

The truth is simple: This book works, but only if you work it. The principles and frameworks I've shared with you have transformed thousands of lives—not because they're complicated or revolutionary, but because they address the fundamental patterns that keep most people stuck.

You already have all the information you need. What happens next depends not on what you know, but on what you do with what you know. It's like having a map to buried treasure—completely worthless if you just hang it on your wall instead of actually following it to start digging.

Most people will close this book and move on with their lives, unchanged. But I suspect you're not most people. I suspect you're tired of knowing what to do without doing it, tired of having potential without results, tired of starting charges without finishing them.

If that's true, then this isn't the end of a book—it's the beginning of a transformation. The real value isn't in these pages; it's in what happens when you close the book and open a new chapter in your life.

So what will it be? Will you be a reader, or will you be an implementer? The difference isn't knowledge—it's action.

Your implementation begins now.